DATE DUE

LIKE SEX WITH GODS

NUMBER THREE
Centennial of Flight Series
Roger D. Launius, *General Editor*

LIKE SEX WITH GODS

AN UNORTHODOX
HISTORY
OF FLYING

Bayla Singer

TEXAS A&M UNIVERSITY PRESS   COLLEGE STATION

The paper used in this book
meets the minimum requirements
of the American National Standard for Permanence
of Paper for Printed Library Materials, z39.48-1984.
Binding materials have been chosen for durability.

∞

Excerpt from "The Hawk's Cry in Autumn" from *To Urania* by Joseph Brodsky.
Copyright © 1988 by Joseph Brodsky. Reprinted
by permission of Farrar, Straus and Giroux, LLC.

Excerpt from *Rig-Veda* from *Hindu Scriptures* by R.C. Zaehner, copyright © 1992.
Reprinted by permission of Everyman's Library.

Library of Congress Cataloging-in-Publication Data

Singer, Bayla, 1940–
    Like sex with gods : an unorthodox history of
  flying / Bayla Singer.—1st ed.
       p. cm.—(Centennial of flight series ; 3)
      Includes bibliographical references and index.
      ISBN 1-58544-256-9 (cloth : alk. paper)
      1. Aeronautics—History. I. Title. II. Series.
  TL516.S56   2003
  629.13'009—dc21   2002152954

CONTENTS

::::

ILLUSTRATIONS

::::

ACKNOWLEDGMENTS

The roots of this work extend back into my childhood, and so my first thanks must go to Dorothy and Irwin Schlossberg, wise parents who indulged and encouraged their daughter's wide-ranging curiosity. Gratitude is also due to all the librarians, teachers, and mentors who shaped my perspective in those long-ago years, and who encouraged me to follow my own pathways.

More recently, when the pathway led to the history of technology, I became indebted to the faculty at the University of Pennsylvania, particularly the History and Sociology of Science Department. Most deeply, to Professor Thomas Parke Hughes, who provided much-needed guidance and support for this very non-traditional student. I hope I have not disappointed him.

The Society for History of Technology has been a welcoming and supportive professional "home," offering shelter to an amazing variety of intellectual approaches. I have learned a great deal from both formal and informal interactions with my colleagues, and their influence may be seen throughout the book. For the opportunity to work on this particular project, I must thank Roger Launius, Chief Historian of the National Aeronautics and Space Administration and editor of the series of which this book is one small part. The collective modesty of the Texas A&M University Press forbids my mentioning the names of all those who supplied encouragement and enthusiasm through the difficult process of actually bringing the book to press, but y'all know who you are, and you have my enduring gratitude for leading me gently through the unfamiliar maze of procedures.

Many amiable friends listened to my enthusiasms, served as sounding boards for my thoughts and conclusions, and even helped gather some arcane linguistic and ethnological tidbits. Librarians at the Palm Beach County Public Library patiently processed scores of InterLibrary Loan requests, without which this book could not have been written.

Larry Eschler, Pamela Laird, and Reba Rodman provided insightful comments on an early portion of the book, and Guillaume de Syon supplied bibliographic suggestions and reviewed my translations from the French. He also generously shared postcard images from his collection, some of which have been used as illustrations for the book. Bonnie Voigtlander, Clyde Voigtlander, Alyce Cresap, and Myles Callum read an early draft of the complete manuscript and supplied helpful insights. Anonymous reviewers for the Texas A&M University Press suggested further refinements. Ruth Horowitz helped enormously in giving the final manuscript coherence and consistency. All mistakes, of course, remain my own.

My husband, Irwin, tried his best to keep me on an even keel throughout.

I hope you have as much fun reading this book as I have had writing it.

LIKE SEX WITH GODS

INTRODUCTION

Human flight is not a simple matter of science and technology. It is a continuing epic of dreams and obsession, of yearning and striving to harness the intellect in the service of the emotions. Humanity's drive toward the heavens has many wellsprings and multiple streams, all of them interacting with and reinforcing the others. Technological ingenuity is simply one outlet for the ancient dream. This book integrates both aspects of this quest, the psychological and the technological, as expressed in art and artifact.

For millennia, people of all cultures have dreamed of flying. Their dreams have had overtones of religion, of liberation and redemption, of sexuality, and of empowerment. Flight is fraught with symbolism, the stuff of legend and myth. Flying has been an end in itself, and a means to other ends. This book explores these complex and varied underlayers of a universal urge, an urge which has not been satisfied by the accomplishments of the twentieth century. Humankind continues to dream of flight: ever higher, further, faster.

The power of these dreams is reflected in the persistent efforts over the millennia to bring them to fruition. From magic carpets and har-

nessed eagles to kites, balloons, and ornithopters, people have devised
an astonishing assortment of mechanisms in pursuit of their objective.
They have risked, and in many cases lost, their lives. The flight of the
Wright brothers marks just one point on a continuing path which extends through the present and into the future, as humanity takes its first
steps into space. The psychological aspects of human flight reinforce
the technological, showing their mutual relationship and reflecting the
complexity of humanity's motivation and ingenuity.

The path from dream to invention has broad implications. Econo-
mists studying capitalist systems emphasize the importance of technological development to the health of the economy and our rising standard of living. What are the driving forces behind technological change?
How can we understand, and perhaps harness or guide, those forces?

Historians of technology agree that invention is part of a process embedded in society and intended to satisfy values held by members of
society. It does not occur in a vacuum; it is not the disconnected prod-
uct of a single mind or of progress along one "correct" path. The dream
of flight, and its fruition, provides one example of this general truth.
The various roots of this development include religion, curiosity, literature and the fine arts, the intellectual playfulness of mechanically minded
people, and the general social attitudes toward inventiveness in general
and flight in particular.

The old proverb says "Necessity is the mother of invention." All too
often, Necessity is construed as simple economic pressure, part of the
drive for survival. As historian George Basalla points out, plants and
animals of all sorts survive very well without invention.[1] The wellspring
of invention might be better sought in play, in imagination, and in the
capacity for abstract thought. The general direction in which imagination flows is provided by the values and social structure of the community, although there is the rare case of imagination "flowing uphill," as it
were, apparently supported only by the sheer persuasive force of genius.

For an invention to become more than a figment of the imagination,
however, the time must be ripe. The social and material environment
must provide a nourishing atmosphere; materials must be available to
construct the invention in a workable manner; there must be rewards
for the inventor, and a mindset favorable to adopting the innovation.
The cultural reaction must be "oh, that's just what we've been looking
for, and didn't realize it" rather than "that might be a clever toy, but it's
not really important." Modern Westerners often assume that if some-

thing *can* be done, it *will* be done, ignoring the very real fact that rejection has occurred, that technological and behavioral choices do not always embrace things that seem alien to cultural values.

All these factors are visible in the story of humanity's long-term and universal fascination with flight.

THE APPROACH

There are many ways to approach history. One is to begin with one event or artifact, and look for antecedents; the operative question then is "how did this come to happen?" This is like saying "I'm here: who are my parents, my grandparents, what is my heritage?" You could imagine this as a group of brooks and streams, combining along the way to form one mighty river. If we start with the Wright brothers and their airplane, we would look backwards in time to see where and when the ingredients were developed, and say "See, here we have investigation into the properties of air, there we have development of small motors, over there we have the discovery of cambered airfoils" and so on. We might then draw some more or less straight lines connecting these points, and call it the history of flight.

This approach makes it much too easy for us to judge each stream or brook by its contribution to the river; to assume that the primary purpose of each little watercourse is to ultimately become part of the river, and if it does not do so then it has somehow "failed." If we think of "flight" as meaning only the airplane, we would dismiss everything that did not lead directly to airplane development, ignoring all the other aspects of flying. This approach invites such summaries as "misguided and eccentric characters ran riot over the field of aviation in the 19th century, while a few wise men strove to keep it on the right lines of development."[2] We would regret the time "wasted" trying to imitate birds, or to utilize human power. We might ignore the balloon, the kite, and the dirigible as irrelevant to the "real" history, as dead ends on the road to the airplane. Or we might notice these things, but consider them quaint minor diversions along the mainstream. Grudgingly, we might concede that they helped keep the dream alive, and provided means for scientific exploration of the atmosphere. They would deserve only a brief mention before our attention turned to the Wright brothers and their contemporaries. We would miss a lot of fun, and some important lessons.

It is also much too easy to get caught up in the image of accumulating waterflows, and ignore the fact that life is seldom so tidy.

Trying to draw a picture of the development of flight is incredibly frustrating. Start with any of the ingredients, and you soon encounter a tangled web. Each of the main sources is a large-scale river in and of itself, with only a small branch or two wandering over to become part of "flying." Religion, for example, can include flying as part of the ritual or as part of the symbolic structure, but the main purpose of religion is not concerned with flying per se. Literature may adopt flying as a symbol of freedom, but literature is concerned with many other things as well. The scientific exploration of the atmosphere provided the foundation for systematic pursuit of "flying machines," but was not primarily dedicated to that purpose. Even hardware such as kites and balloons and gliders and small engines, "lead" toward powered flight capable of carrying people aloft but are not completely dedicated to that end. Some are intended as children's toys, others as ritual objects, still others as sheer intellectual play at a time when actual flight occurs only in the imagination.

We could try another perspective. Begin with the very vague notion of "flying" and see where it leads us. Looking at flight this way, we ask "What has the idea of flying contributed to these other rivers of human thought and action?" What has "flying" meant to religion, to art, to literature, to the scientific and mechanical imagination? And how have these other areas contributed back to the development of physical flight? Some people would not call this "history" at all, even though we would be looking at the whole sweep of the human record through time.

This book tries to take a middle path, looking both at the development of the various ingredients that eventually wound up enabling humankind to physically fly, and at the mutual relationships between flying and other human activities. What were the components of the dream, and how did the dream influence the eventual physical reality? The journey toward physical flight seems to flow, from mystical flight expressed in spiritual terms of communication and love, through magical flight and its attempt to control the supernatural, to our present engineered flight which seems to rely only on the physical but draws its inspiration and driving forces from our emotions and culture. At the same time, metaphorical flight continues to represent a wide range of intangible, abstract concepts.

We approach flying-tales from two directions: their function as myth or symbol, and their function as imaginative groundwork for actual mechanism. Various possibilities imagined for flight have been woven into the flying-tales; sometimes the mechanism is the main focus, at other times it is secondary. Not surprisingly, scholars generally concentrate on their own interests: historians looking for "precursors" of this or that present-day mechanism tend to look only at the means of flight; psychologists, anthropologists, and literary analysts tend to concentrate on the symbolic issues. The result is an artificial separation of motive from method, where both should be considered together.

Most of all, we look at the junction of mental and mechanical circumstances, at the supporting social and material structures that encourage invention. Neither will suffice without the other. The roots of human flight lie both in the desire to do it, and in the imagination and ability to put materials together in effective fashion. For the result to be more than a grownup's toy also requires that the social, cultural, and economic environment absorb the new invention into the mainstream.

It is tempting to read backwards, finding the "origins" of modern technologies in the imaginative musings of ancient writers or artists. Many writers include elements of myth and fable only in order to contrast them with the "sober" scientific history of flight, as if to say that modern approaches have outgrown mere superstition and magic. Look, look, they boast, see how we have matured.

The truth is much more complex: all aspects of past thought about flying, whether mechanical, symbolic, religious, or emotional, contribute in tangled ways to the motivations and imaginations of those who attempt to bring these dreams to reality. The groundwork is laid in the past, for later folk to think "It is desirable, and it may be possible." The creativity and the variety of detail found in the older materials is grist for the mill of those who come later. "It is desirable"—this is the crucial element for eventual success.

Technological evolution mirrors biological evolution. The small increments of change leading to bird flight must have had some value before flight was achieved; natural selection mercilessly prunes useless characteristics, especially when they affect energy and metabolic resources. Why do species of flightless birds continue to develop feathers, when fish confined to lightless caves for generations often lose the very anatomy of their eyes? Also, characteristics that originally served one function are often co-opted by evolution to serve another. Some experts believe that feathers served as insulation before being incorporated into the mechanism of bird flight. Most recently, the suggestion has been made that the "lift" produced by flapping primitive wings was an advantage to running birds, increasing their running speed and helping them rapidly climb trees to escape predators. So far, no single theory has managed to account for all the ingredients of animal flight.[3]

So too with human flight. Kites, balloons, sails, and billowing garments, primitive flapping-wing contraptions doomed to failure, all serve some human purpose beyond their straight-line contribution to the development of powered aircraft. In some cultures, but not all, these technologies become part of the history of aviation. In some cultures, but not all, they are ends in themselves.

Human motivation is complicated. Why does anyone want to fly? Why does anyone want to invent at all? The reasons may be rooted in religion, economics, social status, or playfulness, or the reasons may be buried too deeply for clear expression. Or perhaps "all the above." The youngster who watches the birds just knows that flying is something wonderful, and may grow up to find some way to do it, and to give meaning to it. Magic and superstition may be left behind when science and technology come to dominate our thoughts, but humanity's spiritual and emotional needs must still be served. Again, flying may be an end in itself, or a means to some other goal—riches, glory, sheer physical or intellectual pleasure.

Motivation, ingenuity, the material wherewithal, and social acceptance all are necessary ingredients for the successful pursuit of human flight.

The airplane and the space ship are not really "the end," either; so we will look at ways in which the dream continues, shaped by the results so far. Time is a stream which does not end with us; it continues to flow toward the future.

ORGANIZATION

Part 1 looks at the intangibles, the concept of "flying" and its relationship to the imagination in religion, art, and literature. Chapter 1 describes the inhabitants of heaven, and the symbolism associated with height and flying. Chapter 2 explores the mythical and spiritual accounts of flight as attempts to approach or conquer the heavens. In Chapter 3, we see the association of flight with intellectual freedom.

Part 2 focuses on the mechanics of flying and how the dream was realized by small steps and diverse ways from the 1500s to the present. Each section and even each chapter has cross-connections to the others, and it must always be kept in mind that the division is arbitrary. Thus,

Chapter 4 contains the exuberant speculations of those just beginning to find "invention" an important cultural pastime; Chapter 5 explores mechanisms based on bird flight, and Chapter 6 presents kites, gliders, and parachutes. Balloons and dirigibles, lighter than air, are the subject of Chapter 7.

Chapter 8 follows the dream from the Wright brothers' flight onward into the future, and touches on some ways that the apprehensions of early thinkers have proved all too accurate.

The difficulty we encounter in trying to separate the material into reasonably coherent strands reflects the essentially holistic nature of the story. It has been said that "time is what keeps everything from happening at once"—a linear account tries to keep everything from being said at once, but plucking one strand from the web necessarily involves all the others to which it is related. Our classifications are much like the vertical bar divisions in sheet music; they help us mark time, but "they're not *in the music.*"[4] [Original emphasis.] To help orient readers chronologically, dates and relative chronology are given frequently throughout the book, and a timeline is provided at the back.

Wings, kings, religion, horses, dreams, and myths; balloons, kites, sails, and birds appear and re-appear. At each occurrence, I have tried to provide as much context as appropriate for the moment and for the purpose of the discussion. The timeline, the index, and the glossary may help those who wish to rearrange information; the bibliography and suggestions for further reading may help those who wish more depth on any given topic.

A word of warning: this account is nowhere near complete, nor does it try to be. Whole books have been written, for example, on the artistic expression of the association of flying with sex, or on examples of supernatural, legendary, and mythical flight. Other books have concentrated on the principles of aerodynamics, on balloons and ballooning, or on the "straight-line" history leading to the Wright brothers' historic flight. I have tried for some balance between acknowledging the important material which can be found in almost any history of flight, and exploring the less well-known material at the margins of the direct line. I have emphasized human interest and cultural context, rather than strictly technological contributions. The bibliography contains references to material for further reading, as well as to books and articles directly quoted in the text.

PART I

DREAMS & MYTHOLOGY

CHAPTER 1

DEITIES ALOFT

Humans can run and swim, but not fly. This has been a mystery from prehistory onward. Why is the air forbidden to us? Something so difficult to attain must surely be sacred, spiritual, special. The air is insubstantial, yet can have dramatic and powerful effects; wind and breath partake of the mysterious as well. It is no wonder that most cultures have seen the skies as a home to deities. Thin air, invisible yet powerful, is a natural metaphor for the spiritual and supernatural.

Deities fly, and deities create. Humans intertwine the creative power of sex with their longings for connection to divinity and their yearning to fly, until the strands form a complex web of symbolism and action. The dark side of the supernatural is represented as well, with devils and demons ready to snare the arrogant or unwary. Union with the supernatural, like union with human lovers, can offer torment as well as delight.

Communication between heaven and earth depends on passage through the air. Divine and human ingenuity have been fertile in devising means for accomplishing this; Jacob's ladder, Elijah's chariot, the shaman's "horse" as well as angels, doves, eagles, and ravens. Gifts, too, are a means of communication; the prayers and sacrifices made by humans are intended to convey a message of worship and devotion; deities respond with physical and spiritual gifts to humans.

When the gift is the power of flight, its very nature bespeaks its origin beyond the normal. Saints and kings draw their authority from this sign of divine favor; simpler folk as well offer this evidence of their piety and innocence.

THE BREATH OF LIFE

Air, as one of the four basic elements of the ancients, has been both the home of gods and a god in itself. Earth, fire, and water were domesticated early in human history. Not so the air. Untamed, capricious, powerful, and insubstantial, it remained the stuff of dreams and souls.

Howling storm winds eerily imitate human and animal sounds of distress; the legend of the Wild Hunt, widespread in Britain and northern Europe, tells of homeless souls and slavering beasts running endlessly through the heavens. The hounds of hell run with this pack; sometimes Odin rides at their head, perhaps accompanied by shrieking ravens. Earthbound dogs bay at their windswept cousins, and humans huddle indoors.

Gentle winds stir up metaphors of love, caresses, sweetness, and purity.

Life itself is inextricably bound to air and breath. It is noteworthy that the Hebrew word "ruach" can be translated as either "spirit" or "wind," and it is ruach that moves upon the waters in the biblical Book of Genesis, at the beginning of creation. God forms humans (Hebrew "adam") from the dust of the earth ("adamah"), and blows the "breath of life" ("neshamah," also meaning soul or spirit) into them.[1] Similarly, the Greek word "psyche" and the Latin "spiritus" are used to mean "soul, spirit, breath of life" as well. In the Hindu Chandoya-Upanishad, we find "when fire takes leave, it leaves on the wind. When the sun takes leave, it leaves on the wind. When the moon takes leave, it leaves on the wind. Thus the wind consumes all things . . . When man goes to sleep, his voice takes leave on a puff of breath, and the same is true of his sight, his hearing, and his thought. Thus his breath consumes all things."[2]

Beyond the spiritual associations of the air, the very concepts of "up" and "down" embody a value judgment. Verticality is embedded in our language of aspiration and achievement—"higher power"—"higher forms of life"—"fall from grace"—"fall off the wagon"—"rise to the occasion"—"depths of despair." "Down to earth" means practical, the opposite of idealistic, spiritual, creative, imaginative. Humans have few instincts: one of them is the fear of falling. Is it any wonder that our deities inhabit the skies, and the underworld is a fearsome place?

Height also brings extended vision. The watchtower is an ancient invention. Mountains such as Sinai and Olympus are sacred ground. Sun-gods and other heavenly deities are "all-seeing," particularly when they take the shape of birds. Indian deities representing the dawn and the morning star travel in a sun-chariot and rescue people in distress. The "birds-eye view" is panoramic. Horus the sharp-eyed hawk-headed Egyptian god makes the connection explicit. So does the Hindu god Surya, who can be either the sun or a bird.

Freedom to fly through the air seems the ultimate freedom, implying ultimate power and authority and transcending physical and moral boundaries. Certainly any deity worthy the name would possess such freedom to act and to travel, to observe and control. In the Vedic Indian tradition, the mountains originally had wings, and could fly. Indra, storm and thunder god, cut the wings off the mountains with his thunderbolts; the amputated wings became thunderclouds.[3] No doubt there about who is The Boss.

To be omniscient and omnipotent it is necessary to fly, unless one is a bodiless spirit immanent everywhere. What more natural dwelling place for deities than the skies, the heavens? While some deities live within the earth or in forests, oceans, and other terrestrial locations, by far the majority make their abode in the heavens, and it is to the heavens that favored souls may travel. Not all gods were able to fly at will, however: in one Egyptian legend, a god is sent to a distant kingdom and it takes seventeen months of overland travel to get there![4]

GODS, SEX, AND STORMS

Is the air masculine or feminine? When it comes to gender, the issues become ambiguous and subtle. The gender assigned to the air, and to the deities that represent it, often reflects the attributes and important roles credited to each gender by society. Even when the earth is seen as a fruitful mother, the gender of the sky may not be exclusively masculine. The lower reaches of the air may be seen as more earthly and therefore feminine; the thinner and more delicate upper air may then be considered masculine.

Our survival depends on the fertility of humans, beasts, and grains. Fertility is one of the most ancient mysteries and subject of the most ancient rites. The sexual act is central to early religions everywhere, and remains an important element in modern theologies, East and West. Sexual behavior, or its strict regulation, is intimately linked to community prosperity. The Hebrew Bible thunders against the sexual rituals of the neighboring peoples, "it is an abomination." Other traditions see the sex act as an important form of worship, public or private.

Sexuality in worship may be as straightforward and uncomplicated as "Let's do it, and hope the crops and herds get the idea" or as sublimated and abstract as the concept of the church as the Bride of Christ, with all sorts of variations on the general theme. Intimacy with deities may be a strictly practical matter—your friends are more likely to do favors for you—or it may be a more spiritual yearning. In either case, the most intense form of intimacy we can imagine is sexual, so it is not surprising that we perceive our longings in those terms. Agape shades into Eros without a bump in the road.

Visiting a Roman citizen's home in the first two centuries C.E. you might have seen a winged penis amulet around the matron's neck, or a group of such figurines arranged as a wind chime. Ancient Roman air is gendered female, and one can only speculate on the symbolism, but the small figurines, with their wings, puppylike hind legs, and winsome air, seem quite playful.

Since storm and sun deities are usually masculine and moon deities are often feminine, it is easy to assume that this is a "natural" gender assignment, based on relative strength. We have to be careful, though, because what seems obvious and natural to us may not be anywhere near so clear to others. Even snakes and pillars, so obviously "masculine," have been seen otherwise; aboriginal Australians tell of the snake goddess whose womb produced all animal life, and the pillar in the ancient Near East was often a shorthand form of the feminine Tree of Life, sacred to the fertility goddess Astarte (sometimes known as Ishtar or Ashera). Storms may be seen as masculine for their strength, or feminine for their unpredictability or for the life-giving properties of the rain. The moon's variation may represent more than one kind of human cycle.

Take the Babylonian goddess Ishtar as one confusing example: goddess of love (and war!), she is also the goddess of thunderstorms. Just to muddy the waters further, in some cities Ishtar was masculine, even

Miniature winged penises, Roman, from the beginning of the Christian era. Figurines like these might be worn as pendants on necklaces or arranged as wind chimes.

Courtesy and copyright

© British Museum

within Babylonia. The female Ishtar came to be identified with the Sumerian goddess Innana, who also ruled the storms. Ishtar and Innana are also fertility goddesses, though they themselves never become mothers. Rather, they are young, impulsive (stormy), and beautiful; maidens rather than matrons.

On the other side of the earth, the Inca's supreme creator deity was Viracocha, god of both sun and storms. Viracocha's daughter was the moon-goddess Quilla, and his son was the sun-god Inti, portrayed as a golden disc with a human face. Inca rulers were said to be descended from Inti—divine descent is often an attribute of royalty. It makes government so much easier when local authority is backed up by religion. Legends of kings in many lands included their ability to fly or to command the birds or winds, further evidence of their divine connections. Kings in various Pacific islands were also considered divine, and were not allowed to touch the ground lest their holiness seep away.

The sun is not always male, nor the moon always female. In Japanese mythology, for example, the sun is feminine and the moon masculine. Among the Hittites, a god controlled the storms, but the sun was venerated as a goddess. To the Sumerians, Ishtar/Innana was the daughter of their moon-god, Nanna. The Egyptians venerated both sun and moon as masculine: Ra and Khensu. Hindus also gender both sun and moon as masculine: Surya and Chandra. Chandra, the moon, has other names to suit his various aspects as fertility god, as lord of Soma (the gods' beverage), and others. The phases of the moon, so often seen as relevant either to women's monthly periods or to the life cycle of maiden, mother, crone, in masculine form represent the ages of man: infancy, adolescence, young adulthood, old age.

China too sang to a god of heaven, who rode in a chariot drawn by winged dragons and decorated by feathered streamers. His hymn describes the dark clouds around him, and compares his speed to that of "the horses of the wind." When Pei Ti (also known as Pak Tai) was elected as chief minister to the gods, heavenly messengers brought him suitable robes and shoes, as well as a "chariot of nine colors" to fly him to his new post.[5]

EVIL IN THE AIR

The pervasiveness of evil suggests that demons and malevolent beings can also fly. The familiar Halloween witch on her broomstick is just one example. In the Christian tradition, devils are fallen angels, previously holy beings who rebelled against God and were cast out of heaven. For several centuries, devils were depicted with feathered wings similar to those of the heavenly angels; since about the thirteenth century C.E. they have been shown with bat wings or other grotesque features, sometimes even as hybrid combinations of serpent, bat, and other detested animals.

Ah, bats. Emerging in swarms from their caves at dusk, they seem the very minions of hell. Their faces seem distorted parodies of our own. Their wings are obviously webs between elongated fingers, again a distortion and parody of human features. Their male genitalia are large in proportion to their bodies, and in erection display garish colors and unusual shapes. And as if to emphasize their perversity, they sleep upside down, with their wings like cloaks wrapped around themselves. Their ability to avoid obstacles in total darkness seems supernatural. Dark, mysterious, inhabitants of the night, it is no wonder that bats were familiars of witches and the animal form for the bloodsucking "undead" vampires of European legend. Modern biologists proclaim that bats are innocent, peaceful creatures, feeding mostly on insects or fruit, but su-

perstition and tradition persist nevertheless. As with the gender assignment of sun, moon, and air, the reputation of bats has a cultural basis
rather than a factual one.

Although the scaly winged dragon is sometimes a benign figure in Asian
contexts, in Christian iconography it is usually considered an enemy and
often symbolizes the Devil. On the other hand, the ancient Chinese god
of thunder and lightning, Lei Kung, is usually shown with bat wings. The
Koni people of Colombia (northwestern South America) consider bats
the first animals created, and think of them as spirits of the forest, trans-
formed birds, or shamanic messengers.[6] Again we see that associations
which seem "natural" to some cultures are by no means universal.

Greek mythology contributes a substantial group of ghastly flying
females, in addition to such winged goddesses as Nike (Victory). The
avenging Furies, hideous women with blood dripping from their eyes,
relentlessly pursue those who commit murder and other crimes against
fundamental morality. The Harpies, half woman, half crow or raptor,
may originally have been conceived as ghosts or wind spirits, but are
more familiar as loathsome creatures sent to harass and punish. Medusa was one of three terrifying Gorgons, gruesome women with
dragonlike wings and snakes for hair, whose glance turned humans to
stone. The Greek hero Perseus slew Medusa, and from her blood sprang
the winged horse Pegasus.

INTERCOURSE WITH HEAVEN

As theologian Neil Gillman has pointed out, if there is no communication between humans and their deities, there is not much point in having religion.[7] Humans everywhere send up prayers, and look for signs of
divine communication. At its most intense, communication may be ecstatic and sexual; it is no accident that one four-letter word meaning
"intercourse" is "talk."

The methods of communication between humans and their deities
are as varied as the human imagination. One of the most basic is physical or spiritual ascension to heaven by worthy humans, and has been
part of every religion known thus far. Another method of supernatural
communication is the gift of flight to humans, though whether the source
be benevolent or malicious is often suspect. A third is the descent from
heaven of deities or their messengers, who may take the shapes of humans, animals (usually birds), or some unearthly combination. Although

divine messengers of all faiths can fly, not all are pictured with wings. Of all these methods of communication, birds have the most complicated parts to play.

Since birds naturally inhabit the air, their association with the supernatural seems obvious. Plato, in *Phaedrus,* tells us "The natural function of the wing is to soar upwards . . . to the place where dwells the race of the gods. More than any other thing that pertains to the body, it partakes of the nature of the divine."[8] William Blake, mystical poet of the eighteenth century, sang "Arise you little glancing wings, and sing your infant joy! / Arise and drink your bliss, for every thing that lives is holy!"[9]

Birds have been variously considered to be divine messengers, souls of the departed, symbols of the spirit or of divinity, or otherwise involved in spiritual affairs. The Zoroastrian spirit Fravashi which guides the soul through life is shown with stylized outstretched wings; the five ranks of feathers signify the five divisions of an earthly day, and proper use of the five senses. Zeus took swan-shape to ravish Leda, and as an eagle kidnapped Ganymede. In Sumerian myth, the hero-god Ninurta overcomes Anzu, a monstrous bird, and wins the tablet on which is written the responsibilities of the various deities. The most important Hindu bird is entirely supernatural: Garuda, on whom Vishnu rides. While descriptions of Garuda vary, they usually include some elements of the high-flying or acrobatic birds such as the kite, the eagle, and the falcon. Garuda figures prominently in several Hindu myths, symbolizing the human search for spirituality. We will see more of Garuda in Chapter 2.

Birds are woven into the spirituality of diverse cultures. The very shape of the bird in flight has been taken as a sign of the Cross. Brazilian legend holds that all animals visit heaven to be blessed on the Feast of Our Lady: for this holy occasion, birds carry their wingless brethren. In Japan, one sees freestanding "gates" called torii, literally "bird perches," which originally served as boundaries and gateways between the mundane and the spiritual or divine. The departing soul of a warrior in a Japanese creation myth emerges from his mouth as a crane. The French poet and author Victor Hugo wrote

> *The bird, in Aser woods, seems*
> *A soul in the green boughs*
> *. . . And as if I had a soul*
> *Made of birds' wings.*[10]

The Rape of Ganymede, after a painting by Michaelangelo (now lost).
The calm expression on Ganymede's face and the relaxation of his arms
contrast to the tension in his legs; he does not appear to be struggling.
The eagle's head and neck wrap him protectively.

The allusion becomes more complex when we realize that ancient Egyptians believed the departing soul took the form of a bird, and flew to the afterlife to be judged by Osiris, and that Aser is a synonym for Osiris. Osiris was often represented by a wooden pillar, symbolizing a tree.

Specific species of birds have been assigned particular spiritual roles and attributes. Seeing one of these specially symbolic birds often implies the transmission of some supernatural message, and the believer will look to the circumstances for the particular details. The extreme variation in symbolisms (even of the same bird) gives evidence of humankind's enduring desire to find meaning, and to our ancient preoccupation with birds of all kinds.

In modern times, along the coasts of Great Britain, many fisherfolk believe that after death they return to this world as seagulls, kittiwakes, or gannets. If such a bird appears soon after a death, it will seem to be the soul of the recently departed, perhaps saying a last farewell. Or if the bird appears during times of trouble or crisis, it may comfort people to think that their kinfolk "on the other side" are looking out for them. On some French and British coasts, storm petrels are said to be the souls of harsh ship captains, or of drowned mariners. Shearwaters are sometimes referred to as "damned souls," unable to go to their eternal rest.

The lark might be considered almost pure spirituality: small, nearly invisible against the earth or sky, it is a magnificent obsession to poets who vainly yearn to sing so well. Arising to fly at dawn, singing to welcome the sun, it is no wonder that a group of larks is called an "exaltation." Percy Bysshe Shelley proclaimed to the lark, "bird thou never wert!"

The sacred Hindu literature is rich in birds with spiritual associations, among them Chakora, a partridge which loves the moon and is said to feed on its rays; Chataka, a swallow which drinks only drops of rain as they fall from the clouds; and Nilakantha, a blue jay sacred to Sri Vishnu. Let us set aside what these mean to the devout Hindu, and seek a more general interpretation. The familiar partridge is a timid ground-dweller, the swallow an aerial acrobat, the blue jay an aggressive and intelligent bird. One message to non-Hindus is that all of us, whether practical "ground-dwellers" or idealistic "high-flyers," can be nourished by spirituality and that our own talents are precious and useful in service to something other than, and perhaps greater than, ourselves. Is the meaning "really there," is it "true," have we interpreted the symbol correctly? No matter. The crucial part of this exercise is that we not dismiss the associations as mere superstition, but acknowledge that there is deeper meaning to be found by those who look for it. Humans of all cultures, since the beginning of time, have searched for meaning as best they could. Let us keep that in mind as we explore spiritual heritages.

Pueblo Indians of the American Southwest assigned mythic functions to a great variety of birds; swallows, swifts, hummingbirds, and doves were associated with the rain, the gloriously colored parrot family with the sun, eagles and other raptors with the sky, and so on. The turkey vulture, associated with death, became a symbol and facilitator of purification and rebirth as well. Whether the occasion was the temporary journey of one's soul during a trance, or the final separation of death, Pueblo medicine men would invoke turkey vultures to assist in transition rituals between the spirit world and the everyday.

In the biblical story of the Flood, a dove brought an olive branch back to Noah's ark, as a sign that the waters had receded and that dry land was available. Carriers of ordinary messages, it is not surprising that doves were thought to carry messages between heaven and earth as well.

Doves are often used in Christian iconography to represent the Holy Spirit. Doves may be seen in Christian religious paintings of all eras, peeking out of the clouds or perched on the shoulders of saints or prophets. In some, a dove is portrayed as impregnating the Virgin Mary through her ear, the Word made Flesh (doves were thought to reproduce via "kisses"). In others, the dove may hover about her lap, or be gliding on the breath of God from above. In one legend, a dove is said to have emerged from Joseph's genitals and perched on his head, to designate him as the Virgin Mary's future husband. The sexual associations of the dove are ancient, going back at least to the Assyrians and Greeks. Ishtar, Innana, Venus, it seems all the great fertility goddesses were associated with the milky-white dove. In more recent times, a Bohemian girl might catch a dove, hold it to her bare breast while murmuring a love spell, and then let it fly up the chimney—a vaginal symbol.

Clear erotic connotations have been softened by religious authorities seeking to spiritualize ancient associations. Just as the biblical Song of Songs, presented as an expression of earthly (and earthy) love, has been interpreted as an allegory of God's love for the Hebrews, so the dove has been interpreted as an allegory of God's spirit entering humankind, and the reproductive power associated with the dove's kiss became an allegory of the breath of spiritual life infused into sinful humanity.

Ravens, and their cousins the crows, are among the most intelligent of birds, and it is not surprising to find them playing important super-

Juan de Flandes, The Annunciation, ca. 1508–19. There is a strong diagonal element in the composition, from the angel's upraised hand to the book in Mary's lap. Above the diagonal, the dove representing the Holy Spirit and the lilies foreshadowing the crucifixion offer a spiritual balance to the mass of the figures' bodies.

Courtesy National Gallery of Art, Samuel H. Kress Collection natural roles. At Delphi, sacred to Apollo, a raven symbolized wisdom and science. Odin, chief of the Norse and Germanic gods, depended on his ravens, Huginn (Thought) and Muninn (Memory) to fly around the worlds and keep him informed. It is interesting to note that the first bird Noah sent out after the Flood was a raven, which never returned to the ark. Among the Alaskan Inuit, Raven is the clever trickster god. In the American Northwest, including Alaska, ravens play an important part in creation myths.

As carrion-eaters, crows have a bad reputation in Europe, where they are usually seen as prophets of death. In Europe and in other cultures where black represents death or despair, black-colored birds are a spiritual puzzle, since birds in general are symbols of life, freedom, and spirituality. Black birds often become multivalent symbols of both death and rebirth, despair and hope, of soul and body. For instance, the blackbird was often placed in depictions of the Virgin and Christ Child to foreshadow the crucifixion. Other times, the blackbird represents the forces of evil, as when one flew in front of Saint Gregory and threw him into agonies of sexual temptation.

Eagles are frequent symbols of majesty, if not outright divinity. Strong and swift, the eagle nests in high and inaccessible areas such as gods might inhabit—indeed, most of the Greek gods lived on Mount Olympus. Jupiter, the Roman god of rain, thunder, and lightning, is associated with eagles, as is his Greek counterpart Zeus. Roman emperors, claiming divine ancestry, adopted the eagle as their rightful sign. The eagle has been the emblem of several European states up through modern times. The United States of America shows a bald eagle on its national Great Seal, and on several coins. In the Hebrew Bible, before the revelation on Mount Sinai, God reminds the Israelites that he brought them out of Egypt "on eagles' wings."[11] The phrase is clearly intended to reinforce the impression of God's power.

Cranes, those stately and long-lived birds, graceful in flight and mating for life, have inspired observers both East and West to associate them with divinity and virtue. In China, the crane's powerful wings are said to convey departed souls to heaven, and the pious to higher levels of spirituality. The Immortals are often shown as riding on cranes.

Early Asian agriculturists looked to crane migration as indicators of the season: planting was done as cranes went to their breeding areas in the spring, and the cranes returned at harvest time. The vigorous, lively dance of courting cranes, with its circular or spiral motion, became associated with the sun and the coming of spring, with cycles of fertility and death. The dance is widely imitated in Asian cultures, to comfort the spirits of the dead.

In Japan, cranes are said to live a thousand years, and a relatively recent tradition has developed of folding a thousand paper cranes to express wishes for health or peace. The connection between health and the crane's longevity seems clear; is it too cynical to suspect that the connection with peace originates in their marital fidelity?

In Greek and Roman myth, the crane was associated with Apollo both in his role as sun-god and as patron of poets. (Anyone who has heard the raucous noises made by cranes must wonder about that poetry association.) Europeans saw the crane as vigilant and loyal, standing guard with a stone in its claw so that if it fell asleep, the sound of the falling stone would waken it. Early Christians associated the virtues of cranes with those of life in a monastery, guarding the faith.

We see here two distinct, although related, reasons why birds were used as models in early and late Western attempts at human flight. First is their obvious success at flying, and second is their symbolic association with positive spiritual qualities. Even when would-be flyers turned to engineering rather than magic as their preferred technology, the deep symbolisms of birdflight remained part of their mindset. In their youths, they watched birds and longed to join them. Physical, spiritual, and emotional freedoms were the goal; engineering or magic merely the means to that end.

If one imitates God, one is godly; if one imitates saints, one is saintly; if you imitate birds, which have such rich symbolic meanings, do you not also dress yourself in those same symbolic meanings?

SEXUAL SYMBOLISM IN FLIGHT

Freud reminds us of the sexuality associated with birdflight:

> When we consider that inquisitive children are told that babies are brought by a large bird, such as the stork; when we find that the ancients represented the phallus as having wings; that the commonest expression in German for male sexual activity is vögeln ["to bird": Vögel is the German noun meaning "bird"]; that the male organ is actually called "l'ucello" ["the bird"] in Italian—all these are . . . from a whole mass of connected ideas, from which we

learn that in dreams the wish to fly is . . . a longing to be capable of sexual performance. . . . Thus aviation, too, which in our day is at last achieving its aim, has its infantile erotic roots.[12]

In our own times, the vulgar gesture known as "the finger" is also called "the bird," and the male organ is nicknamed "cock" in several languages, East and West. Freud insisted that the dream of flight is erotic, with the body as phallus. Erotic or spiritual, the drive is very strong. Indeed, the erotic and the spiritual have been associated from earliest times, and it is only a very short conceptual step from earthly fertility ritual to mystical union with the deity.

An ancient type of dedicated holy man, the shaman is found around

Man riding a cock, Greek plate ca. 521–510 B.C.E. The man's anticipatory smile and the gentle caress of his hand on the cock's neck reflect the visual pun. Although they do not seem to be hurrying, the composition is off-center and the man's feet are jammed against the rim of the plate. Lovemaking should not involve undue haste, yet has a definite course.

Courtesy Metropolitan Museum of Art

the world, from the nomadic tribes of northern and central Asia to South American native peoples, from Australian aborigines to African herdsmen. Clothing himself in feathers and skins associated with his familiar spirits, dancing to the hypnotic beat of the drum, the shaman symbolically ascends the axis of the earth until he "flies" upward into the spirit world. The details of his ritual dress may differ from one group to another, but there are always complex symbolic functions for each element. Calling on the symbolic speed and stamina of the horse, the grace and strength of the birds, and the guiding spirits who have offered to assist him, the shaman's ritual combines the physical with the spiritual. He may physically ride a pole as if it were a horse, he may climb a tree or ladder, the beating drum may even be called his "horse" as he is carried away in ecstasy and communicates with the spirit world.[13]

Echoes of these symbolic elements are found almost universally in other traditions. In Taoism, for instance, the immortals are portrayed as dressed in feathers, and even in modern times Taoist priests are called "feather guests" or "feather scholars." Buddhists who have achieved certain levels of enlightenment are portrayed as floating above the earth, sometimes seated on lotus flowers. The Hindu tradition includes Garuda, the bird which Vishnu rides, as well as many other flying deities, spirits, and demons. The guardian cherubim of the Hebrew ark of the covenant are winged, and the terrifying militant celestial beings of Ezekiel's vision were winged as well. Divine messengers traveled up and down Jacob's ladder, an activity reminiscent of the shaman's ascent to the spirit world. The similarity is not surprising since there are a limited number of options for reaching heaven—one either flies, rides, or climbs. "High places"—hills, mountains, even the famous biblical Tower of Babel— serve as meeting places for humans and their gods.

Zoroastrians tell of a pious man sent as a messenger to heaven, three hundred years after the prophet had established the religion, to inquire whether the people were performing the commandments in the proper manner or if they had fallen into error and hence impurity. Arday Viraf, the messenger, traveled only in spirit, his soul separating from his body after appropriate prayers and under the influence of a sacred narcotic. One step at a time, he climbed up to each of the four heavens; the first step took him to the "star track," the second to the "moon track," the third to the "sun track." Each step upward represented an increase in brightness and a higher level of good living on the part of those who were not Zoroastrians. The fourth heaven shone with "the radiance of

Garôdmân the all-glorious," and was reserved for pious Zoroastrians alone. When he returned to his body, the assembled witnesses eagerly questioned him, but he insisted on first things first—food and drink! After which, he reassured them as to the acceptability of their rituals and religion, describing the rewards of the righteous and the punishments of evildoers.[14]

Horses also have a special place in the celestial symbolism, perhaps because of their swiftness and strength. Wherever the horse is known, it is regarded as the noblest of draft and riding animals, a fit mount for divine beings and suitable to draw divine chariots. While deities are certainly capable of flight by their own powers, it is generally considered more befitting their dignity and sovereignty for them to ride, either in a suitable vehicle or directly on a supernatural animal.

The winged horse Pegasus may be the most familiar, but he's not the only myth in the stable. Horses symbolize the Sun in the ancient Vedic texts of India. Horses also draw the sun's chariot in Greek and Roman mythology. Odin, chief of the Norse and northern European deities, rides his eight-legged horse Sleipnir (surely an eight-legged horse is swifter than one with merely the usual four); Odin's handmaidens the Valkyries

Odin on Sleipnir, detail from a standing stone found on the Island of Gotland, Sweden. The figure is very stylized and hard to interpret. This image is displayed on many websites, including
http://www.pitt.edu/~dash/mythlinks.html

ride their horses above the battlefield, picking up heroes who have died in combat and transporting them to Valhalla. King Solomon of biblical fame is said to have owned "the horse of the wind" and "the horse of the clouds." The prophet Elijah ascends to heaven in a fiery chariot, drawn by fiery horses. There is an ancient Arab legend that God created the horse from the belly of the South wind. Mohammed rode a winged mare, Buraq, through six heavens, and entered the seventh on a flying carpet.[15]

There are sexual overtones to the symbolism associated with the horse, as well. The shaman's pole at once represents both the axis of the universe and the "horse" that carries the shaman into a writhing religious ecstasy hardly to be distinguished from the sexual. For cultures intimately involved with the cycles of birth and death, mortally concerned with fertility among themselves and their crops or livestock, the pole will certainly evoke phallic imagery as it is held erect between the shaman's legs. Mounting and riding a horse also evoke sexual associations. Shakespeare expressed it for us, as the Dauphin of France speaks of his horse as flying: "When I bestride him, I soar, I am a hawk: he trots the air; the earth sings when he touches it; the basest horn of his hoof is more musical than the pipe of Hermes ... he is pure air and fire; and the dull elements of earth and water never appear in him, but only in patient stillness while his rider mounts him."[16] The dialog then extends the image of "riding" to sexual intercourse, and the Dauphin claims his horse is his faithful mistress, allowing none but him to ride. One has only to think of the rhythm of the horse's movement, and the tactile sensations involved, to understand the metaphor.

Jacob's ladder and the shaman's pole (or tree, or ladder), essence of verticality, also represent the Tree of Life, link between heaven and earth. Named Yggdrasil ("fearsome horse"!) in Norse and Germanic mythology, the Tree sheltered the fountain Mimir, source of wisdom. Odin paid an eye for a drink from Mimir. An evil serpent gnaws at the roots of Yggdrasil, perhaps in mythic recognition that sexuality is a force for both good and ill.

Both the Tree of Life and the Tree of Knowledge are featured in the Genesis account of the Garden of Eden, the original dwelling place of Adam and Eve. The focus of the Genesis story is entirely different from that of Odin, however. The serpent in Eden is a tempter of humans, rather than a threat to the Tree itself. Odin the chief god seeks wisdom; Adam and Eve are humans, and their motives are complex. Expulsion

Buraq. This image is typical of those found commonly in Muslim countries. When the figure of Mohammed is included, he commonly wears a veil; it is prohibited in most (but not all) Muslim traditions to depict the face of the Prophet.

from Eden, rather than the loss of an eye, is the price paid; and it is not at all clear whether Adam and Eve gained wisdom or some other kind of knowledge.

The world-tree shows up in the Hindu *Rig-Veda*, as well:

[2] What was the primal matter (adhisthana)? What the beginning?
How and what manner of thing was that from which
The Maker of All, see-er of all, brought forth
The earth, and by his might the heavens unfolded?

[3] His eyes on every side, on every side his face,
On every side his arms, his feet on every side—
With arms and wings he together forges
Heaven and earth, begetting them, God, the One!

[4] What was the wood? What was the tree
From which heaven and earth were fashioned forth?
Ask, ask, ye wise in heart, on what did he rely
That he should [thus] support [these] worlds?[17]

Heaven and earth are bound together by the Tree; climbing it will surely bring you to heaven. Notice the abundance of images here: God *forges* the world, *begets* the world, *forms* it from the wood of a tree. No one word, no one phrase can convey the essence of God or God's creation. Each symbol is multivalent, shimmering between meanings as an optical illusion shimmers between images, but still insufficient. The mystery and complexity are simply too difficult to express. Climb the tree, embrace the tree, feel its substance, reach for communion and union with God in heaven, *experience* what you cannot put into words.

God is portrayed here as having "eyes on every side, on every side his face, . . . his arms, . . . his feet . . ." Surely the personification of an omniscient and omnipotent being! Why does God use both "arms and wings" to forge and beget the universe? Why arms rather than hands, and is this word the choice of the original author or a rough approximation by the translator? And what mythic, symbolic purpose could those wings be serving? Do they instill the breath of life? Do they beat the rhythm of the seasons? Do they fan the spiritual flames of the sacred forge? Or do they tell us that manual skill alone is not sufficient? All answers are "correct" in that they display facets of the greater truth glimpsed within the symbol.

FLIGHT BY ASSOCIATION

Cultures worldwide and throughout time have agreed on this: the ability to fly has important spiritual qualities, and at the very least, for humans, signifies more-than-human status. It can be a gift from the divine, a snare set by the forces of evil, or an achievement after deep and perhaps morally suspect study. The act is always full of meaning, either way.

Most dramatically, the transition from human to divine or immortal status is marked by flying to heaven. The Hebrew prophet Elijah ascends in a fiery chariot, Mohammad rides Buraq, Jesus is resurrected from the dead. At about the same time that Pei Ti was elected as chief minister to the gods, a bit over five thousand years ago, the legendary Chinese emperor Huang Ti became immortal and ascended to heaven on a dragon, or perhaps on a creature with the body of a horse and the wings of a dragon. This creature was strong enough to carry Huang's wives and ministers as well. Some officials of lower rank tried to come along by grabbing hairs of the dragon's beard, but the hairs did not hold and the hangers-on fell to the ground.

Huang Ti had earned his promotion by introducing a large number of useful artifacts and teaching his people new skills and concepts: writing, coinage, the bow and arrow, wooden houses, boats, and governmental institutions. Silkworm culture, the spinning of silk thread, and the weaving of silk textiles are credited to his wife or wives, who also were carried to immortality in heaven. It is not specified what his ministers did to deserve being taken along, but presumably they gained merit by helping to establish good government.

Much more recently, in the second century c.e., Chinese legend tells of another pious man, Tung Yung, who was rewarded by "The Spinning Damsel" (a goddess) with two sons. One of the sons had fleshy wings in his armpits. When this son was full grown, he unfolded his wings and carried his father up to heaven to "rejoin" his mother.

Flight can be given as a gift from the gods to those deemed worthy, without being accompanied by the gift of immortality. The gift may be a one-time event, or more long-lasting. Evil spirits may also confer the power of flight to their devotees; the familiar image of witches riding broomsticks is just one example. The divine association of kings is often signified by their ability to fly, or to harness the denizens of the air; saints, sages, prophets, shamans, and yogins[18] demonstrate their spiritual powers by traveling through the air.

There is nevertheless often some ambiguity in particular cases, as to whether the gift of flight is of divine or demonic origin or simply the result of intense study and arcane natural knowledge. When misunderstandings occur, the flier may be physically attacked or subject to ordeals or religio-judicial trials.

In the Christian tradition, saintly flight is associated with chastity, while flying witches and warlocks include perverse sexuality in their rituals. Beyond the phallic symbolism of the broomstick, the "Witches' Sabbath" is said to have included orgiastic abandon, bestiality, and sexual congress with the Devil himself, for both men and women.

The claim that the ability to fly had been gained by purely secular means was viewed with deep suspicion well into the nineteenth century.

Scientific American reported in 1850 that a woman who had ascended in a balloon from Lisbon and attempted to land in a rural area was greeted as a demon: some villagers fled, others fell to their knees in prayer, yet others gathered weapons and offered defiance to the devil.[19]

Christianity offers many examples of flight as a sign of divine favor. Saint Thomas Aquinas is said to have hovered three feet in the air during his ecstatic devotions before the crucifix at the church of Saint Dominic in Naples. Fasting, praying, and purging oneself of gross materiality were the most common avenues to mystical flight. Saint Margaret of Hungary, Saint Bernard, and Saint Catherine of Siena are among those whose religious zeal earned them the power of levitation.

Franciscan monk Saint Joseph of Copertino (not to be confused with the father of Jesus) earned his privilege in another way. He was physically and mentally handicapped, and had a sweetly childlike disposition. His birdlike flight seems to have been the result of a spiritual simplicity and delight in praising God. He flew so many times—more than a hundred flights and levitations are attributed to him—he earned the name "aviator saint."[20] One Christmas Eve at Copertino, Joseph "first began to dance about as a result of his great joy, and then . . . flew like a bird through the air from the middle of the church to the top of the high altar . . . where he calmly remained . . . for about a quarter of an hour without knocking over any of the lighted candles . . . and without setting alight any part of his vestments. The shepherds [playing flutes and pipes before the altar] were astonished beyond measure."[21] On another occasion, having flown up to a tree branch in his ecstasy, he was unable to get down after he recovered. The saint who flew and perched in a tree like a bird had to be rescued like a cat, with a ladder.[22]

EAST AND WEST, OLD AND NEW

We long for union, or at least communication, with our deities. Lacking any physical means to this end, we turn to symbolic ones. Sex, religion, flying, dragons, horses, birds, and bats are parts of a symbolic web tying us to heaven. To paraphrase an axiom from mathematics, "things connected to the same thing are connected to each other." The particular details may vary with place, culture, or religion, but the elements are universal.

CHAPTER 2

ARTIFICIAL WINGS
AND THE
IMITATION OF GOD

W hat would it mean, to domesticate the air? Physical flight, freedom to move about in the heavens, is just one part of it. Mastery must include the spiritual, emotional, and symbolic aspects of the air as well. Thus, a human's ability to fly can be taken as a sign of other masteries: perhaps the result of deep study, of extreme piety, or of black magic. Conversely, when the spinners of legend wish to attribute great power or honor to their subjects, we hear tales of flying.

Western cultures have used flight as a metaphor for romantic and spiritual love through symbol and myth. The construction of artificial wings by mythological tinkerers and smiths (such as Daedalus and Wayland) have provided cautionary tales consistent with the theology of the ambient culture. These myths are teaching-stories, conveying richly woven examples of behavior and its consequences.

Freedom to move through the air also signifies other freedoms: to move in three dimensions; to move with speed unhindered by connection to the earth; to escape from captivity; and in a metaphorical sense to move from corporeal physicality to bodiless spirituality. We break our bonds, and speak of letting our imagination fly free, of flights of fancy, of being "free as a bird."

As flying represents the ultimate in freedom, a caged bird is the ultimate symbol of captivity. In the words of the poet William Blake,

> *A Robin Red Breast in a Cage*
> *Puts all heaven in a Rage.*[1]

The images used by poets are not arbitrary. They speak to us and are filled with meaning precisely because they express so well our own thoughts.

MYTH AND SYMBOLISM

The word "myth" is seriously misused in popular speech. We look at simplistic versions of ancient stories, unaware of the deeper meanings they held for the people who believed them, and we scoff that such things could never have happened. We use distorted and superficial summaries to prove to ourselves that we are superior to such superstitious, primitive folk. If our own religions were subjected to such treatment, they would look little better.

Americans tell stories which embody our secular myths: Washington and the cherry tree, the Pilgrims and religious freedom, Abraham Lincoln and the log cabin, the rags-to-riches stories of Thomas Edison and Henry Ford. "If they aren't true, they ought to be." Our secular myths are so deeply embedded in our thoughts that we do not recognize them as such, even when reality fails to measure up. Democracy, freedom, honest government, even-handed justice, equal economic opportunity— these concepts are embodied in myths which guide our aspirations and benchmarks against which we measure events and behavior.

Far from being simple fiction or easily dismissed pieces of folklore, myths are serious attempts to symbolize complex abstract and spiritual values. Ambiguity is often at their core, reflecting the fact that life cannot usually be represented in stark black-and-white clear-cut terms. Mircea Eliade, eminent historian of religion, commented, "one characteristic which is specific to a symbol [is] its *multivalence,* which is to say the multiplicity of meanings which it expresses simultaneously. This is why it is sometimes so difficult to explain a symbol, to exhaust its significations; it refers to a plurality of context and it is valuable on a number of levels."[2] Myths are symbols in narrative form. If we read only the literal story, we have missed the point.

WINGS AND ARROWS OF THE SPIRIT

The flight of arrows across sexually charged space has long been a symbol of both desire and physical union. Eros shoots piercing arrows into those he would afflict. The correspondence is explicit in a painting by Lucas Cranach the Elder, of a grumpy toddler *Amor* (Love) holding his arrow close to his body in an unmistakable erect position.[3]

For Christians, Love's arrow gained another meaning. Christianity, in contrast to Greek religion, sought to separate spiritual from carnal love. For ordinary folk, the sheer jump to physical celibacy was too difficult, so physical love was gradually sublimated into the spiritual. Physical love was seen as a metaphor for the spiritual quest, and desire was deflected from human beings to God himself. Gian Lorenzo Bernini's sculpture of *Saint Theresa and the Angel,* in which the (smugly?) smiling youthful male angel stands holding an arrow ready to plunge into a fainting, ecstatic Theresa, illustrates this beautifully.[4]

Poetic literature from the Middle Ages and the Renaissance resounds with a complex metaphor: Love gives us wings, we make the choice between flying to earthly or spiritual love. In an agonized series of poems written after the death of Laura, his beloved-from-afar, Petrarch sees himself scolded by Amor. Amor claims that Petrarch always had wings but failed to use them properly; if he had done so, he would have ascended to Heaven to lie beside Laura in pure, chaste bliss. Flight is "an expression of both sexual and spiritual longing."[5] Dante's *Divine Comedy* teaches a parallel lesson: Beatrice, symbol of spiritual love, teaches Dante to use his wings for upward, spiritual flight rather than base descent into earthly lust.[6]

In most societies, the sacred and secular are not separated; all of one's life is subject to religious values and regulations. In that sense, as Eliade points out, "all symbolism begins as religious symbolism."[7] Ananda Coomaraswamy extends that concept when he insists that art which conveys no meaning is literally "in-significant" and not worthy of the name.[8]

The capacity for abstract thought, religious or secular, depends on symbols. How else to represent the intangible and unseen?

The myths embodying and teaching abstract concepts are older than the words to name those concepts. Eliade offers as an example, "The words expressing the concepts of *transcendence* and *freedom* [were defined] relatively late in the history of philosophy" yet our ancient systems of myth and religion deal intimately with these fundamental issues. In his words: "many symbols and myths relating to 'magical flight' and celestial ascent are used to signify these spiritual experiences [transcendence and freedom]"[9] and " . . . the desire for absolute freedom ranks among the essential longings of man, whatever his cultural period and his form of social organization."[10] This desire is a fundamental part of what makes us human in the first place, and we use the idea of flying—symbolized by wings—to express our longing.

Eliade observes that symbols and myths retain their power long after the words have been found, and long after the cultures which hold them dear can no longer be called "primitive." In his words, ". . . in folk-lore, in the history of religions and in mysticism; . . . the imagery in question [flight and ascension] was always that of transcendence and freedom . . . upon the different but interconnected planes of the oneiric, of active imagination, of mythological creation and folk-lore, of ritual and of metaphysical speculation, and, finally, upon the plane of ecstatic experience, the symbolism of ascension always refers to . . . 'liberty of movement', freedom . . . "[11]

Wings still carry us to spiritual and emotional heights.

FLYING HIGH

The sense of freedom is central to thoughts of flying: physical, spiritual, or intellectual freedom may be sought in the skies. Myths involving flight reflect this, whether they speak of simple physical escape, the ability to fly as a sign of spiritual advance, or the transformation of the soul into a bird.[12]

When we look around at flying-tales, we are immediately overwhelmed by their abundance and variety. The sheer ingenuity of the human imagination is staggering. How can these tales be presented without washing the reader away in the flood? All too often we are given mere flat catalogs of beliefs and stories, without any indication of their significance or symbolic context for the cultures in which they arose. This takes the form of "All cultures have the same myths, with minor differences" or "The Egyptians believed this, the Chinese believed that, the Indians something else."

Classifications which sort by such superficial features as "with or without wings" or "riding on animals or carried in a vehicle" necessarily miss the point. To lump together, for example, the ascent to heaven of the Chinese emperor Huang-Ti[13] aboard a dragon with that of Jesus after the Crucifixion, and simply classify them both as "mystical" with the note that such ascents are associated with spirituality and the achievement of immortality, is to lose most of their significance.[14] The differences carry important messages.

Even those accounts which trace a story from one geographical location to another, detailing the adaptations made along the way but giving no interpretation of why the changes were made, leave out the truly important aspects of the journey.

Unfortunately, cataloging or simple description is the predominant mode of reporting in comparative accounts. It mirrors the mindsets of the people doing the reporting. In some instances, the classifiers truly believe all religions (or "belief systems") to be equivalent and are intent on showing similarities. In other cases, the flatness reflects an attempt to be "scientific" and "nonjudgemental," to avoid privileging one belief system over another. Other reasons for the lack of context may be ethnocentrism or perhaps a simple denial that these stories or beliefs could have any function beyond mere entertaining folktale or superstition. Indeed, the myths are usually described in such simplistic terms that it is all too easy to believe "that's all there is."

European and American scholars, acknowledging our cultural debts to Mediterranean and Near Eastern sources, have mostly focused on mythologies which we believe have directly contributed to our own patterns of thought. As a result, there is abundant interpretative material about some mythologies available for those who read European languages; for many others, including most of the African, Asian, and Oceanic cultures, such studies remain to be written.

Ignorant as we are, perhaps the superficial categories are the best we can do for the present. They do have the virtue of showing that the same full range of potential mechanisms for flight has occurred to societies around the world. No single culture has a monopoly on spiritual, technical, or mechanical imagination. Here you will find just a sampling of this variety.

The book you hold is as guilty as the rest in not providing context for non-Western myth. The best I can hope for is that you will realize what is missing, and not dismiss the potent mythologies of alien cultures with "Oh, how strange" or "Oh, how quaint," or worst yet, "Oh, how primitive." We will take an in-depth look at some familiar myths and literary works as examples of the richness which can be hidden in them. I would like to persuade you that similar richness must lie within other myths we know less intimately.

The myth of Daedalus and his son Icarus is perhaps the most familiar of the myths about flying. In its simplest form, the myth reminds humans of their folly in trying to reach the abode of divinity by using mundane means. Icarus flies too near the heavens, the wax holding the feathers to his wings melts from the heat of the sun, and he plunges to his death before his father's horrified eyes. When we look more closely, however, we see multiple meanings in the story.[15]

The word "Daedalus" literally means "skilled artificer" in Greek, and the mythical character represents all tinkerers and inventors.[16] Sometimes Daedalus is portrayed as a human, sometimes as a demigod. In this particular instance Daedalus had been commissioned to design and create a maze in which Minos, King of Crete, could hide the Minotaur, the half-bull, half-human offspring of his wife's infidelity. A further complication is the fact that the bull had been a gift from Poseidon, god of the sea, intended as a sacrifice. When Minos failed to sacrifice the bull, Poseidon caused Minos's wife to lust after it. Thus, the very existence of the Minotaur is a result of the king's defiance of the gods.

To feed the Minotaur, Minos demands that young men and women be sent as tribute from Athens. Daedalus confides the secret of the maze to the king's daughter, and she helps the young Athenians escape. As punishment, the king imprisons Daedalus and Icarus, who then escape via Daedalus's further ingenuity. Artificial wings are to be their vehicle to freedom, but Icarus flies too near the sun.

Clearly, one important element of this narrative is the interplay of technology with human values both admirable and ignoble. Another important element is *hubris,* the arrogance of humans who wish to join, defy, or compete with the gods. Related to *hubris* is the question of control or mastery, of self-discipline and skill.

Daedalus the human engineer and designer is also a metaphorical reflection of Hephaestus, the Greek god of blacksmithing and mechanical invention (the Romans called their smith-god Vulcan). In some stories, Daedalus is credited with being the father of sculpture, particularly sculpture which imitates life; the arms, legs, and eyes of his statues are alleged to move. Hephaestus himself is also supposed to have crafted women automata (robots) of gold to serve him. In another myth, sculpture is said to have sprung from the "seed" of Hephaestus, spilled on the ground after Athena (goddess of wisdom) defended herself vigorously against his attempt at rape. An alternate version has Hephaestus and Athena collaborating willingly in the creation of sculpture.

A common element in these origin-myths is the association of sculpture with both intellect and artifice, as well as with the incomplete or inadequate creation of biological life. Daedalus, as the human mirror of the divine Hephaestus, ties heaven and earth together. The association of Daedalus the engineer with flight, with sculpture, with questions of morality are all part of the multiple layers of meaning incorporated within the mythic structure as a whole.

There are many versions of each myth, from different geographic areas and different times. Each version serves the purposes of the folks who use it, and each group shapes and reshapes the myth to respond to their own concerns. We, too, select from the story-buffet, preferring myths that speak to our own longings. We retell the story that has Daedalus and Icarus flying with artificial wings from Crete, and ignore the version in which "wings" are simply a poetic metaphor for the sails on a ship.[17]

The mythic association between flying and the creative imagination that we find in the Daedalus and Icarus story is strengthened by the story of the winged horse Pegasus. With a stroke of his hoof Pegasus brings forth the Hippocrene spring, whose waters are a source of poetic inspiration. The deeper and darker roots of creativity are suggested by Pegasus's own origin; he arose from the blood of the snake-haired Gorgon, Medusa, after she had been beheaded by Perseus.

The story of Bellerophon, prince of Corinth, and his relationship to Pegasus brings us full circle back to the issue of *hubris*, of the dangers of arrogantly "flying too high." With the aid of Athena, Bellerophon had tamed Pegasus and used him in the performance of heroic adventures. One such adventure was the slaying of the Chimera, a fire-breathing monster that had the head of a lion, the body of a she-goat, and the tail of a dragon. When Bellerophon in his pride tried to ride Pegasus to the top of Olympus, to join the gods, Pegasus threw him off and Bellerophon thereafter wandered disconsolately about, pursued by misfortunes. Pegasus was given a permanent place on Olympus bringing Zeus's thunderbolts to him.

Nathaniel Hawthorne retold the story of Bellerophon and Pegasus for children, including among his characters a shy and delicate child who believed in Pegasus when everyone else, including Bellerophon, had given up hope of ever seeing the winged horse. Hawthorne ended his tale with the words "But in after years that child took higher flights upon the aerial steed than ever did Bellerophon, and achieved more honorable deeds than his friend's victory over the Chimaera. For, gentle and tender as he was, he grew to be a mighty poet!" [Exclamation mark in original.][18] We can see multivalence here: the "flight" of Pegasus carried Bellerophon to adventure and heroic deeds; carried the young boy's imagination to heights of poetry; carried the instruments of the chief god's primary function.

Another Greek flight-myth focusing on the danger of *hubris* is the story of Phaëthon. A demigod, son of the sun god Helios and the nymph Clymene, Phaëthon demanded as proof of his noble birth that he be allowed to drive the sun-chariot across the sky one day. It is easy to imagine the young man, proud of his parentage, and the mocking taunts of his skeptical companions. We have all been through this, we all know the cruelty of childhood and adolescence. We can almost hear the conversation between Phaëthon and his father. Helios reluctantly granted permission (every parent knows the feeling!), but Phaëthon was unable to control the spirited horses which drew the chariot. He approached too near the earth, scorching fertile land into desert; then too near the heavens. Zeus felt compelled to slay the young man in order to save the world from destruction.

We should be careful to differentiate between simple "imitation" of the gods, which seems to be permissible in Greek thought, and the overweening pride which leads to *hubris*. It is not Daedalus himself who is punished, but Icarus. Similarly, Phaëthon and Bellerophon are tolerated and even encouraged, until they overstep themselves.

Another, more subtle subtext of these flight myths is the issue of responsibility and control. Icarus and Phaëthon are too immature, too lacking in self-control to be entrusted with dangerous technology. Neither one of them recognizes or acknowledges his limitations, a fatal flaw. It is not the technology itself, but human misuse of it, which leads to disaster.

PLAYING GOD

In sharp contrast is a story from India about a weaver who loves a princess. His friend, a carpenter, makes a wooden airship in the form of

*Garuda statue in Puri-Ubud, Ubud, Bali. The intricate detail is
typical of Balinese woodcarving. In various Hindu traditions, representations
of Garuda vary widely, from bird-headed human to almost
completely bird-like creature.*

Courtesy Sharon Millman

Garuda, the bird on which the god Vishnu rides. The weaver dresses to impersonate Vishnu and flies on the Garuda-airship to the princess's rooms on the seventh story of the palace. The seduction is complete; who could resist such a courtship, and so noble a lover? The princess believes herself the consort of a god, and her father the king is delighted to be allied with Vishnu. Thinking that his daughter's liaison gives him special privileges, the king becomes arrogant toward the neighboring kingdoms. They resent this, and perhaps not fully convinced of the Vishnu alliance, rise in armed resistance. The king calls upon the pseudo-Vishnu, who feels doomed one way or the other; surely the king would execute him if the deception became known! The young weaver decides to maintain his disguise and go down fighting. He helplessly and hope-lessly takes to the air on the mechanical Garuda with a bow and arrow. The real god Vishnu, fearing that a defeat of the impersonator will re-duce his own credibility, enters the weaver's body and achieves victory. Afterwards, the weaver confesses. He is not punished either by Vishnu or by the king. Rather, the king honors and rewards him, giving him the princess in marriage and endowing him with a large estate.[19]

Since all of these stories have rich symbolic meanings, as they are retold the narrators often make "improvements" to suit the customs and values of their audiences. Even today, classic stories are retold in mod-ern terms; producers give us Shakespearean plays set in more recent periods to help us see that the meanings of the stories are timeless, and Shakespeare himself mined still older works. Eugene O'Neill reset the ancient Greek tragedy of Electra in the American Civil War, as *Mourn-ing Becomes Electra.*

Changed motifs and emphasis can be clearly seen in film versions of *Frankenstein.* In Mary Shelley's 1818 book, the monster begins as a gentle, benign creature who learns hatred only when he is cruelly mistreated by those who can see his ugliness. (A blind old man treats him kindly.) The monster becomes murderous only after Victor Frankenstein, in a be-lated fit of remorse at his previous act of creation, destroys the female he had promised to create as a trade for the monster's promise to retreat from all contact with humans. Shelley's emphasis is on innocence be-trayed, and on the consequences of many varieties of human behavior. Her book was strongly influenced by scientific investigations of electric-ity in the half-century before she wrote; Franklin's kite had shown that heaven's lightning was the same stuff that could be produced by rub-bing fur or amber, and Luigi Galvani's twitching frog legs made a direct link between electricity and life.

Heaven's lightning brought to earth, and shown to be an animating life force; could scientific analysis of the soul be far behind? All this seemed to promise exciting new ways for humans to "play God," with all the philosophical and moral choices that entailed.

In film versions, the monster is usually presented as being vicious from the beginning, an object lesson in the evils associated with the *hubris* and arrogance of imitating God in the creation of life. The films give the handsome young Dr. Frankenstein a grotesque assistant not present in the original book; the assistant's appearance and repulsive personality are intended to represent the twisted motives and inevitable doom of Frankenstein's experiments. These changes in the storyline are not simply adaptations to the film medium, they are fundamental alterations in the meaning of the story itself. "Playing God" is no longer a morally neutral activity, to be shaped for good or ill; it is an absolute evil with no shades of possible human benefit, no further moral choices to be made.

The Greek myth of Zeus in the form of an eagle kidnapping the handsome young prince Ganymede may have been the model for a popular Buddhist tale, the subject of many paintings and sculptures all along the trade route called the Silk Road, which reached deep into China.[20] Zeus was notorious for infidelity to his wife Hera, but this is one instance in which he brought his human lover home with him. Ganymede became cup-bearer to the gods of Olympus, displacing Zeus's own daughter Hebe.

In the Buddhist version, a bodhisattva takes the form of a Garuda in order to abduct a married woman with whom he has fallen in love. I wonder what prompted the Buddhist storyteller to make these particular substitutions: instead of a god, he gives us a human destined for enlightenment; instead of an eagle, the new version has a supernatural bird taken from the Hindu tradition; and instead of a handsome young prince, a married woman! The homoerotic elements in the Ganymede story were acceptable to Greek society; stealing a woman already married is generally frowned upon in all cases. What are the new symbolic associations of the revised story? We may find a clue by looking more closely at the Garuda element.

Imitation of Garuda occurs frequently. In one tale, the wife of a rich man's son was kidnapped by a powerful king. Her husband enlisted five young friends to help reclaim her. One friend is the son of a rich man, one of a physician, one of a painter, one of a mathematician (!), one of a carpenter and one of a smith. The carpenter's son constructed a mechanical Garuda, and the painter's son decorated it to resemble a live bird. Their scheme is successful; the rich man's son reclaims his bride and flies off with her, back to his companions.

In a Sanskrit version of the story, there are only three young men rather than six—one brave, one possessed of vast knowledge, and one proficient in magic. All three are courting a Brahmin's daughter. She is kidnapped by an ogre, and the mechanical Garuda is used in her rescue. Neither of these versions involves any hint of disapproval for arrogance or presumption in imitating divine attributes.[21]

Look again at these tales, seemingly so simple. What a different color and texture they acquire when one realizes that the bird Garuda symbolizes the ascent from the material plane to the spiritual. Suddenly, the young men become archetypes and symbols themselves, representing known social groups or values, and the woman who is kidnapped and rescued (or the princess who is wooed and won) seems to represent their souls. The kidnapper may represent the nagas, serpents who are Garuda's traditional enemies; or he may represent "lesser gods" who distract worshippers from Vishnu. While the Bhagavad Gita proclaims that the ability to worship at all is a gift from Vishnu even when directed toward the lesser gods, Vishnu declares "Mine come unto me;" the truly faithful revere Vishnu alone. Those who worship the lesser gods "pass with those they worship," fading away as all material things must do.[22] Those who effectively imitate Vishnu reap great spiritual rewards.

"Riding Garuda" implies a journey toward God. The effectiveness of the mechanical Garuda further teaches that we are capable of constructing our own vehicle to Heaven. Yet it is not enough merely to construct the vehicle, we must also use it wisely, or the rescue is incomplete. And if a soul is diverted from its true goal by a false Garuda, into the service of an otherwise admirable personage (even a bodhisattva) who is yet not fully enlightened, that too is a loss of potential. Suddenly, what appeared to be a simple adventure tale is revealed as a profound theological statement.

Indian tales also mention other forms of air travel, in mechanical airships attributed to Greek manufacture, the secrets of which were forbidden to non-Greeks. The Greeks had a high reputation in India for mechanical ingenuity, and it is possible that this fame was exaggerated to include yet more marvelous contraptions than had actually been made. Certainly, there are no Greek accounts of such airships in their own land.

If we look for mythic elements in these Indian tales of Greek airships, we find considerations of oath-breaking, of loyalty, of marital fidelity, and of priorities. When Indian rulers demand to know the secrets of airship manufacture, all these issues arise for the men who hold this knowledge. In each case, the artisan refuses to share the secret, though his livelihood, his life, or his spouse be forfeit. We may not learn much about the real Greeks from these myths, but we have no doubt about the ideals held by the Indians.

In Norse mythology, as with Indian tales, there is also no issue of *hubris*. Mortal men who die valiantly in combat are brought up to Valhalla, the abode of the gods, by the warrior female Valkyries, there to feast and make ready for the final combat between the gods and their adversaries. There is a clever smith in the Norse tales, Volund (also called Wayland or Wieland), who is imprisoned and crippled by a greedy, angry king. Volund crafts artificial wings and escapes; there is no divine punishment for imitating the gods. Volund does have revenge, unlike Daedalus; before escaping, he rapes (and impregnates) his captor's daughter and slaughters her brothers, making their skulls into jeweled cups for the king's table.

Volund's leg tendons had been cut by the king who imprisons him; both Hephaestus and Vulcan, smith-gods of Greece and Rome, were lame. The widespread mythic image of the crippled smith may hint at a darker truth; perhaps the earthly smiths or artificers were so important to their towns or villages that they were deliberately maimed to prevent escape, as a bird's wings might be clipped. The practice may then have become ritualized and legitimated by the myths. An alternative interpretation offers the notion that a cripple may still be useful to his society although he cannot hunt or farm. Which is "true"? For moderns, the second lesson is more acceptable no matter what the original might have meant. The very ambiguity of myth allows it to be instructive across the ages and across cultures.

The Finnish smith deity, Ilmarinen, is not crippled, although he seldom receives the rewards promised for his efforts. His name derives from the Finnish word "ilma" for air or wind, and he is sometimes cast as a thunder god or wind god as well as a smith. Perhaps, as some scholars insist, the connection lies in the blast of air from the smith's bellows as he forges; only one more step of the imagination takes us from the stormy wind and the blast of the smith's bellows to the breath of life. Ilmarinen too, like Daedalus and Hephaestus, fashions a woman from metal, but she remains cold and lifeless. Were the Finns wiser, in maintaining a sharp distinction between the organic and the artificial?

We can see the limits of the smith's control over his creations in the story of Ilmarinen's wooing, rune 19 of the epic Kalevala. Ilmarinen wishes to marry "the Fairy Maiden of the Rainbow, of Night and Dawn the Daughter." She welcomes him, as he has already forged a magical treasure called the Sampo as a wonderful gift for her. When Ilmarinen comes to claim her, however, her mother, Louhi, sets Ilmarinen three "impossible" tasks to be done.

Ilmarinen asks his intended bride for advice on how to accomplish each in turn. The first task is to plow a field of vipers "without touching beam nor handles;" he forges a magic plowshare and harnesses a horse of fire. The second is to muzzle a certain wild bear belonging to Tuoni, god of death; he forges a steel muzzle. The third and most difficult task is to catch "the monster-pike" in Manala, the Death-land.

This third task is qualitatively different from the first two. It is the only one for which Ilmarinen creates a free agent, and that free agent has wings.

> *Then the suitor, Ilmarinen,*
> *The eternal artist-forgeman,*
> *In the furnace forged an eagle*
> *From the fire of ancient wisdom;*
> *For this giant bird of magic*
> *Forged he talons out of iron,*
> *And his beak of steel and copper;*
> *Seats himself upon the eagle,*
> *On his back between the wing-bones,*
> *Thus addresses he his creature,*
> *Gives the bird of fire, this order:*
> *"Mighty eagle, bird of beauty,*
> *Fly thou whither I direct thee,*
> *To Tuoni's coal-black river,*
> *To the blue deeps of the Death-stream,*
> *Seize the mighty fish of Mana,*
> *Catch for me this water-monster."*

Only in this third task does Ilmarinen encounter active opposition, and he falls into mortal danger; the magic artificial eagle rescues him, captures the monster pike (on the third try) and eats most of it, leaving only the head for Ilmarinen. Ilmarinen has issued orders, but the details are left to the bird's interpretation, and it goes well beyond the simple instructions when it eats the "mighty fish of Mana."

Ilmarinen scolds him for spoiling the evidence, whereupon

> *. . . the bird of metal talons*
> *Hastened onward, soaring upward,*
> *Rising higher into ether,*
> *Rising, flying, soaring, sailing,*
> *To the borders of the long-clouds,*
> *Made the vault of ether tremble,*
> *Split apart the dome of heaven,*
> *Broke the colored bow of Ukko,*
> *Tore the Moon-horns from their sockets,*
> *Disappeared beyond the Sun-land,*
> *To the home of the triumphant.*[23]

The bio-technological construction is clearly an independent entity here; even the god-hero Ilmarinen's powerful magic cannot control it. The mighty bird shakes and splits the heavens, breaks the rainbow, displaces the Moon, and disappears. Think about that for a moment: What are the implications for the gods' other free-agent creations, the humans? What does it mean that "the home of the triumphant" is "beyond the Sun-land"? Defiance of the gods is quite a different case here than it was in Greek mythology.

Each myth—Daedalus and Icarus, Helios and Phaëthon, Pegasus, Ilmarinen, Volund, Garuda, and all the rest—embodies and teaches the deep truths and values of the societies they represent. Each displays some relationship between the gods, the heavens, and humankind. These truths are ambiguous, full of nuances and shades of meaning, rather than being expressible in sharply drawn sound bites. The listener or reader is first drawn in by the drama of the story itself, and only later comes to realize the lessons it teaches.

KINGS AND WINGS

Legendary kings, supreme rulers, surely had—or sought—dominion over the sky, through wisdom or brute force. From Etana in Sumer to Solomon in Israel, from Alexander the Great in Macedonia to Kai-Kawus in Persia, and from Bladud in Britain to Shun in China, there echo tales of aerial exploits. Flying seems as necessary and natural to heroic kings as their crowns.

Myth and legend often shade into one another. Such a tale is that of Etana's journey to heaven. It begins with a primeval conflict between "the" eagle and "the" serpent, traditional enemies. In the Sumerian myth, interestingly enough, the eagle is the offender and the serpent an innocent victim. After the eagle eats the serpent's children in violation of solemn oaths he and the serpent had sworn to each other, Shamash the sun-god advises the serpent how to trap him. The eagle disregards his own son's warnings and is crippled by the serpent and cast into a pit to die. Etana, the first recorded king of Sumer, rescues the eagle (with Shamash's advice) and earns his permanent gratitude. When Etana's wife is suffering in childbirth, the eagle offers to carry Etana up to heaven to obtain medicinal herbs from the gods. Etana clings to the eagle, "breast to breast . . . his hands on the quills of his wings." Why Etana trusts the oath-breaking eagle is not explained.

As they rise toward the heaven of Ishtar the mother-goddess, the eagle bids Etana "look down at the earth, and see how it is." Each time Etana looks, there seems to be less dry land and more water, until "the earth is submerged, and all is ocean." Etana is overcome by the sight: "I see how the earth has vanished. . . . My friend, I wish not to ascend to heaven. Halt, I pray thee, that I may return home to the earth."[24] It is not the air or the height that daunts Etana in the end, it is homesickness for dry land.

What a strange preview of the Earth's actual appearance from space, the "big blue marble," mostly water! It is an even stranger concept when you look at a map of Mesopotamia (in modern Iraq). Not even from the top of the highest local mountains would you get the impression that the seas surround the land. Where might the Sumerians have migrated from, that the sea so dominated their thoughts? Etana was no sailor, but he shared the sailors' ancient fears.

Ancient Hebrew and Arabic legends demonstrate King Solomon's wisdom, and favor in God's eyes, by recounting his fluency in all animal languages and his ability to command the animal kings. Among them is Ziz, king of the birds, who swiftly obeys all Solomon's instructions and carries him wherever he wishes to go (an echo of godlike power and dignity). Ziz also acts as a vassal to Solomon, sending his own subjects on missions to serve Solomon's desires. Is something lost, that might be seen by the sharp-eyed inhabitants of the air? Ziz will make sure that the birds do their best to find it. Solomon domesticates the air by exerting sovereignty over the birds.

Alexander the Great of Macedonia, he who smote through the Gordian knot and who after years of stunning military success wailed that there were no more worlds to conquer, had a clever idea. He fastened spears to each of the four corners of his chariot, and harnessed eagles in such a way that they could almost but not quite reach the raw meat atop each spear. Thus as they tried to eat, they would lift up his chariot and he would assault heaven itself. Not surprisingly, there are conflicting reports of the outcome.

The great Persian poet Firdausi tells a similar story about Kai-Kawus, an early shah, adding the elegant touch of a glass of wine in the shah's hand as he traveled upwards. Alas, the eagles could not reach the heavens, but became faint and had to return to earth.[25] Firdausi wrote at the turn of the eleventh century c.e., and does not pretend to know the truth:

> He bound a lamb's leg from every spear-head
> Brought four strong eagles, tied them to the throne,
> And took his seat, a cup of wine before him.
> The swift-winged eagles, ravenous for food,
> Strove lustily to reach the flesh, and raising
> The throne above earth's surface bore it
>   cloudward.
> Kawus, as I have heard, essayed the sky
> To outsoar angels, but another tale
> Is that he rose in this way to assail
> The heaven itself with his artillery.
> The legend hath its other versions too;
> None but the All-wise wotteth which is true.
> Long flew the eagles, but they stopped at last,
> Like other slaves of greed. They sulked exhausted,
> They dropped their sweating wings and brought
>   the Shah,
> His spears and throne down from the clouds to
>   earth. . . .
> Instead of sitting on his throne in might
> His business then was penitence and travail.
> He tarried in the wood in shame and grief,
> Imploring from Almighty God relief.

No divine punishment for hubris here, but personal disgrace and disappointment. Humans cannot rise to heaven by their own devices.

Long before King Arthur, Britons were ruled by King Bladud, whose legends are particularly hard to untangle. The many versions vary wildly in their details. Bladud is credited with founding the city of Bath, and dedicating the medicinal springs to Minerva, but that is beside the point for us. Bladud may be descended from Bryttys (or Brutus), after whom the British might be named. Bryttys is said to have sailed to Britain from Greece sometime in the twelfth century B.C.E., stopping at an island where priests of Diana regularly jumped off a tower as part of her worship, hoping that their "wings" would work. (Ovid, writing at the beginning of the Christian era, describes the island and the rituals, but somehow fails to mention Bryttys.) Or maybe the priests threw suspected thieves off the tower, and those who were saved by their billowing clothing from death on the rocks were declared innocent. Or maybe the tower was dedicated to Apollo. And maybe Bladud himself studied magic, prepared wings for himself, and in 852 B.C.E. jumped off Apollo's tower in Trinovant (now London), his death ending his twenty-year reign. It is pretty certain that Bryttys and Bladud were something special, and so surely they must have made some attempt to fly—or so the legend-spinner's reasoning goes. Apollo being the most intellectual of the gods, it is only fitting that Bladud should have come to a tragic end by crashing into Apollo's temple.[26]

Early in China's recorded history, we find Shun, whose tradition places him in the years 2258 to 2208 B.C.E. Shun's mother died when Shun was young, and his father remarried. Unlike the stereotypical European tales of a wicked stepmother and weak-willed father, however, it was Shun's father himself who took a dislike to the son of his first wife. The father hatched several plots against Shun, but Shun miraculously escaped each one, with his filial piety and exemplary behavior undiminished. Finally Shun's virtue brought him to the attention of the Emperor, Yao, who sent his two daughters to teach Shun "the art of flying like a bird."

An ancient Chinese record recounts: "Shun's parents . . . made him plaster a granary and [they] set fire to it . . . Shun donned the workclothes of a bird, and flying made his escape." Another version may be more plausible to moderns: "Ku Sou bade his son Shun build a granary and ascend it, and thereupon set the structure on fire. Shun, who stood on top of the tower, spread out two large reed hats which he used as a parachute in making his descent, and landed on the ground unscathed." When their plot failed, Shun's parents tried another, sending him down into a deep well and heaping stones on it. "Shun donned the work-clothes of a dragon and crawled out of the well." Shun's skills and virtue paid off: he married the emperor's daughters, and eventually became emperor himself.[27]

These legends serve mythic functions, as examples of virtuous behavior or extraordinary powers that give shape and meaning to the national personality. If a useful myth is not handy, we are likely to make one up, as parson Weems invented the story of George Washington and the cherry tree. The ability to fly, or to command the inhabitants of the air, is a quality almost universally attributed to the greatest heroes.

MAGES AND SAGES

The borderlines between magic, religion, and technology are not always easy to find. It boils down to the question, "Who's in charge here?" Do we compel spirits to obedience through magic, do we apply knowledge of natural phenomena to achieve our goals, or are affectionate deities inclined to give us what we ask for when we go through the proper polite forms? Magic and technology seek mastery, religion offers possibilities. The boundary between magic and religion is especially blurry, since priests from time immemorial have offered wonders on demand as evidence of their divine connections and favor.

One powerful magic principle is that of similarity. Voodoo dolls, for instance, gain their power from their likeness to their subject. The heart-shaped leaves of the plant *digitalis purpurea* were used for heart ailments from medieval times and perhaps earlier. Does the fact that we moderns use digitalis for heart ailments prove that the principle of similarity is scientifically correct? No, because the principle does not hold up when applied to some other cases. Liverwort, for example, resembles the liver but it has no medical effectiveness at all.

Outward appearance is just one part of similarity; symbolic connections are even more important.

Symbol often becomes so closely associated with the thing symbolized that the two seem synonymous. The horse *is* the wind, and the wind *is* a horse; the bird *is* the soul, the Holy Spirit *is* the dove. Not so long ago, as human history runs, it was widely believed that names had some intimate correspondence with the thing named. Ananda Coomaraswamy points out that all art is symbolic, and insists that art and theology are fundamentally the same thing. When we manipulate the symbol, we manipulate the thing—or the deity—it is connected to.[28]

Belief in the power and reality of symbols is still deeply embedded in our psyche. We behave toward the symbol as we would behave toward that which it represents. Pictorial arts have their origin in similarity-magic, and still serve religious and spiritual ends in all societies we know. Modern scholars find it necessary to remind us that "the menu is not the meal" yet when the flag is burned or stepped on, or a crucifix is immersed in urine, or an icon of the Madonna is decorated with dung, people take to the streets in vigorous protest. Athletic teams become such powerful symbols that fans often resort to violence in their behalf.

Magic is definitely a "technique," a way of domesticating the supernatural in the same way that crafts and sciences domesticate the material world. With magic, humankind asserts mastery over the supernatural. There are definite procedures to be followed: certain equipment, particular spells, exact timing, carefully prepared recipes, prescribed movements and personnel. If the desired result is not forthcoming, there must be a fault in the spells, in the recipes, or in some other detail—failure cannot be due to the will of the spirit being commanded, since that will must bend to properly performed magic.[29] Indeed, we might as well call magic a part of technology, one that seeks to harness supernatural rather than physical forces.

From earliest times, magic and technology have co-existed, cooperatively and mostly interchangeably, both of them tools for bringing an unruly world under our dominion. Knowledge of the spiritual world is theology; mastery over it is magic. Knowledge of the material world is science (for millennia, classified as part of philosophy); mastery over the material world is technology. And to what end did we compel the spirits? For material reward, just as we compel biology, physics, and chemistry to serve us by technological means. We bend both spiritual and material techniques to our will, to improve our quality of life.

In the context of magic, the gift of flight is not freely given by God or gods, but forced from them by humans. "If we knew the right magic, we could fly" is not so different from "if we could build the right machine, we could fly." The one seeks to utilize the spiritual, the other looks to the material. For most of our history, both types of mastery were equally appealing and valid. Learned men, "mages," were expected to study both the spiritual and material worlds.

One thought-provoking example comes from fifteenth- and seventeenth-century Chinese illustrations of a classic text from the second century C.E. The illustrations show a self-propelled wheeled flying cart carrying two individuals of the mythical Chi-Kung people. The wheels are toothed, and closely resemble a waterwheel. In the earlier drawing, the clouds seem to be pushing against the wheel. Did the artists think of air as a fluid driving the cart? Was this an imaginative application of a technological idea which simply did not become physical reality in the Far East?[30]

Archytas, Greek philosopher and mathematician, is said to have constructed a wooden dove which could fly, though it could not lift itself off the ground. The Dove of Archytas has confounded scientists and engineers for millennia. Descriptions are maddeningly indecipherable in modern terms, and it is nearly impossible to tell whether the whole tale is a complete fiction or might just possibly contain some plausible grain of truth. Histories of aviation usually include the Dove, along with wide-ranging speculations as to what might have been its mechanism and motive power. Older commentaries especially were prone to "throwing around them an air of mystery and secrecy well calculated to delude the unlearned into the belief that it required the aid of a spiritual agency, which could only be acquired by those whose learning entitled them to hold communion with saints and demons."[31]

Roger Bacon, often called the father of modern science, claimed, "It is certain that Ethiopian sages have come into Italy, Spain, France, England, and those Christian lands where there are good flying dragons; and by an occult art that they possess, excite the dragons, and drive them at top speed through the air. . . . " Where might Bacon have gotten such an idea? Possibly from the "Letter from Prester John," which was circulating in Christendom at that time. The "Letter" was fiction, and Prester John a pure legend, but that was not apparent in Bacon's day. There were serious rumors of a Christian king, variously called John Presbyter or Prester John, in lands to the east of Palestine, and when the "Letter" appeared it was taken literally. Among other things, it speaks of wondrous things to be seen in and around India, including dragon-tamers. As for the good flying dragons in such Christian lands as Italy, Spain, France, and England, Bacon was liable to credit reports without looking too deeply into their origins; he knows, for instance, of an expert who has completely thought out the way to make a flying machine that works, though no one has seen it.[32]

For those who look to the future, science fiction writer Arthur C. Clarke offers his law: "Any sufficiently advanced technology is indistinguishable from magic." A man flying through the air with artificial wings is clearly making a technological attempt; we know the natural principles he is using. Or do we? One of the most common magical principles is imitation or similarity; that is the basis for copulation as fertility rite, for example. Is our aviator imitating the birds as an exercise in magical similarity, or because he thinks he understands the philosophical (scientific) principles of birdflight? Look at the white-knuckled passengers on an airliner; how many of them know and trust the principles at work?

To fly when supported only by spells is clearly magic. Or is it? If you climb into an airplane cockpit, invoke the spirits of flight, press certain buttons in a predetermined sequence, run through a checklist, speak certain words, wait til the red lights all turn green, and pull back on the yoke, is that magic or technology? If you construct wings that look like birds' wings, cover them with feathers, and flap mightily, is that applied science or similarity-principle magic? Gustav and Otto Lilienthal began in this way, imitating stork wings, and they are counted among the pioneers of modern aviation.

If we have no idea what principles are involved, we cannot tell the difference between technology and magic; it could be either one. As far as the white-knuckled airline passengers are concerned, if they had been raised in a society that claimed that the principles of magic are effective, they would not hesitate to ascribe their flight to magic.

What could be the foundation for the story of Kibaga, brought to us by explorer Henry M. Stanley? Kibaga was a Ugandan warrior who used efficient bombardments from the air to achieve his victory. He was rewarded with a wife from the conquered tribe, who eventually betrayed him to his death. Kibaga flies of his own power, rather than riding any mechanism or animal. Were the composers of this legend thinking of religion, magic, or technology? As Berthold Laufer comments, "If this tradition had been recorded in recent years, we should be inclined to trace it to the influence of World-War stories spreading to Africa, but it was recorded . . . in 1871 when there were no Zeppelins and aeroplanes in sight."[33]

When we look back at pre-Renaissance days, the picture gets terribly muddied when we see heroes and deities use mechanical means to fly. Mercury's winged helmet and heels, Ilmarinen's magical bird, the imitations of Vishnu's Garuda, all imply techniques that could be learned and used by mortals. The Greek demigod Perseus (his father was Zeus, his mother a mortal princess of Argos named Danaë) receives winged sandals and other magical equipment from nymphs; folklore abounds with tales of flying carpets, seven-league boots, and other magic-technology. It is no wonder that people try jumping from towers with wings of their own manufacture!

A more recent painting by Swedish artist Hans Baldung-Grien illustrates the synergy and the distinction between natural and artificial flight. It depicts Mercury, life-size, standing on a hill overlooking a valley. He is wearing the usual winged helmet and sandals, but the wings are lifeless, grey-colored, obviously stylized and artificial. His crotch, however, is covered in gloriously colored feathers which are growing from his own flesh, and he has a similarly colored small tail of feathers at the base of his spine. The contrast between intrinsic, organic, life-giving flight and the artificial flight represented by the helmet and sandals could not be more explicit. Yet it is the artificial symbols, the helmet and sandals, that are used to identify the god as Mercury and distinguish him from the other gods.

In these cases, no clear distinction is made between mechanical and "supernatural" flight. Both types occur in the context of religion, and both types are also attributed to intense study and learning. In the Christian tradition we have the story of Simon Magus, a magician attracted to Christianity by the superior quality of Jesus' miracles. Simon is interested only in the supernatural powers to be harnessed, not in the spiritual values of the religion itself. In all the various versions, the grand finale comes in Rome, when Simon demonstrates his power to fly. Saint Peter, watching, prays until the demons supporting Simon let go and Simon falls to his death.

MYSTICISM, MONEY, MASCULINITY, MOUNTAINS

Willie Sutton was asked why he robbed banks. "Because that's where the money is." Climbers insist they want to reach the tops of mountains "because they're there." It might be said that people want to fly just because it ought to be possible—a challenge, a "mountain." So are the womblike depths of the sea, but they do not call to us in the way that the heavens do.

Flying is a challenge, but not just because the air exists. Through the ages, the dream has been fed by other dreams: of spirituality, of fame and fortune, of benefit to humanity, of personal achievement, of virility. To meet this challenge, to accomplish this dream, we have called into service every spiritual and physical resource we have: magic, religion, science, and technology.

CHAPTER 3

TRAVEL TO EXTRAORDINARY KINGDOMS

ravel brings us to strange places, none stranger than when we fly. What a wonderful wide spectrum of symbolic functions flight has served in art and literature: creative, escapist, utopian, spiritual, satirical. We have Pegasus and the Hippocrene spring of poetic inspiration, high-flying imaginations, interplanetary flight to absurdity in Voltaire's *Micromegas* and to science and mathematics in Kepler's *Somnium.* We have Cyrano de Bergerac's fanciful and pungent *Flight to the Moon,* and the intellectual adventure of Jules Verne's "science fiction." We have arrows of love and longing, spiritual flights and earthy desires. All these and more employ flight as a symbolic vehicle.

CREATIVE FREEDOM

The word "poet" derives from the Greek for "maker, creator." Drink from the Hippocrene, the wellspring of imagination drawn forth by the hoof of the winged horse Pegasus, and you become a poet, a maker, whose words can then fly of their own accord. Again, flight represents the ultimate freedom: creativity, the fundamental attribute of the creator. A maker of words—a craftsman in language—perhaps most closely approaches the creativity of the Holy One of Christians and Jews, whose Word brought forth the universe. The *Rig-Veda* of the Hindus describes the winged celestial musicians, the Gandharvas, as the archetype for human poets.[1] Plato agrees, "the productions of all arts are kinds of poetry, and their craftsmen are all poets."[2]

Unrestrained, soaring flight symbolized the ultimate freedom of the soul. Giordano Bruno, monk and freethinker of the sixteenth century, titled this poem "Philosophical Flight." The unknown translator kept the sonnet form of the original, but had to torture the English a bit in order to do so. The antique flavor suits it, though, and repays the effort of the attentive reader:

> *Now that these wings to speed my wish ascend,*
> *The more I feel vast air beneath my feet,*
> *The more towards boundless air on pinons fleet,*
> *Spurning the earth, soaring to heaven, I tend:*
> *Nor makes them stoop their flight the direful end*
> *Of Daedal's son; but upward still they beat.*
> *What life the while with this death could compete,*
> *If dead to earth at last I must descend?*
> *My own heart's voice in the void air I hear.*
> *Where wilt thou bear me, O rash man? Recall*
> *Thy daring will. This boldness waits on fear.*
> *Dread not, I answer, that tremendous fall:*
> *Strike through the clouds, and smile when death is*
>   *near,*
> *If death so glorious be our doom at all.*[3]

Come look again at Daedalus and Icarus. See Daedalus, the careful engineer, artful sculptor, and loving conservative parent, fashion wings for his son and instruct him in their use. See adolescent Icarus, heedless and ambitious, exultant in his new abilities, fly exuberantly toward the sun regardless of consequences. Here is an eternal tension between rationality and emotion, enacted in every generation and every society.

Emotion calls to emotion. "Tis better to have loved and lost, than never to have loved at all." Those who see poets as misunderstood outcasts, possessed and driven by implacable and insatiable muses, find Icarus a perfect mythological symbol. Bruno was a monk, but could not cage his thought. "Dread not ... that tremendous fall: Strike through the clouds, and smile when death is near, If death so glorious be our doom at all." The imagination must fly, come what may.

The French Romantic poet Théophile Gautier put it well, in the nineteenth century: "The fate of Icarus frightened no one. Wings! wings! wings! they cried from all sides, even if we should fall into the sea. To fall from the sky, one must climb there, even for but a moment, and that is more beautiful than to spend one's whole life crawling on the earth."[4] As these poets saw it, Satan, Prometheus, and Icarus took parallel risks in challenging God. The challenge to society was implicit in this vision; the poet, the maker, the creative person in all fields (and some named such men as Napoleon and the scientist Cuvier among the poets), was necessarily doomed to be a misfit. Yet the poet was helpless in service to his muse, his "genius." Victor Hugo described the creative force as a speeding hippogryph, half horse, half eagle, and the suffering poet as taken for a wild ride:

> *Terror-stricken, he shrieks, you fly on relentlessly.*
> *White-faced, exhausted, mouth agape, overcome*
> *   with the speed of your flight*
> *He hunches in fear;*
> *Each step that you take seems to dig his grave.*
> *Finally, the destination! . . . he leaps, he falls,*
> *And is once again King.*[5]

Another French Romantic poet, Leconte de Lisle, admonished:

> *Better than the hunt of eagles . . .*
> *Man! leap up into the resplendent air.*
> *The old earth, beneath, keeps silent and dwindles.*[6]

The modern Russian poet Joseph Brodsky mirrors Icarus with a hawk who has passed above a wind-shear plane into air that is too thin to breathe, and who cannot descend:

> *What am I doing at such a height?*
> *He senses a mixture of trepidation*
> *and pride. Heeling over a tip*
>
> *of wing, he plummets down. But the resilient air*
> *bounces him back, winging up to glory . . .*
> *. . . So once again*
>
> *he turns and plunges down. But as walls return*
> *rubber balls, as sins send a sinner to faith, or near,*
> *he's driven upward this time as well! . . .*
> *Still higher! Into some blasted ionsphere!*
> *That astronomically objective hell*
>
> *of birds . . .*
> *Not with his puny brain but with shriveled air sacs*
> *he guesses the truth of it; it's the end.*[7]

As the bird falls into the rushing winds, his body is torn apart and precipitates the first snowfall; children on the ground call out in delight, "Winter's here!" Again we see the Romantic vision of helpless sacrifice, this time for the production of beauty. The hawk, like the poet or the intellectual, must follow his nature and fly, whatever the consequences; the benefits to others are strictly incidental.

ESCAPE FROM AUTHORITY

Flights of fancy, in literal and metaphorical senses, allowed authors to offer critiques and alternatives under the guise of whimsical entertainment. The miracle of language and the power of words was recognized in many cultures; the proper words could summon gods to one's bidding. Knowing a god's "true" name was equivalent to controlling the god's actions. Mere mortals were even more to be controlled by words, seduced by sweetly constructed falsehoods. Hence the need for those who would challenge the existing powers to pretend that they spoke of faraway places, "not here." Modern politicians call this sort of pretense "maintaining plausible deniability."

By "flying away" and placing stinging absurdities in a clearly imaginary setting, the authors could lodge their tongues firmly in cheek and deny that any correspondence or contrast with their own social or political environments was meant. "Flight" to faraway places worked hand-in-hand with the poet's free-flying intellect; what more natural place for such flight than the moon and outer space? What could be further from "here" than the insubstantial heavens and the unreachable heavenly bodies? Even better, the biting commentary supposedly coming from the realm of Divinity and Truth would sting all the more.

Widely acknowledged forefather of the genre is Lucian of Samosata, who flourished in the second century c.e. Lucian traveled throughout the Roman Empire, eventually settling in Athens to write pointed satires of the superstitions and philosophical beliefs of his time. It was more than a thousand years before other satirists followed him into the fictional heavens.

Two of Lucian's satirical works, *The True History* and *IcaroMenippus,* include a trip to the moon. Lucian begins *The True History* by pointing out the fine quality of his work, particularly "the veiled reference underlying all the details of my narrative; they parody the cock-and-bull stories of ancient poets, historians, and philosophers; I have only refrained from adding a key because I could rely upon you to recognize as you read." Lucian continues, "My subject is, then, what I have neither seen, experienced, nor been told, what neither exists nor could conceivably do so. I invite my reader's incredulity." What he really invites is his readers' educated guesses as to the objects of his satire, while insisting that nothing is to be believed and no harm is meant. If he were standing in front of us, he would bat his eyelashes and smirk.

In *The True History,* Lucian speaks in the first person, describing how his ship is lifted by a mighty whirlwind and carried to the moon. His crew first encounters a river of wine, complete with huge footprints in the ground and a sign "Dionysus was here." At the head of the river are grapevines whose "upper part was a woman, complete from the loins upward." The vines invite kisses, and some "made further amorous advances; and two of my comrades who yielded to these solicitations found it impossible to extricate themselves again from their embraces; the man became one plant with the vine, striking root beside it. . . . " Could there be a clearer description of helpless addiction?

The remainder of the crew are captured by Endymion, ruler of the moon, who is at war with Phaëthon, ruler of the sun, over the right to colonize a barren land which lies between them.[8] (Fighting over "barren lands" and other useless pieces of real estate would seem to be an enduring human tendency.) Lucian provides ample absurd detail about the composition of each army and the conduct of the battles. Readers in his day would likely have recognized such contingents as the Garlic-men, the Millet-throwers, and "from the North, . . . 30,000 flea-archers." The flea-archers are accompanied by the wind-coursers, who move "through the air without wings; they effect this by so girding their shirts, which reach to the ankle, that they hold the wind like a sail and propel the warriors ship-fashion." Eventually, a peace treaty is concluded, and Endymion allows the earthlings to return home.

It should be noted that the sail-shirts of the wind-coursers would sound plausible to Lucian's readers, a touch of homey practicality amidst the absurdities. Further development of this concept, from the sixteenth century onward, would eventually lead to the invention of the parachute. For the moment, it is enough to point out that our ancestors were acute observers, and no dummies when it came to ingenuity. As I have heard a physics professor say, Why do we think we can look down on people who built the pyramids with hand tools?

In *IcaroMenippus* the protagonist disdains to use the wax which proved the downfall of Icarus. Menippus, the hero, uses one wing of an eagle and one of a vulture, considering these the only ones suitable to bear the weight of a man. We are immediately struck by the contrast between the two birds, one usually considered to represent the noblest aspirations of humanity and the other an ignoble carrion-eater, universally despised. The effect is surely intentional; the fact that Menippus must snare two birds, and discard the unused wing of each, draws our attention to the contrast and to its allegorical significance.

The distinction is alluded to only once in the text, when Menippus is on the moon and trying to see some detail on the Earth. The philosopher-physicist Empedocles suggests that Menippus exercise the arm to which the eagle's wing is attached, so that the sight in the corresponding eye should sharpen until it resembles that of the eagle. Thus Menippus is able to see the essential pettiness of earthly vanities and values. Lucian is employing a two-pronged attack, as a high-minded eagle-eyed analyst who yet also sees his prey as dead and rotting. The eagle's eye reveals humanity's faults; we can only imagine what would happen if the vulture's qualities were invoked.

We can also savor Lucian's slyness in naming Menippus as his character; the actual philosopher Menippus lived about three centuries earlier, and was famed as a satirist in his own right. Exotic settings, such as a descent into Hades, were a specialty of Menippean satires. How appropriate to put Menippus on the moon, and put satire in his mouth!

Menippus/Lucian mocks the entire community of philosophers and pseudoreligious. He begins the tale by recounting his frustration with philosophers and his determination to seek truth in Heaven. His approach is another touch of practicality, like the sail-shirts of the windcoursers. Attaching the bird wings to a sturdy leather harness, Menippus makes "experiments, first jumping up and helping the jump by flapping my hands, or imitating the way a goose raises itself without leaving the ground and combines running with flight." He next launches himself over the Acropolis, and having landed safely begins longer flights: "I took to starting from Parnes or Hymettus, flying to Geraea, thence to the top of the Acrocorinthus, and over Pholoe and Erymanthus to Taygetus." Once sure of his skills, he flies to Olympus and above. There he meets characters who challenge his science, his morals, his theology, and his philosophy.

At the conclusion of his wanderings about Heaven, Menippus encounters Zeus, who declares all the squabbling sects of philosophers and theologians to be hypocrites. If they were honest, Zeus tells him, these men would confess "I consider it superfluous to sail the sea or till the earth or fight for my country or follow a trade; . . . I am a Momus who can always pick holes in other people's coats; if a rich man keeps a costly table or a mistress, I make it my business to be properly horrified; but if my familiar friend is lying sick, in need of help and care, I am not aware of it. . . . "

These elements—absurdity, plausibility, denunciation placed in the mouths of fictional characters—we will see again in other fantastic voyages. Often the element of plausibility is incorporated into the mechanics of flight, either borrowing from folklore or utilizing the accepted principles of the time. Flight thus serves two purposes: placing the action in some physically remote location and providing some anchor to reality while at the same time indicating an element of fantasy. Flight is not really the main subject, but rather an important literary tool. Occasionally the plausible elements will be convincing enough to fool a scholar. One respected historian comments that another, studying this same subject of ancient flight "has a tendency to take the legendary material too seriously."[9]

The book that gave its name to an entire genre deserves mention in this lineage, although it does not deal with aerial flight: Sir Thomas More's *Utopia*. The name is derived from the Greek words for "no place," and has come to signify an impossible ideal society. The book was written in Latin, and circulated among scholars in 1516. It was not translated into English until 1551, sixteen years after More's execution in 1535, and four years after the death of his sovereign, Henry VIII. More's Utopia is a republic on an island protected by a harbor with treacherous rocks at its mouth; its location is not discussed. In describing the desirable aspects of Utopia's government and of its society as a whole, More levels severe criticism at church and state in his native England. All is put in the mouth of a traveler, Raphael Hythloday, who acknowledges that his comments would be unwelcome to the ears of authority. Alas, he spoke truly; Sir Thomas More's integrity was unacceptable to Henry VIII, who had him executed for treason (that is, for disagreeing with Henry).

Johannes Kepler, almost a century later, knew that he had to be careful. Church politics was intimately entangled with secular politics, and both worked to the detriment of scientific freedom. Taking a stand on certain scientific points was equivalent to taking a religious and political stance. Not only was this a matter of potential charges of heresy and treason, but since scholars were dependent upon patronage, it was an everyday matter of one's livelihood as well. Clear statements might risk alienating potential sponsors by seeming to espouse a rival cause, yet one did often want to engage in some dialogue with colleagues in distant locations. Hiding one's thoughts from the unlearned, and scattering hints for the knowledgeable, was one way to deal with this problem.

Galileo and Copernicus, Kepler's contemporaries, had run afoul of the establishment by insisting that astronomy be revised, and with it the place of humans in the universe. Kepler's contribution to astronomy was equally controversial; by insisting that planetary orbits were not circular, he implicitly attacked the notion that the heavens were perfect.

For centuries, the contrast between the perfect heavens and the obviously imperfect earth had been an important theological point for Christians. With earth at the center of the universe, and Hell at the center of the earth, all the sublunar world was characterized by pollution, corruption, and change. The heavens, beyond the moon, were perfect and unchanging, the proper abode of pure spirits and God Himself. It followed that the "crystal spheres" in which the heavenly bodies were embedded, and the paths of all celestial objects, simply had to be the most perfect geometrical forms—the sphere and circle.

The souls of humankind were cluttered and polluted by the earthly matter, their bodies. Their destination after death was determined by the degree to which they had either purified themselves or allowed themselves to be further defiled and corrupted.

Thus the physical axis from earth to heaven was seen as a reflection of the spiritual journey necessary for fallen humankind to reach salvation, and as evidence of God's universal plan. The moon, at the boundary between the lower and upper regions of the universe, was of a mixed nature. Pockmarked and showing phases, it resembled the changing sublunar region. White, shining, set in the sky, it symbolized hope in the perfectibility of humankind, if only they would yearn toward the Divine. To think of it as nothing more than a bit of rock, a world like the earth—no, no, the entire order of the cosmos would be overturned.

In 1593, as a student in his early twenties, Kepler began a work he was later to call *Somnium, Sive Astronomia Lunaris (A Dream about Lunar Astronomy)*. It was not printed until several years after his death, although handwritten copies had circulated since 1610, when he lent one to a visiting nobleman. Under the guise of a visit to the moon, Kepler presented arguments for a sun-centered astronomy and the concept that the moon was a world of the same sort as the earth. Both of these were highly controversial ideas which could be dangerous if broadcast carelessly. Challenging the accepted astronomy was tantamount to challenging the Church itself. Trials for heresy, even if they did not result in a death penalty, were not pleasant experiences.

In 1600, Giordano Bruno was burnt at the stake for, among other things, suggesting that other worlds orbit other stars, and that those worlds are surely inhabited, since God provides abundance and God's creativity is infinite. If those beings had fallen like Adam and Eve, God's grace would require that a saviour offer them redemption; speculation as to whether God might have more than one "begotten Son" to send to those other beings was not something that the church cared to encourage. Fallen or not, the very concept of other inhabited worlds called into question the fundamental principle that earth-born humankind was the central element of the universe, for whose benefit everything else had been created. Such thinking was a Pandora's box of heresy, and the church desperately wanted to keep that box tightly closed.

Nine years later, Galileo published *Sidereus Nuncius (Starry Messenger)*, describing his observations using his improved version of the telescope which had recently been invented in Holland. The demonstration that the heavens were not perfect, and that Jupiter had moons which definitely did not circle the sun, caused an uproar in the church. In his later work, Galileo carefully used an imagined dialogue among fictional characters to present his new ideas about physics and astronomy. The technique was an old one: two thousand years earlier, Plato had presented Socrates' thoughts in similar fashion. In the dialogue format, several points of view might be argued by the various characters, and the "truth" seemed to appear by virtue of logic, rather than being the opinion of the author. Unfortunately, the least intelligent of Galileo's characters seemed modeled on a certain person of high rank in the church, and Galileo found himself in very hot water once again.

Kepler went a step further than Galileo, to distance himself from the controversy. By arguing with the man in the moon, and further presenting the whole discussion as a dream, he hoped to be able to say, in effect, "Oh no, I didn't mean you, sir, Holy Father, your Honor, your Highness, your Majesty, how could I possibly have meant you? And everyone knows that dreams are not always what they seem." Even so, Kepler tried to keep some sort of control over the manuscript by loaning it only to persons he trusted. Alas, a copy found its way back to Kepler's hometown, and was read by "people in the barbershops."

Kepler may have expected trouble for himself from church and state; he was not prepared for a vicious attack on his mother. Most of the book was unintelligible to the average layman, since it was highly technical geometry and calculations. The story that framed the geometry, however, seemed easily decipherable and lent itself to accusation. The hero's mother summons spirits with an incantation, the hero is obviously modeled on Kepler himself, therefore Kepler's mother must be a witch.

Kepler's mother was indeed an "herb-doctor," and reportedly an unpleasant person with several powerful enemies in her town. They seized on Kepler's apparent acknowledgment of his mother's black art, added some testimony from townsfolk she had allegedly bewitched, and from 1615 to 1621 attempted to have her burnt at the stake. Falling short of this, she was brought to the torture-room, shown the horrifying equipment for torture and earnestly entreated to confess her sins. In spite of her terror, she insisted on her innocence, falling to her knees in prayer. This was as far as the authorities were willing to pursue the matter, and she was released. The traumatic episode may have hastened her death, which followed shortly thereafter.

Greatly shaken by this ordeal, Kepler began to write a series of footnotes to the *Somnium,* explaining his intentions and decoding his allegory. When complete, the footnotes were much longer than the original text. (For a non-mathematician, they are also more fun to read.) In one footnote, Kepler bitterly comments that the hero, Duracotus, is meant to represent science, and his mother, Fiolxhilde, represents ignorance:

> I wished, too, to hint that Science is born of untaught experience . . . and that so long as the mother, Ignorance, lives, it is not safe for Science, the offspring, to divulge the hidden causes of things. . . . The object of my *Dream* was to work out, through the example of the moon, an argument for the motion of the earth. . . . I believed that Ignorance was by then sufficiently extinct and erased from the memory of intelligent men. But the spirit struggles in a chain of many links, and the ancient mother is still alive in the Universities. . . .[10]

It should be noted, however, that "Ignorance" in the *Somnium* is responsible for summoning the daemons (from the Greek word meaning "to know") who convey the story's hero to the moon. This is not what we moderns call "ignorance," which implies a complete lack of knowledge. Ignorance for Kepler includes "untaught experience," otherwise known as empirical knowledge, and is not to be completely rejected. Only when information is organized according to logical principles can it be called "science." Science is a child of *both* ignorance and reason, and draws on empirical knowledge as well as intellectual analysis.

The tone of Kepler's footnote contrasts sharply with the ebullient enthusiasm evident in his 1610 letter to Galileo, in which he predicts "Provide ship or sails adapted to the heavenly breezes, and there will be some who will not fear even that void. So, for those who will come shortly to attempt this journey, let us establish the astronomy: Galileo, you of Jupiter, I of the moon."[11]

Kepler's choice of the moon as the destination for his fictional journey had a complex origin. It was absurd enough to protect him, it was a good place to demonstrate the new astronomy, and it expressed the restless, exploratory spirit of his times. The great sea voyages of what we now call "The Age of Exploration" were less than a century behind him. New worlds, new lands, new understanding of nature—what might not lie ahead? What a magnificent challenge to the creative thinker, the maker, the poet.

In spite of the dangers, Kepler had published several scientific treatises on astronomy, without the distracting technique of a fictional framing narrative. Why did he feel it necessary to clothe his lunar exercise in this way?

Kepler may originally have had a political purpose in mind. If so, it would be doubly dangerous to speak plainly. He begins the narrative frame of the *Somnium* by invoking the legendary Queen Libussa, a major positive figure in the political myths of Bohemia and central Europe, and then shifts his focus to the fictional mother Fiolxhilde (representing ignorance). By doing so, he may have meant to hint to his learned readers that they should be aware of relationships between ignorance, science, and politics as suggested by the persuasive geometrical and mathematical reasoning presented under this veil of fiction. He may have hoped that the pure light of reason and science would forestall or avoid the violent political consequences of dissension due to ignorance.

Any such hopes were dashed by the reception of the 1610 manuscript. We have no way of knowing why he persisted in this direction, preparing the footnotes and finally in 1630 attempting to publish his *Somnium* with the fictional framing still intact. Perhaps his letter to Matthias Bernegger in 1623 offers a clue: "Would it be a great crime to paint the cyclopean morals of this period in livid colors, but for the sake of caution, to depart from the earth with such writing and secede to the moon?"[12] If such were his intent, however, it is hidden beneath so many layers of geometry that the modern reader will scarcely guess at its existence.

Speech was a bit easier in Protestant England at this time, but Bishop Francis Godwin saw fit to put his lunar narrative in the mouth of a Spaniard, at that time England's traditional enemy. His book, *The Man in the Moon,* is not as sharply focused as Kepler's. Godwin, in the guise of his narrator Domingo Gonsales ("the speedy messenger"), spends about a quarter of the book recounting his adventures in various parts of the earth and bragging about his nobility. Gonsales seeks to escape from one island by training geese to lift a vehicle capable of carrying him. He describes his procedure step by step, perhaps in conscious echo of Lucian of Samosata's IcaroMenippus. He makes emergency use of this vehicle when attacked, but the geese, instead of responding to Gonsales's reins, carry him to the moon.

Godwin's book was written in English, and the first edition appeared in 1638, after Godwin's death. The lunar society he describes is utopian, with no person suffering want. Crime and disease are unknown, and the lunarians thus have no need for doctors or lawyers. Their language is pure musical tone. Even morality is perfect: "I know not how it cometh to pass by a secret disposition of nature there, that a man, having once known a woman, never desireth another." Those who are born "imperfect" are sent away to the earth; the usual place of exile is North America, but "Sometimes they mistake their aim, and fall upon Christendom, Asia, or Africa."

Cyrano de Bergerac's *Other Worlds: The Comical History of the States and Empires of the Moon and the Sun,* published in 1650, is much more clearly satirical. The author was born Savinien Cyrano in 1619, and adopted the name "de Bergerac" from a small estate owned by his father.[13] Most nonspecialists today hardly realize that he was a real historical person, knowing of him—and his nose—only through the popular play written in the late nineteenth century by Edmond Rostand, or from more recent movies.

Cyrano begins his first-person tale among a group of drinking companions, a situation extremely familiar to the author. They are speculating as to the nature of the moon, and offer several absurd possibilities; they greet with hilarity his declaration that it is a world like ours. He determines to go there and see for himself. The first method he tries is to cover himself with jars of dew, so that the morning sun should draw him upwards. It does indeed, but so quickly and in such a direction that he fears to miss the moon entirely. Accordingly, he breaks some of the bottles until he begins to descend. The earth has revolved under him in the meantime, so he lands in New France, Canada.

The modern reader might completely ignore and take for granted the sun-centered astronomy implied here, but it was surely a signal to Cyrano's contemporaries. After all, if the earth were the center of the universe, the motion of the sun, not of the earth, would change day into night and vice versa. Subtly but clearly, Cyrano establishes his theology and politics.

In spite of his first failure, Cyrano persists in his desire to visit the moon, and prepares a machine he believes adequate to take him there. Unfortunately, the device proves insufficient and he tumbles to earth.

Having salved himself all over with beef marrow for his bruises, he tries to return to his machine, only to find that it has been fitted with rockets for a fireworks display to intimidate the local savages. Appalled, he attempts to save it at the last moment, only to be lifted along with it by the rockets as they are set off. The rockets bring him only partway to the moon, and he is pleasantly surprised to find that the moon was sucking at the marrow smeared on his body and pulling him along the rest of the way, as his machine plummets to earth. (The tendency of the moon to suck marrow was a widely held belief of his day.)

The inhabitants of the moon, who call themselves "men," cannot at first believe that Cyrano is a man, since he does not resemble them: they travel on all fours, he on his two legs; they subsist on vapors and aromas, he requires solid food, and so on. They are further convinced that he is subhuman once they learn to communicate with him, since Cyrano's description of his home customs seems to them completely absurd. Cyrano, on the other hand, is delighted with most customs he encounters, particularly the fact that the coin of the realm is original verses, whose valuation is proportionate to their quality: "Thus when someone starves to death it is never anyone but a blockhead and witty people always live off the fat of the land."[14]

As Cyrano is passed from one lunar country to another, he tries to prove anew that he is human. Offering his captors and hosts the cream of earthly philosophy and theology only convinces them that he cannot think for himself, since the principles he expounds are so obviously false. "When they finally saw that all I could jabber was that they were no more learned than Aristotle and that I had been forbidden to argue with anyone who denied his principles, they all unanimously concluded that I was not a man but possibly some type of ostrich. . . . "[15] In another situation, Cyrano is astonished to see that the bronze badge of honor worn by the nobles is in the shape of male genitals. In our world, he exclaims, the mark of nobility is to wear a sword! His hosts find it incredible that the instrument of destruction should be honored more than that of procreation. When Cyrano argues Christian theology with another moon native, he again becomes an object of derision when he cannot support his statements with logic. Everywhere he turns his customs and thoughts are subject to ridicule. Cyrano returns to France, only to be arrested as a sorcerer. He escapes prison and reaches the sun, where his reception is quite similar to that he had on the moon. At last, he comes to the country of the birds, where to be a man is a capital crime, on account of mankind's debased and barbaric nature. He is not punished, because it is obvious he is only a dumb brute, totally lacking any of the higher moral qualities and incapable of distinguishing right from wrong.[16]

All of these matters were the stuff of titillating rebellion among some French freethinkers of the mid-seventeenth century, but could not be seriously presented in public without danger from the established church and state. Even Voltaire, writing a hundred years later when the humanistic, secular philosophical movement called the Enlightenment was much stronger, felt it prudent to clothe his thoughts in absurdity and to locate them far away from his home. The established order had reason to fear the Enlightenment; the principles developed by these philosophers later provided the foundation for both the American and the French Revolutions.

Voltaire (born François Marie Arouet) had tasted firsthand the injustice of the French class system. In 1725, when he was just under thirty years old, Voltaire made a sarcastic remark to a minor noble and was whipped and beaten by the noble's lackeys, while other nobles whom Voltaire had thought his friends simply stood by and watched. Voltaire was then thrown in the Bastille for two weeks before being sent into a two-year exile from France. He spent those two years in London, just in time to read *Gulliver's Travels,* another set of fantastic voyages to lands inhabited by strange beings whose characteristics offer sharp contrast to the author's home.[17]

As Voltaire had learned, it was politically and physically dangerous to openly challenge the powers that be. He usually set his satires in faraway places, and in 1752 he published the story "Micromegas," which describes the travels of "an Inhabitant of the World of the Star Sirius" to Saturn and thence to earth. The Sirian, a "young man" not quite two hundred fifty years old, was eight leagues tall (the Sirian is tall indeed; a league is three miles). Voltaire, mocking the mathematicians, and with a nod toward the pretensions of small states, calculates that the globe which produced such a prodigy "must necessarily have a circumference just twenty-one million six hundred thousand times greater than our little earth. Nothing in nature is simpler and more ordinary. The states of certain sovereigns in Germany and Italy, which one can circle in half an hour, compared with the empire of Turkey, of Muscovy, or of China, give only a very feeble picture of the prodigious differences that nature has placed between all beings."

The Sirian's first stop in our solar system is at the planet Saturn, where he encounters men who seem to him short-lived and petty, with a lifespan of only fifteen thousand earth years. The Sirian converses with a Saturnian philosopher for a while, and they decide "to make a little philosophical journey together." It will not surprise you to hear that they are astounded that anything so small as an earthling human can speak, let alone reason, and they have great pity for our "smallness" and general deficiency in mental and physical qualities.

The earthling philosophers whom the travelers encounter do not give a very good report of their philosophy or theology. When asked what they do, one philosopher replies "We dissect flies, we measure lines, we assemble numbers; we agree about two or three points that we understand, and we argue about two or three thousand that we do not understand." And a bit later, when asked about the earthling soul, another philosopher quotes Aristotle. The Sirian complains that he does not understand Greek too well, and the philosopher confesses that he does not either. "Then why do you quote a certain Aristotle in Greek?" "Because it is essential to quote what we do not understand at all in the language we understand the least."

Finally, a theologian of the Sorbonne proclaims that the travelers, "their persons, their worlds, their suns, their stars, everything was made solely for man." The two giant travelers are so convulsed with such laughter at this incredible arrogance that the earthlings, who had been perched on the Sirian's thumb, "fell into a pocket of the Saturnian's breeches" and were fished out with great difficulty. At this point, the Sirian promises to prepare

> a fine book of philosophy, written very small for their use, and that in this book they would see the final word about things.

> Indeed, he gave them this book before he left; they took it to Paris to the Academy of Sciences; but when the Secretary opened it he found nothing but a completely blank book.

> "Ah!" he said, "that's just what I suspected."[18]

And, of course, to this day we have not yet found "the final word about things."

MODERN MYTHS

The tradition of fantastic voyages continues, however, in the genre we call science fiction, although the term "technology fiction" more closely describes the actual subject. Flight itself is not the main topic, as it had not been for Lucian, Kepler, Cyrano, or Voltaire. Flight is simply a useful means to other goals.

Most technology fiction is set in outer space, resonating with the old associations of freedom, frontiers, and spirituality. Spirituality? Yes. What else can we call the moral dilemmas faced by the characters as they grapple with new situations and experiences? Technology fiction is part of our mythology, a vehicle for moral exploration and cultural instruction in our mostly secular society.

Technology fiction has two main currents: the prediction of future technological advances and exploration of the social effects and implications of new technology. A third current, purely focused on adventure and escapism, using the "science fictional environment" simply as background, need not concern us here except for the degree to which it encouraged dreams of space. The grandfather of this third branch of science fiction (also called "space opera") is Edgar Rice Burroughs, whose first novel, *Dejah Thoris, Princess of Mars,* appeared in 1912 and was an instant bestseller. Burroughs followed it with several sequels, and branched out into setting his stories in another faraway place—Africa, home of his best known character, Tarzan. Ironically, the Tarzan series is more obviously satirical, presenting vivid contrast between the moral jungle creatures and the class-conscious and dishonest English society.

Modern technology fiction is generally considered to have begun with Jules Verne, in the mid-1800s. His book, *From the Earth to the Moon,* published in 1865, is a comic masterpiece, satirizing national stereotypes and the foibles of "scientific" men alike. Like Kepler's *Somnium,* Verne's book also provides a great deal of the scientific information available at the time. Unlike the *Somnium,* however, its main purpose is to entertain rather than instruct. Nor does Verne have to fear the wrathful power of church and state; by the mid-nineteenth century the church no longer insisted on the central position of the earth, and governments had learned some tolerance.

Set in Verne's own immediate future, the novel follows the Baltimore Gun Club as they proceed to fire an enormous cannon shell toward the moon. The project was intended to cheer up the Gun Club members, since they believe that with the end of the American "Federal War" (usually called the Civil War) there will be no more employment for artillery experts. These men, of whom "it was calculated by the great statistician Pitcairn . . . that throughout the Gun Club there was not quite one arm between four persons, and exactly two legs between six," nevertheless greet the new gun project with unbounded enthusiasm. (The anatomical calculation does not exactly require advanced mathematics; the "great statistician" is invoked to set the tone of extreme scientific exactness followed through the rest of the novel.)

An excitable Frenchman wires the Gun Club president that he is on his way to America to ride inside the projectile to the moon. As the story unfolds, the Gun Club president, who had been an outstanding designer of artillery, and his arch-rival who had excelled in producing armor plate, join the Frenchman on the voyage. Their dialog en route provides much of the scientific information with which Verne embellishes his story, while the Frenchman consistently complains that his head aches from all the mathematics and serious theory.

Verne puts a great deal of precise calculation into his story, perhaps to satirize the nineteenth century concept of "science as measurement" and to spoof the stereotype of scientists as calm, objective men. Verne does not, however, calculate at all the force of gravity acting on the gentlemen in the projectile as it is shot from the cannon at "escape velocity," twelve thousand yards per second. Had he done so, as Arthur C. Clarke has pointed out, it would have quite ruined the story; the resulting twenty thousand "g" would have smeared the valiant explorers into a thin film before they ever left the muzzle of the cannon.[19]

Today's technology fiction includes travel and colonization in space, because humankind still dreams of expansion and of exploring the universe. Military implications have often been cited as the principal stimulus for space programs, especially during the Cold War between the United States and the former Soviet Union, but they are not the only factor. The best of the genre, as with the best of all literary genres, presents well-rounded characters and complex moral situations. Outer space has become a playing ground for inner conflict, a fit locale for our society to examine itself, and a worthy successor to Lucian of Samosata's Moon.

Long before the Cold War the men who would be space and rocketry pioneers were inspired by early technology fiction.[20] They even named the robotic arms and hands used for remote handling "waldoes," a tribute to Robert A. Heinlein's classic character, Waldo, in the book of the same name. Waldo is a stereotypical social-outcast genius who invents the device and channels all his bitterness and frustration into obnoxiously rubbing the world's nose in his mental and financial superiority. Rather than being a "98-pound weakling," Waldo himself is grossly overweight and needs to live weightlessly aboard an orbiting space station. The book is usually bound with its sequel, *Magic, Inc.,* in which Waldo undergoes a spiritual renewal and rejoins the human race.

Technology fiction continued to be popular among young engineers. There is a report that one man claimed to be able to locate the top-secret research installations of the Cold War by pinpointing places where per-capita subscriptions to *Astounding Science Fiction* magazine were much higher than the national average. One might point to technology fiction as a kind of mythology for engineers, as it developed scenarios involving humans and the achievement of their dreams.[21]

Emotional support for the space program has long outlasted any military rationale. The space program exerts a strong grip on the American psyche: both the visionary and practical aspects of the American self-image are deeply, almost viscerally, engaged. Jules Verne would not have been surprised; his description of enthusiasm for the Gun Club's project could be lifted wholesale to apply to the space program.

Jules Verne, H. G. Wells, and their colleagues in the late nineteenth and early twentieth century fed a growing market for literature which attempted to explore the implications of the new industrial era, and which also offered some framework for understanding the increasingly opaque science and engineering that supported it. Although many now denied that deities resided in the heavens, a strong undercurrent of hope remained that answers to human problems might nevertheless be found beyond the moon. Walter M. Miller's tale of a post–nuclear holocaust world *A Canticle for Liebowitz* ends with people and animals entering a spaceship two-by-two, a new Noah's Ark, aimed at making a new start elsewhere in the universe.

In the 1920s, the problem of radio static reinforced the idea that a wiser "elder race" might reside nearby: scientist-inventors Gugliemo Marconi and Nicola Tesla thought the observed extraterrestrial radio static might originate on Mars. As Susan Douglas observes, "There was a hunger [for contact with distant, otherworldly beings]. . . . [I]t would be reassuring; it would be religious."[22] This "will to believe" applied to devils as well as angels, however, as became evident in the panic response to Orson Welles's 1938 radio broadcast of H. G. Wells's *War of the Worlds;* thousands of listeners believed that an invasion from Mars was actually happening.

At some point between the Second World War and the end of the Korean conflict, the notion became commonplace that the transition from technology fiction to reality could be accomplished for spaceflight as it had been for atomic energy. The public appetite for space-oriented technology fiction grew. From the 1930s onwards, spaceflight became a staple of American movies and television, offering free rein for the imagination as well as titillating fear. The phrases "bug-eyed monsters" and "flying saucers" entered the national vocabulary, along with such heroes as Flash Gordon and Buck Rogers.

More recently, we have the enduring popularity of the various *Star Trek* television series and the runaway success of the *Star Wars* movies. As these fictions have developed, the moral issues presented through them have ranged from toleration for different cultures to personal identity crises and the clash of conflicting values. *E. T.* touched hearts as had *Peter Pan,* a tale of lost children in a strange land one could only reach by flying. In turn, that enthusiasm fed public support for the space program.

In 1992, congressional debate on proposed cuts in funding for a space station elicited examples of the impassioned arguments which have become almost standard for such situations.[23] The military threat from the former Soviet Union had collapsed, but the space station remained high on the American agenda.

Supporters of station funding at current or increased levels insisted that a glittering, though by its very nature nonspecific, future would be foregone forever if any cuts were made. Economic, educational, scientific, medical, and psychological benefits were all invoked. Although direct statements of the form "keep the dream alive" constituted only a small percentage of the arguments presented, that concept was clearly the bedrock of support for the station.

Station opponents rebutted with depositions from leaders in the medical, scientific, and business communities which contended that the space station has been diverting, and continues to divert, funds from other essential activities (including existing aeronautical and medical research, as well as such social programs as education, vocational training for the unemployed, and veterans' health care). After the laundry list of justifications was thus dealt with, response to the "dream" component was essentially "we cannot afford it," never a notion congenial to Americans. The amendment was soundly defeated. Despite the American reputation for hard-nosed practicality, it remains a nation committed to dreams and to flights into the unknown.

WAKING DREAMS

Throughout history, the symbolic use of flight has reinforced the physical perception of actual flight. Achievement feeds the dream, and the dream reinforces the drive toward the heavens. Even when flight or space seems to be merely background for the author's or artist's main points, it is not chosen arbitrarily. The heavens have symbolic resonance which gives weight and substance, and flavor, to the discussion.

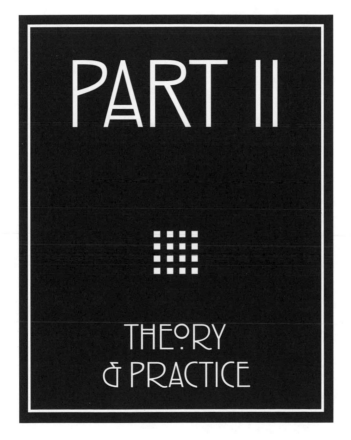

PART II

THEORY & PRACTICE

CHAPTER 4

EXUBERANT
SPECULATIONS

How could humans master the art of flight? By magic, by philosophy, by craftsmanship? By imitating or harnessing birds? By floating in the air as ships float on the sea? With human muscle power, or some engine? As early as the 1200s, Roger Bacon prophesied that "philosophical" means would someday be found for powered flight. Gradually, the focus shifted from the magical or supernatural to the mechanical, although the shift was by no means uniform either in time or geographical area.

SERIOUS PLAY

"Play" is a shimmering, elusive concept. We think of children's play as innocent and aimless, yet in most cases it is directly related to skills that adults need. Adult play may be equally serious, involving experimentation, variations on a theme, development of a skill. Often, we speak of "play" in terms of flexibility or adaptability—a play on words, playing with an idea, the "play" in a steering mechanism. The Wright brothers took up aerial gliding as a "sport"—their word—yet brought to it the full force of their considerable intelligence, adapting, extending, and applying the scientific knowledge of their day.[1]

Around the world, as we have seen, and throughout recorded time, humans have "played" with the idea of flight. Among the proposed mechanisms for flight were flying carpets and airborne chariots, the harnessing or riding of real or mythical flying beasts, seven-league boots, and artificial wings. You would expect that pursuit of an actual mechanical aircraft would be similarly widespread. But no. This happened only in the context of Western Christianity. Why? The answer has been sought as part of the larger question, Why was Western Christendom so favorable, so supportive, you could almost say so obsessed, with machines of all sorts?

Between the middle of the first Christian millennium and the middle of the second, a profound change had occurred in the Western European mindset and lifestyle. Part of the change is called the "Scientific Revolution," but the change is deeper and much more widespread than that.[2]

Across the full range of activities, from philosophy and the arts to agriculture, crafts, and trade, the emphasis and values shifted. Attention turned from the mystical and spiritual to the materialistic, rational, and physical; from qualitative, imprecise expression to quantitative and precise measurement; from a natural perception of time in solar and astronomical terms to an artificial division of equal hours, and months counted in days rather than by lunar cycles; exuberant and disorganized daydreaming gave way to patient, systematic approaches.

In the case of human flight, mystical motivations submerge and other motives take the foreground: glory, fortune, social status, camaraderie. This is a matter of emphasis, not replacement; the older motivations do not disappear. Alfred W. Crosby and Lynn White, Jr., trace the shift in mindset without falling into the trap of projecting present attitudes onto the past. Their language is carefully non-judgmental; Crosby respectfully calls the ancient worldview "the Venerable Model," and White, a pioneering historian of medieval technology, is equally respectful of the Eastern indifference to technological improvements.

Crosby begins by asking how the Western European "bumpkins" (his word) so greatly outstripped their more civilized Eastern cousins in only a few hundred years. He rightly dismisses as "hilariously unlikely" the Social-Darwinian notion that "those members of the human species most subject to painful sunburns were the most recent, highest, and in all likelihood, final twigs on the exfoliating tree of evolution. Pale people were the brightest, most energetic, most sensible, most aesthetically advanced, and most ethical humans"[3] Yet, he asks, tongue firmly in cheek, "What other explanations are there?"

Sometimes when we ask "Why," history responds simply "Why not?" Then we can only put events in perspective, and gain insight rather than rigorous explanation. For example, Crosby suggests that the flood of information reaching Europe in the Middle Ages gave Europe intellectual indigestion and triggered the Renaissance and its shift toward quantification. However, the "older" civilizations already possessed that information, and had not gone numbers-crazy. Even the inventors of the "Arabic" numerals, who certainly also participated in long-distance trade, in advanced mathematics, in music, and in so many other civilized pursuits, did not have the explosion in new science and technology—and in new theology—that the West enjoyed from about the fourteenth century onwards.

It was the shock, the overload, the sheer quantity and diversity of information and new concepts that sent the Western Europeans into intellectual overdrive. The advanced civilizations of the Near and Far East were accustomed to having their intellectual tools and extensive stock of knowledge, and took them for granted. Early Christian Europe had looked more to spiritual matters, and had turned its back on the physical world. When it was suddenly brought back to earth, it had to work harder, and thus became stronger. This is the essential part of Crosby's argument.

More than that, we look for a synergy, a combination of factors, which supplied fertile ground and guidance for the intellect. The flood of information surely played a part, but Western Europe could just as easily have ignored it all, rejecting it as irrelevant and un-Christian. Medieval Eastern cultures were in no hurry to adopt Western technologies; they had different priorities, a different notion of what was important.[4] We need to think about the Westerners' sense of playfulness and their willingness to push the envelope, to take an idea or technique to its limits and see what could be done with it.[5]

Perhaps the stage was set around the turn of the first millennium of the Common Era, or even a bit earlier. Lynn White, Jr., argues that the accelerating pace of European technology began "as early as the 9th century" while "after the 7th century, Byzantium showed amazingly little concern for engineering improvements."[6] White sees Christian ethics as an important ingredient, and notes a "cultural" difference between the Eastern and Western Christian outlook on life: the West was active, versus a predominantly contemplative mood in the East. He uses Eastern and Western illustrations of the Creator to support his point; only in the West is God shown with building tools, actively taking part as if He were an engineer or craftsman. This difference begins to appear about the turn of the millennium, and reflects or embodies the growing importance of technology in Western Christendom.

Which is cause, which is effect? Let us rather consider it a mutually reinforcing collaboration, a "beneficial" cycle. Bees pollinate flowers as they gather nectar for honey; the plants that attract the most bees have the greatest likelihood of reproducing themselves, and the bees that are most effective in collecting and transferring pollen then find themselves with a greater number of flowers for their harvest of nectar. The evolution of plants favors more attractive flowers, and the evolution of bees favors improved organs for collection of pollen. Both the plants and the bees profit thereby. Technological evolution is conscious, and once it is put into motion it proceeds more rapidly than biological evolution. Strong motivations bring forth strong efforts, as the brightest minds turn their attention to the most intellectually and emotionally rewarding fields. The extension of craft skills into new avenues also presents new possibilities to the imagination.

There are two separate but related streams in this Western Christian mindset. One is the association of technology with virtuousness and religion, the other is the importance of measurement and precise numerical quantification. Let us take a closer look.

Religious art was not simply a beautification of church and prayerbook; it was primarily intended to provide visual instruction for the pious life. It can instruct us, as well. In the Utrecht *Psalter,* printed sometime between 816 and 834, the illustration for Psalm 63 shows evildoers sharpening swords with old-fashioned whetstones on one side of the picture while the virtuous use the crank-driven labor-saving grindstone (verse 10 of that psalm reads "May those who seek to destroy my life . . . be gutted by the sword"). Advanced technology is an aid to the Godly; the sinful do not recognize its value and are deprived of its use.[7] Moral validation adds to other motivations driving talented men to invent and adopt new mechanisms.

Religious values are also inherent in the actual forms and acts of worship. Saint Joseph, the father of Jesus, was a carpenter by trade. For centuries he was not particularly respected, suffering the indignity of being considered the patron saint of cuckolds, the model of a complaining, hoodwinked husband. No relics were saved, no churches named in his honor. Few boys were baptized "Joseph" until the 1300s. White chronicles the change: "In 1399 the Franciscans adopted his feast . . . and the Dominicans quickly followed their example. It was introduced into the Roman breviary in 1479 and became a commemoration in the entire Roman Catholic Church in 1621."[8] White suggests that the rise in attention to Saint Joseph mirrors the growing respect for manual labor, for craftsmanship, and for material technology in general, in the medieval West. The attitude toward nature becomes more activist/aggressive in the West, beginning in the ninth century. Instead of calendars showing months and seasons as stiffly posed figures holding symbolic attributes, they now feature dynamic illustrations of seasonal activities such as sowing, reaping, harvesting acorns, and slaughtering pigs.[9] All these chores are aided by new technologies.

This morality of mechanism is not evident in that period of Eastern Christianity. Clocks, for example, were not permitted inside Eastern churches; the faithful were to concentrate on eternity, an infinite and indivisible symbol of the omniscient and omnipotent single God. In the West, however, when the regularly ticking mechanical escapement was invented in the fourteenth century, elaborate clocks were put both inside and outside Western churches to demonstrate and proclaim the order, regularity, and predictability of God's universe.[10]

Once again, as with the gender of the sun, moon, and storms, we see different meanings for the same symbol—in this case the mechanical clock. Symbols are what we make of them. The clock can be a symbol of God's lawfulness, or of a blasphemous division of God's unity. The iconic symbols and the forms of worship of Western Christendom reflect the shift toward giving mechanical things, and inventiveness, a high spiritual and moral value. This value then supports and encourages talented people to turn their imaginations toward the physical, toward activities we now would call science and technology.

CONTROLLING INTERESTS

Among the four Cardinal Virtues of Christendom, *Temperantia,* or Temperance, is most relevant to our story. Temperance turns one's mind to number, to quantification, which in turn supports the modern "scientific" style of invention. The rise of Temperance, like that of Saint Joseph, is emblematic of the shift from "The Venerable Model" to "The New Model." Just as folks selected among the myths of Daedalus, new circumstances led to new selections and emphases among the saints and their attributes.

Temperance is often portrayed in religious art. Between the ninth and the thirteenth centuries, she gradually emerges from the bottom of the saintly totem pole, slowly rising in prominence. By the fifteenth century she was supreme among the virtues in the Western Church.[11] The church may have been simply keeping up with attitudes among the aristocracy. Courtly poetry sang of moderation, *mesure,* as the Virtue opposing lawlessness, the source of all human evil. "Dante's teacher wrote in the late thirteenth century . . . 'Here stands Temperance / Whom folk at times / Call Measure'" and "The Master [Aristotle] says that all the other Virtues are inferior to Temperance." White points out that "the fact that neither Aristotle nor any other author known to us had ever said it in just this way makes the misquotation all the more significant. . . . "[12]

Pictures of Temperantia look bizarre to modern eyes. Intended as educational rather than merely ornamental, they include symbols of her various qualities. By the fourteenth century she is usually shown with a clock on her head and wearing a horse's harness, its bit in her mouth and the reins in her hand. The mechanical clock, with its regularly ticking escapement, represents measured control and dominance over the very passage of time. It also symbolizes self-control; a writer in 1400 proclaimed "just as the clock is worth nothing unless it is regulated, so our human body does not work unless Temperance orders it."[13] This regulation is moral as well as physical. As for the harness, once again, the horse symbolizes our own brutish instincts, and Temperantia can help us master these. She often holds a jug, from which she pours water into a cup of wine to "temper" it; appropriate balance in life is a sign of wisdom. Other symbols of wisdom and control may be added according to the artist's fancy.

Temperance is associated with measurement as well as with control. In 1560, Pieter Breugel (or Breughel) the Elder jams his painting of

Temperantia with symbols of her influence. Astronomers measure the moon and stars; builders use compasses, a plumb bob, a mason's square; gunnery officers, merchants, and accountants use mathematical tables; children are instructed in literacy, the better to learn the new complicated tools of daily living; an artist incorporates perspective, a mathematical technique, in his painting; musicians are performing and people singing from sheet music which included recently developed notations for pitch and rhythm. Temperantia herself wears the usual horse harness (bit, bridle, reins) and spurs—she is both controlled and controlling. She has a clock on her head and eyeglasses in her hand. She stands on the vane of a windmill.[14]

In sharp contrast, in the East neither Islam nor Christendom displayed any interest in new technology. About 1444, a learned Byzantine cleric wrote to suggest that the Despot of Morea (present-day Greece) send young men to study Western technology, particularly their water- and windmills. By that time, these mills were no novelty in Europe; they had been seen by visitors from the East, but ignored.[15] The Emperor of China turned away offers of trade with Europe with the remark that his realm already had all that was needed.

Europe, but not the East, had developed "a technological attitude toward problem solving."[16] Science alone was not enough to stimulate technology: Arabic science was the most advanced in the world, yet Islam remained indifferent to any mechanical innovation.[17]

In Europe, from the fifteenth century onward, mechanically creative men played with ideas and possibilities, including suggestions for flight. Their sketchbooks show their sheer delight in creativity, their exuberant enthusiasm for mechanical novelty. The cycle fed itself; each mechanical advance trained more artisans in woodworking and metalcraft, raising the level of skills which then could be put to use in more complex ways. Creative minds then had a greater vocabulary of mechanisms to play with.

Creative men asked the question: If such a thing could be accomplished at all, how might it be done? What are the necessary ingredients? And they began to assemble those ingredients and explore their properties. They turned them this way and that, in their mind's eyes and in sketches. Some of their contraptions were simply preliminary play, not meant as serious finished products. Some avenues led in rambling ways to eventual success in flight, while others led elsewhere, sometimes branching toward devices whose distant family relationships are now the domain of specialists.

SCIENCE VERSUS NATURE

Western science has a distinct tinge of masculine gender. Nature is seen as female, and the scientist sets about to wrest her secrets from her, to open her innermost parts to his gaze and manipulation. In many ways, to be a scientist is to play god, claiming for oneself the knowledge of mysteries and the ability to control and shape matter to one's will. Technology likewise is gendered masculine, and females are stereotypically ill at ease with it, or distinctly subordinate and apologetic about their roles.

From the Middle Ages onwards, scientists were described as those "who would 'master,' 'disrobe,' and 'penetrate' a feminine Nature."[18] This attitude is particularly prominent in the case of nuclear physics, as radioactivity affects both the flesh and the reproductive capabilities of living things. Nuclear radiation is invisible, but inevitably the comparison is made with visible light from the heavens, with the rays of the sun. As the sun warms and nourishes or strikes and kills, so too nuclear radiation may be used for good or ill. Here was a way for humans to control a "life force" as their forbears had sought to control the gods.

Des Aviatiker's letzter Augenblick

*The maiden in flowing white garments, with her suggestion of a halo, holds
the olive wreath of victory just out of reach as the skeletal figure of death
brandishes his scythe and displays an hourglass to show that
"The Aviator's Last Moments" have arrived.*

Courtesy Guillaume de Syon

"Modern Transport to Heaven, via Zeppelin's Airship."

Courtesy Guillaume de Syon

As nuclear physics has its links to the sun, flying has its links to the heavens and all that is associated with them, including sexuality. The line from winged phalluses to balloons, dirigibles, and airplanes is not direct, but it is present.

Female pilots were rare in the early days of aviation, and soon were excluded from commercial cockpits altogether. The very name "cockpit" suggests the masculinity of the domain. Women appear as flight attendants for early airlines, garbed to resemble nurses and charged with the tender care of apprehensive passengers.[19] Their continuing role as stewardesses was aptly summarized in the phrase "coffee, tea, or me?"

American warplanes were called "she," and given female names; bombs were known as "eggs." U.S. Air Force Gen. Curtis LeMay vividly described bombs inside aircraft, "electronic snakes packed into every inch of a bomber's body, monstrous treasures 'throughout the stiff flesh.' Most impressive of all was the nuclear bomb, that 'baby . . . clinging as a fierce child to its mother's belly.'"[20] Eventually, for planes of the U.S. Strategic Air Command, the female names were discarded, and the pinups traditionally gracing the aircraft were replaced by another image: the SAC logo of an armored fist holding one olive branch and three thunderbolts—an even more direct invocation of pagan mythology.[21]

MIXED MOTIVATIONS

Human flight evoked mixed emotions, even in prospect, before there was any effective human-carrying flying machine. Benefits often seemed outweighed by threats. In one Chinese legend, the emperor Ch'eng T'ang (reigned 1766–54 B.C.E.) ordered that a flying chariot be destroyed; he evidently feared that such an innovation would destabilize his society and threaten his reign.[22] More than three thousand years later a Jesuit, Francesco Lana de Terzi (1631–87 C.E.) suggested one possible reason:

> For who sees not that no city would be secure from surprise attacks, as the airship might appear at any hour directly over its market-square and would land there its crew? The same would happen to the courtyards of private houses and to ships crossing the sea, for the airship would only have to descend out of the air down to the sails of the sea-going vessels and lop their cables. Even without descending, it could hurl iron pieces which would capsize the vessels and kill men, and the ships might be burnt with artifi-

cial fire, balls, and bombs. This might be done not only to ships, but also to houses, castles, and cities, with perfect safety for those who throw such missiles down from an enormous height.

Nevertheless, Lana de Terzi proposed his own design for a flying machine, lifted by four large copper spheres emptied of air. The copper was to be so thin that each sphere would weigh less than an equal volume of air, thus providing the lifting force. He anticipated objections:

> Difficulties might be experienced owing to the . . . great pressure of the outer air trying to . . . compress the vessel, and if not break it, at least flatten it.

> To this, I reply, that it might so occur if the vessel were not round, but being spherical the air could only compress it equally on all sides, so that it would rather strengthen it than break it, which has been shown by experiments with glass vessels . . . round vessels of glass, although very thin, do not break . . . [23]

Lana de Terzi acknowledged that his design might "sound like unto a fable," but assures us that he has "conferred on these matters with many sage and well-instructed persons who have not been able to find any errors in my discourses." Only his "vow of poverty prevented [his] expending 100 ducats, which sum at least would be required to satisfy so laudable a curiosity." He is so certain of his theory and design, that if richer persons should make the attempt and "any error of construction should prevent a successful outcome," there is "no doubt I could show them how to correct any such errors."[24]

His attitude is all too familiar to modern ears; no matter how dangerous a new technology might be, some engineer will nevertheless consider it a "laudable curiosity," a worthwhile novelty.

Another cautionary tale from the past is recounted by E. Charles Vivian, writing a history of aeronautics in 1921:

> In one of the oldest records of the world, the Indian classic Mahabarata, it is stated that "Krishna's enemies sought the aid of the demons, who built an aerial chariot with sides of iron and clad with wings. The chariot was driven through the sky till it stood over Dwarakha, where Krishna's followers dwelt, and from there it

hurled down upon the city missiles that destroyed everything on which they fell." Here is pure fable, not legend, but still a curious forecast of twentieth century bombs from a rigid dirigible . . . [25]

In the *Thousand and One Nights* (also known as *The Arabian Nights*), a tremendous bird called a Roc hurled huge boulders at Sinbad's ship.[26] This image is echoed by Jonathan Swift in his famous *Travels into Several Remote Nations of the World,* more popularly known as *Gulliver's Travels,* where bombardment from the air is used by the Laputan king as a way to maintain his rule and discipline rebellious cities. The military implications of flight seem to have been obvious to just about anyone.

The story of the friar Bartholomew Guzman, or Bartolomeo Gusmán, finds its way into just about every history of aviation that looks to the years before the Wright brothers. This enterprising monk petitioned the king of Portugal, claiming to have invented a flying machine capable of carrying passengers for long distances, and begging for an exclusive patent. The king was only too happy to oblige, issuing a proclamation on April 17, 1709:

> Agreeably to the advice of my Council, I order the pain of death against the transgressor [anyone but Guzman who builds a flying machine]. And in order to encourage the petitioner to apply himself with zeal towards improving the machine which is capable of producing the effects mentioned by him, I also grant him the first Professorship of Mathematics in my University of Coimbra, and the first vacancy in my College of Barcelona with the annual pension of 600,000 reis during his life.[27]

Alas, Guzman was unable to enjoy the fruits of his patent. The Church in Rome sternly requested him to desist from his heresy, and when he protested that human flight was not sacrilegious, the Holy Office of the Inquisition carted him away, never to be heard from again.

Thirty years earlier, Bishop John Wilkins titled his book *Mathematical Magick: or, the WONDERS That may be Performed by Mechanical Geometry.* "WONDERS" is the largest word on the title page. Addressing his readers, he explains that he calls the whole discourse "Mathematical Magick" (and puts those words in an antique "blackletter" font, to contrast with the more modern typeface of the main text) "because the art of such Mechanical inventions as are here chiefly insisted upon, hath been formerly so styled; and in allusion to vulgar opinion, which doth commonly attribute all such strange operations unto the power of Magick."[28] This in 1680, shortly before Isaac Newton published his major scientific work, *Philosophiae Naturalis Principia Mathematica,* usually just called "the *Principia.*" The division between science and pseudoscience was not as clear in those days as we now make it; Newton himself, the very poster boy for rigorous scientific thought, dabbled for years in alchemy. Wilkins writes in English, and proposes usefulness; Newton writes in Latin, for the edification of his scholarly colleagues.

Wilkins named his book's two sections for ancient engineers: *Archimedes* deals with power, *Daedalus* explores mechanical motion. Since anything that moves has to have some source of power, the two sections are related. Indeed, we find the second section beginning with notice "of the contrivance of several motions by rarified air. A brief digression concerning Wind-guns." The next chapter describes "a sailing Chariot, that may without horses be driven on the land by the wind, as ships are on the sea." Clearly, men had begun to play with unusual combinations of power and vehicle.

Three of Wilkins's chapters deal directly with flying. He begins with the "*volant Automata,* Archytas his Dove, and Regiomontanus his Eagle. The possibility and great usefulness of such inventions." The next chapter is a systematic consideration of "the Art of flying. The several ways whereby this hath been, or may be attempted." Finally, "a resolution of the two chief difficulties that seem to oppose the possibility of a flying Chariot."

Wilkins makes a valiant attempt to explain Archytas's Dove. As a good historian, he considers the objections already given and counters them one by one. Cardan, says he, objects on the grounds that the mechanism would be too heavy. Wilkins maintains that "it is easie [*sic*] to contrive such springs and other instruments, whose strength shall much exceed their heaviness. . . . Nor can he shew any cause why these Mechanical motions may not be as strong (though not as lasting) as the natural strength of living creatures."[29] Other objectors get similarly short shrift.

Regiomontanus's eagle is another tough case, though it is supposed to have been constructed just two hundred years before Wilkins rather than two thousand. While the dove of Archytas is reported to have been powered by a "spirit," Regiomontanus's artifact is simply named rather than described. In fact, some versions call it an iron fly rather than an eagle. Fly or eagle, it is almost certainly pure legend.

The mechanical wonders Wilkins has himself observed lead him to an open mind about others; "to distrust them without a stronger argument, must needs argue a blind and perverse incredulity."[30] Superstitious, ignorant folk are not the only ones who will believe in miracles! A modern author points out that if you want an example of someone who believes in things unseen, talk to a nuclear physicist.[31] If Wilkins can think of a way something can be done, he is willing to allow that someone else might have actually done it, or certainly will do it in the future.

While the ancients thought the dove's motions to be produced by "some included air," Wilkins thinks its motion might be "better performed by the strength of some such spring as is commonly used in Watches; this spring may be applied unto one wheel, which shall give an equal motion to both the wings; . . . it is easie to conceive how the motion of flight may be performed and continued."[32] Wilkins has no doubt this will lead to human flight "than which there is not any imaginable invention that could prove of greater benefit to the world, or glory to the Author."[33]

He warns, however, that "nothing in this kind can be perfectly determined without a particular trial. . . . [I]n these practical times, unless a man be able to go to the trying of things, he will perform but little." Wilkins himself, however, offers only the theory, "for the encouragement of those that have both minds and means for such experiments."[34] Money is definitely an issue: he notes that Aristotle had a generous allowance from "his pupil Alexander" for the employment of "Fishers, Fowlers, and Hunters," who were to bring in creatures for Alexander's education. "The reason why the world hath not many *Aristotles* is, because it hath too few *Alexanders*."[35] [Italics in original.] Teachers the world round will enthusiastically agree; Alexander was an eager student, and there are all too few of those, rich or poor.

What else besides money stands in the way? "Inventions or attempts [at flying] . . . are so generally derided by common opinion, being esteemed only as the dreams of a melancholy and distempered fancy." Quoting an early Catholic theologian, "therefore none will venture upon any such vain attempt . . . unless his brain is crazed. . ."[36] Tales of human flight are dismissed by our learned forbears as exaggerations, as ornaments of legend (as we have seen with the stories of kings and saints who fly) rather than literal truths. The scientific Wilkins quotes the Greek historian Diodorus (first century B.C.E.), for example, who admits the "Historical truth" that Daedalus merely flew "in a swift ship" rather than through the air. Wilkins suggests that "the Ancients durst not so much as mention the art of flying, but in a fable."[37] Here is a turnaround! Moderns should be believers, abandoning the ancients' "perverse incredulity"! Technology has opened our eyes to mechanical dreams, where the ancients could see only fable.

If Wilkins is a representative sample of the educated class, they were optimistic: wonders had to be plausible, but plausibility had new horizons. All sorts of things might be possible with the new mechanisms, "some such spring as is commonly used in Watches." Thousands of years between the sail and the kite, but for Wilkins it was commonsensical to imagine the spring that drove a watch to be useful in making an artificial bird! Roger Bacon, in the 1200s, might have been ahead of his time, but Wilkins in the 1600s assumes that his suggestions are reasonable and need no special argument. They are offered as supporting evidence, a foundation to be built on, rather than as hypotheses to be proven. The rapid cascade of technological miracles has given rise to a new exuberant belief in endless possibilities.

Wilkins, ever systematic, offers four general classes of possible human flight:

1. By Spirits or Angels
2. By the help of fowls
3. By wings fastned [*sic*] immediately to the body
4. By a flying Chariot.[38]

In the first group, reports of Daedalus, Elijah, Simon Magus, and other supernatural flyers are summarized, "but none of these relations may conduce to the discovery of this experiment . . . upon *natural* and *artificial* grounds."[39] [Italics in original.] Artifice is to harness nature, to serve humanity without supernatural assistance. Humankind will not have to achieve saintliness or dance on the edge of damnation in order to fly.

As for training birds to lift a human's weight, Wilkins thinks "it is not certainly more improbable than many other arts, whereto the industry of ingenious men has instructed these brute creatures. And I am very confident, that one whose genius doth enable him for such kind of experiments . . . might effect some strange thing by this kind of enquiry."[40] Such confidence, all the stronger for having a basis in reality! No superstition this, no primitive uncritical acceptance of miracles, but rather a dazzling optimism born of personal experience and observation.

Moving right along to his third method, wings attached to the body, "if we may trust credible story, it has been frequently attempted, not without some success." Wilkins lists the exploits of "a certain English monk called *Elmerus* ... and so another from Saint *Mark's* steeple in Venice; another at *Norinberge;* and ... a Turk in *Constantinople* ..." but soberly warns that inexperience led these pioneers to broken arms or legs. He suggests then that one who wishes to try this method be "brought up to the constant practice of it from his youth."[41] After all, "it is not more incredible, that frequent practice and custom should inable [*sic*] a man for this, than for many other things which we see confirmed by experience." Rope-dancers, acrobats, and tumblers are his evidence, as are "certain *Indians,* that they are able when a horse is running in his full canter, to stand upright on his back, to turn themselves round, to leap down, gathering up any thing from the ground, and immediately to leap up again, to shoot exactly at any mark, the horse not intermitting his course. ..." [Italics in original.] If men can achieve stunts like that through practice, what is the big deal about flying?[42]

On reflection, though, Wilkins notes that human arms

are but weak and easily wearied, therefore the motions by them are like to be but short and slow. ... It were therefore worth the inquiry to consider whether this might not be more probably effected by the labour of the feet, which are naturally more strong and indefatigable. In which contrivance the [motion of the wings] should be from the legs ... so as each leg should move both wings, by which means a man should (as it were) walk or climb up into the air. ... Which conjecture is not without good probability ... [43]

Most useful of all is the much more comfortable Chariot, "this contrivance being as much to be preferred before any of the other, as swimming in a ship before swimming in the water." Several persons may labor together, taking turns, so that the motion would be "more constant and lasting" than if one person worked alone. Two questions must be faced, however: whether something so heavy may be supported by such a thin medium as air, and "whether the strength of the persons within it may be sufficient for the motion of it?"[44]

Wilkins insists that it may be difficult, but cannot be impossible, to find suitable proportions of weight to size for the mechanical flying chariot. "As it is in those bodies which are carried on the water, though they be never so big, or so ponderous (suppose equal to a City or a whole Island) yet they will always swim on the top, if they be but any thing lighter than so much water as is equal to them in bigness; So likewise is it in the bodies that are carried in the air."[45] Wilkins does not rely on scientific principle, but offers experience to support his claim: there is "a fowl in *Peru* called *Condores,* which of themselves kill and eat up a whole Calf at a time. Nor is there any reason why any other body may not be supported and carried by the air, though it should as much exceed the quantity of these fowl, as they do the quantity of a fly." [Italics in original] Scale presents no problem to Wilkins. The ratio of his flying chariot to the size of a condor may be as the condor compared to a fly—yet both condor and fly have the freedom of the air, why shouldn't that future "contrivance"?[46]

He makes equally short work of the second question. Once the thing is in the air, "the motion of it will be easie, as it is in the flight of all kind of birds, which being at any great distance from the earth, are able to continue their motion for a long time and way, with little labour or weariness." Wilkins supposes that gravity (or "Magnetick virtue") becomes less at higher elevations, so that the chariot once aloft will need little power to keep it there. The "divers other particulars" necessary to success must wait for experiments; and those, Wilkins leaves for the interested reader. The difficulty will "add a glory to the invention."[47] The difficult we do at once; the impossible takes a little longer!

Here is technology fiction indeed, though Wilkins offers it as sober scientific thought. All objections are brushed away as either "perverse incredulity" or the mewlings of the incompetent. Grant that a thing is possible, and some clever mechanic will produce it sooner or later.

Looking backward from the comfortable distance of the late nineteenth century, balloonist John Wise of Philadelphia opines

> We find here that for the space of over 400 years one generation after another conceived more or less fully the principles and truths of a theory without any real success toward its consummation in practice. The idea thrown out by Roger Bacon of atmospherical buoyancy, it does seem from history, had become the favorite theory with the most philosophical portion of the advocates of the doctrine that flying through the air could be accomplished by human beings. The other portion, who were evidently more of a mechanical turn, contended that it must be accomplished, by the aid of artificial wings, on the bird principle. Now, that it is not philosophically disproved that man may fly by the aid of artificial wings is evident, for it would be no more at variance with the laws of nature than it is for him to swim in the water like a fish.

While Cuperus upon the one hand, in his treatise on the "Excellence of Man," contends that the faculty of flying by the use of artificial wings fastened to the body of a man can be attained, Borrelli, a Neapolitan mathematician, asserts that, after having examined the subject with great nicety, in a comparison of the strength of the muscles of a man to the muscles of a bird, it is impossible to fly by means of wings fastened to the body. Under this view of the subject, we may safely steer a middle course, neither denying the one nor positively assuming the other, but leaving to the age of improvement in which we live to decide, by actual experiment, what may be accomplished by both plans.[48]

We should note that at the very moment Wise wrote this, scientists and mechanics on both sides of the Atlantic were entangled in such experiments. The one option Wise does not mention, fixed-wing aircraft, proved to be the most promising and ultimately successful. We are getting ahead of our story, though.

FLYING FACTS AND FABLES

How can we untangle the possible historical facts from the legends built upon them? Only with the utmost care, and full understanding that we are very likely to be mistaken. John Wise summed it up in 1873:

> ... plausible accounts and mathematical deductions ... are interspersed among the romantic and fabulous stories which seem to have been built upon them. It was often difficult to find out who the real or original authors were, and whether they were writing from personal knowledge or from hearsay. In regard to most of them ... the inventors of these flying machines mainly attribute the particular excellence of their discoveries to some patron saint's spiritual power, notwithstanding they used many wheels and pinions [gears] in their aërial apparatus.[49]

Spiritual power may have been more effective than Wise was willing to admit, but as inspiration and motivation for the inventors rather than as a physical force sustaining aircraft.

CHAPTER 5

HUMAN-POWERED FLIGHT

ORNITHOPTERS

T he imitation of birdflight had a powerful grip on the imagination of inventors. If only the power of human arms and legs could be multiplied, perhaps by levers and sails, it might be possible to travel through the air. Then in the late nineteenth century when small motors became available, they too were pressed into service. The old dreams did not die, however, they seldom do; when powered flight was achieved, human-powered flight was simply relegated to the world of serious sport.

THE "TOWER JUMPERS"

Towers and other high places were much in demand as starting points for wing trials. It is always easier to keep going than to get started, and artificial flight is no exception. The first one that historians count as successful was that of Eilmer, a monk in the abbey at Malmsbury, who "in his early youth had hazarded a deed of remarkable boldness. He had by some means, I scarcely know what, fastened wings to his hands and feet so that, mistaking fable for truth, he might fly like Daedalus, and collecting the breeze on the summit of a tower, he flew for more than the distance of a furlong. But, agitated by the violence of the wind and the swirling of air, as well as by awareness of his rashness, he fell, broke his legs, and was lame ever after."[1] Thus the story is told by a fellow monk, William, of the same abbey, who very likely had it at only second or third hand from monks who had heard the tale from Eilmer himself and perhaps from others who had witnessed this "deed of remarkable boldness." In modern measure, Eilmer's flight covered more than six hundred feet, longer than two football fields. Even allowing for some exaggeration, that is quite an accomplishment.

We have to do some historical analysis to arrive at an approximate date for this feat. Since Eilmer is described as a "youth" when he attempted his flight, yet old enough to construct his wings, he was probably at least a teen but less than twenty-five years old. While we do not know his exact date of birth, we do know that he saw Halley's comet in both 989 and 1066; his flight would likely have been sometime between 1000 and 1010 C.E.[2]

What in the world possessed him, to try such a stunt? It is not likely he had heard of similar attempts by others; there were very few of those, and a country boy in England would not be aware of them, except possibly the legend of Bladud, founder of Bath, who had crashed into London almost two thousand years before. Perhaps it was the turning of the millennium; perhaps a boyish desire to distinguish himself before he became just one more of the brethren at Malmsbury.

He might have known the Daedalus legend, and maybe thought to demonstrate the greater power of Christianity in contrast to paganism. At that time, as so often even today, physical power was thought to be a mark of divine favoritism; if God was on your side, what need you fear? He may have been inspired, or at least encouraged, by Isaiah's promise of "those who put their trust in the Lord . . . shall raise wings as eagles."[3]

And in any case, adolescent boys and girls tend to think that they are immortal. Only once he was actually aloft did he feel "awareness of his rashness," much like those cartoon characters who run off a cliff and only fall when they realize that they are unsupported in midair.

At about that time, too, there was a radical change in the way Jesus' ascension to heaven was portrayed by the pious in England and Europe. Where previously Jesus arose in great dignity, perhaps floating on a cloud accompanied by angels, in England of Eilmer's time Jesus begins to be shown rocketing up to heaven; he goes so quickly that he is barely seen in motion, only his feet remain at the top of the frame, and his disciples' garments flutter in his wake. This imagery might have inspired Eilmer to attempt a rapid rise as well.[4]

There was also a change in the depiction of God. Before 1000, God is shown creating the earth by sheer power of thought; after 1000, we begin to see God holding scales and a drafting compass, "measuring" the earth and judging it. In later illustrations, only the compass, premier instrument and symbol of the engineer, appears in God's hand. Perhaps Eilmer was influenced by these changes in religious perception, and inspired to use physical means to achieve a spiritual goal.[5]

Eilmer's exploit is the earliest example of human flight taken seriously by modern historians. His feat resounded through the centuries, although anyone who has tried to puzzle through medieval English letters will sympathize with Ralph Higden, who in 1352 misread the "Ei" as "O" and the "m" as "iv", thus transforming Eilmer's name into "Oliver."[6] Nevertheless, Bishop John Wilkins in 1648 cited Eilmer/Oliver as having accomplished winged flight, and Eilmer is still honored as a pioneer.

Other tales of intrepid flyers are less well documented, and may be entirely fictional. Abul Quasim ibn Firnas (the "Wise Andalusian") made a fatal attempt from a cliff in Spain in 852 or 875 (reports vary as to date). An unnamed "Saracen" leaped from the hippodrome in Constantinople in 1161. The Saracen seems to have fared better than most, since an eyewitness claimed that "he soared like a bird and seemed to fly in the air [across the hippodrome]."[7]

Unhappy outcomes did not faze their successors, all sure that they had finally perfected the apparatus. About 1490, Giovanni Battista Danti, an Italian mathematician, attempted to fly over Lake Trasimeno.[8] Some twenty years later, a certain Father Damian, physician to the Scottish king, boasted that he could fly on homemade wings and arrive in Paris sooner than the embassy which had been dispatched to France. Alas, his leap from Stirling Castle resulted in broken legs, which he blamed on having some hen-feathers in the wings—since chickens were more attracted to the barnyard than to the sky, it was unavoidable that their influence would prevent him from achieving his boast.[9] The histories are full of similar stories, often with drawings of the hopeful contraptions. The devices look pitifully inadequate and absurd, but one must remember that drawing to scale was not a concern.

Imprisoning folks in towers seems to have been popular among early kings, offering opportunities for imitations of Daedalus. King Shapur I (reigned over the Persian Empire 241–72 C.E.) shut up his prize architect in a tower so he could not produce such fine work for others, but the clever man fashioned wings of wood and made good his escape.[10] Rodrigo Aleman, a Spanish sculptor imprisoned in another tower, made wings from the feathers of birds he had eaten, but his jump was unfortunately fatal.[11] Aleman's feat may be pure legend; the cathedral from which he is supposed to have jumped (Plasencia) has no tower.[12] Like Regiomontanus's eagle, however, the story persists and contributes to the total mythos of flight.

Robert Hooke, a respected scientist and experimenter of Newton's day, claimed to have flown an ornithopter, but did complain about the difficulty of remaining in the air.[13] His flight was more probably a glide than an actual powered flight, but it is certainly hard to tell from the records.

Tower-jumping was not limited to sages, showoffs, and sculptors: in 1742, a relatively enlightened time, the Marquis de Bacqueville devised a set of wings which he attached to his arms and legs, and attempted to fly across the Seine.[14] And in 1781, Karl Friedrich Meerwein, architect to the prince of Baden, proposed a flapping-wing glider.[15]

FLYING MODELS, TOYS, AND AUTOMATA

Before people strapped wings on themselves, they designed imitation birds for amusement and study. In the early days, these models were unusual enough to be the delight of kings and emperors East and West. What better way to impress your sovereign with your mechanical and intellectual skills, or with your occult knowledge, than by producing an artificial bird? What better way to develop designs and study aeronautics, than by producing a small-scale flyer?

Chinese tradition recounts the marvelous artificial flying birds made by Kungshu Phan and Mo Ti in the fourth century B.C.E., which flew for three days before coming down. We can only guess what tidbit of reality might be at the heart of these tales, which were written down long after they were supposed to have happened.

A certain amount of skepticism and doubt was already expressed in the first century C.E. by one Wang Chhung,[16] who wrote "If such a thing had the shape of a bird, how could it fly for three days without resting? If it could soar, why only for three days?" Wang Chhung goes on to note that Kungshu Phan is supposed to have lost his mother in a flying wagon he built for her that simply flew completely away; if Kungshu Phan could make such a long-flying wagon, Wang Chhung asks, why did his artificial bird not stay aloft for an indefinite time as well?[17]

The "birds" of Kungshu Phan and Mo Ti may have been kites, since the Chinese symbol is ambiguous, but there is no question about the bird made by the great astronomer Chang Heng, who was a little younger than Wang Chhung. This bird had a spring-driven mechanism in its belly, which enabled it to fly for some considerable distance. Wang Chhung himself seems to make reference to the contraption, musing in his memoirs after being dismissed with some disgrace, "Yet linked wheels may be made to turn of themselves, so that an object of carved wood may be made to fly all alone in the air. With drooping feathers I have returned to my own home; why should I not adjust my mechanisms and put them in working order?"[18]

The European counterpart is the "flying dove" demonstrated by Archytas of Tarentum in the fourth century B.C.E., just about the time of Mo Ti and Kungshu Phan. Archytas's amazing bird is not described until several centuries after it was supposed to have flown, and just as with the "birds" of Mo Ti and Kungshu Phan, there are important unanswered questions about its mechanism. Some accounts suggest that Archytas used expanding gas, perhaps steam or compressed air, as its motive power; others that there was some sort of launcher and then the model continued as a glider.

Joseph Needham, comparing the Chinese and European tales, comments that the Dove of Archytas seems to fit better with the much later style of the Alexandrian "mechanicians" who worked with pneumatic devices and suggests "conceivably, therefore, the account . . . may refer to a light model with glider wings . . . with a narrow backward-pointing outlet, through which a jet of steam could issue, as in Heron's aeolipile."[19]

Johann Muller, also known as Regiomontanus, is supposed to have created an iron eagle—or perhaps an iron fly—to welcome the Emperor Charles V to Nuremburg. Regiomontanus lived in Nuremburg from 1471 to 1475, and it is hard to tell which Charles V might be the one involved; all the ones listed in histories and encyclopedias were not alive in

Regiomontanus's lifetime (1436–76).[20] Yet the story is repeated by most of the writers describing "the history of aeronautics from earliest times," which suggests that they were simply copying from their predecessors. Even so, the legend persists and has influence on the minds of those who read it. Legends need not be true to be powerful.

Bats, those detested and sometimes feared inhabitants of the night, were not usually imitated, and batwings are often associated with the devil. The one outstanding exception is the work of Leonardo da Vinci, who used both bird and bat wings in his sketches of flying machines. Batwings did not have such negative connotations in non-Western cultures, but feathers still seem to have been preferred, as evidenced by the Taoist honorific "feather guest" for example. When humans dreamed of wings, those wings had feathers.

SERIOUS BIRDWATCHERS

Leonardo da Vinci understood the fluid nature of air and the forces of lift and drag. While he was a keen and accurate observer of birdflight, he sought to do more than simply copy the anatomy and motions of birds. His goal was to extract general principles which could then be used in developing machines to aid human flight. Those principles would have to be mathematical; da Vinci insisted "no knowledge can be certain, if it is not based upon mathematics or upon some other knowledge which is itself based upon the mathematical sciences. Instrumental, or mechanical science is the noblest and above all others the most useful" and "let no man who is not a mathematician read the elements of my work." Specifically, in his codex *On the Flight of Birds:* "A bird is an instrument working according to mathematical law, an instrument which it is within the capacity of man to reproduce with all its movements."[21] There are some clues that Leonardo actually tried the experiment, but the only report we have is from Jerome Cardan, the son of an acquaintance of Leonardo's: "Leonardo da Vinci also attempted to fly, but misfortune befell him from it. He was a great painter."[22]

It has been said that Leonardo's designs could not work because he did not understand the limitations imposed by the weight of materials and the energy available from human muscles. By the 1600s, though, these problems had been thoroughly discussed and analyzed. In mocking the persistence of ornithopter-type designs, many historians cite Giovanni Borelli's 1680 "proof" that human power alone could not sustain flight.[23] Borelli certainly brought all the available science to bear on the question, but we may be excused if we, like many of his contemporaries and later dreamers, fail to be convinced. History is so full of examples of the experts confounded that it seems the more "impossible" a feat is proclaimed, the more any given dreamer becomes convinced that the very act of rejection proves the validity of his or her plan to accomplish it. "They laughed at Columbus," goes the thought, "and they're laughing at me; therefore I must be as right as Columbus was." And there is always the very human desire to show up the experts and gain glory. Accomplishment against great odds seems the sweeter victory, whether those odds are a physical or "scientific" challenge.

In the mid-1600s, Tito Livio Burattini built at least three complex ornithopter models, each in the form of a flying dragon. They attracted the serious attention of contemporary scientists, including Christiaan Huyghens, better known to us for his work on optics.[24] Like many others of his day (most notably including Isaac Newton), Huyghens was also interested in dynamics, the principles governing motion. Physicist Robert Hooke also dabbled in ornithopter design and construction, as we have noted. Flying machines made excellent subjects for both theoretical and experimental exploration.

Emanuel Swedenborg, in the next generation, followed a career path which seems strange in modern terms. Younger son of a prominent Swedish bishop and theologian, as a young man Emanuel traveled to Britain and the European continent with a letter of introduction to the brightest minds of the age. His father and elder brother had also traveled and established impressive reputations, which opened doors for him in London, Paris, the Hague, and elsewhere. His friends and intellectual mentors included a long list of prominent astronomers, mathematicians, and physicists. Returning to Sweden, he began to publish a scientific journal called *Daedalus Hyperboreus*[25] in which he presented both his own work and that of others.

After devoting himself to natural science for three decades, in 1744 he abruptly abandoned scientific work and devoted himself to theology, writing several books and eventually founding a new Protestant denomination.[26] As he wrote to a friend, "I was first introduced by the Lord into the natural sciences and was thus prepared; and this from the year 1710 to 1744, when heaven was opened to me."[27]

To our modern Western eyes, this would be considered an abrupt change from one mindset to another, from a secular and scientific—

"rational"—perspective to a religious and mystical one. But in the eighteenth century, the lines were not so clearly drawn. For some philosophers, science and religion were completely contradictory perspectives and to embrace one was to forsake the other. But for those like Swedenborg, science and religion were complementary, supporting and reinforcing each other. It is also probable that Swedenborg, like his father before him, saw his scientific activities as part of his service to God. In theoretical mechanics, he sought the "soul" of matter; in anatomical research he looked for the location of the biological "soul."[28]

At the age of twenty-seven, already accepted in rarified intellectual circles, Swedenborg published a well thought-out design for an ornithopter. He carefully specifies that the construction materials be as light as possible while sturdy enough to hold together and support the pilot. Calculations based on birds and kites establish the minimum size of the "sails" to guide and support the contraption. He notes, for example, "that the wind can lift up very heavy materials, so that when it blows against a gate with force, it can blow it open even though two men be pushing against it, when yet it is often 16 square ells in extent. How, then, would it act on a surface of 150 square ells, with the wings helping along?"[29] He offers the example of kites and birds, which once aloft "swim in the air and with all their weight rest on their wings without moving the least feather for several minutes. In the case of kites, made of paper and wood, we see a similar property, in that they keep themselves up in the air without sinking down in the least." Once an ornithopter was in the air, perhaps human strength would be enough to keep it there.

His general description of the vessel displays his careful reasoning. He begins by specifying "if we follow living nature, examining the proportions that the wing of a bird holds to its body, a similar mechanism might be invented, which should give us hope to be able to follow the bird in the air." Not only the proportions of the wing to the body, but of weight to volume and of shape, are considered:

> First, let a car or boat or some object be made of light material such as cork or birch bark, with a room within for the operator. Second, in front as well as behind, or all around, set a widely stretched sail parallel to the machine, forming within a hollow, or bend, which could be reefed like the sails of a ship. Third, place wings on the sides, to be worked up and down by a spiral spring, these wings also to be hollow below in order to increase the force

and velocity take in the air and make the resistance as great as may be required. These, too, should be made of light material and of sufficient size; they should be in the shape of bird's wings or the arms of a windmill or some such shape, and be tilted obliquely upwards and be made so as to collapse on the upward stroke and expand on the downward.

Swedenborg goes on to consider the dynamics of the machine in flight:

Fourth, place a balance or beam [*vectis*] below, hanging down perpendicularly to some distance and with a small weight attached to the end, pendent exactly in line with the center of gravity—the longer this beam is, the lighter it must be, for it must have the same proportion as the well known [Roman] *vectis* or steelyard. This would serve to restore the balance of the machine whenever it should lean over to any of the four sides. Fifth, the wings would perhaps have greater force, so as to increase the resistance and make the flight easier, if a hood or shield were placed above them, as is the case with certain insects. Sixth, when now the sails are expanded so as to occupy a great surface and much air, with a balance keeping them horizontal, only a small force would be needed to move the machine back and forth in a circle, and up and down. And after it has gained [sufficient] momentum to move slowly upwards, a light movement and an even bearing would keep it balanced in the air and would determine its direction at will.

He does admit there might be some bugs in the system at first: "although when the first trials are to be made, you may have to pay for the experience and must not mind an arm or a leg."

Swedenborg's crisis of faith was sudden, resulting from a series of dreams in 1743 and 1744. The explicit sexual content of these dreams may be related to Swedenborg's feelings of guilt about his ambition to be recognized for his scientific work. He draws analogies between his former "love of the sex" while he was primarily studying science, and the chaste spiritual love and search for a soulmate (he remained unmarried) associated with his return to theology and metaphysics. In one dream, for example, he finds that a desirable woman "had teeth where I wished to penetrate" and interprets this to mean that he should turn away from secular (scientific) pursuits and devote himself to religion.[30]

Between the 1780s and the twentieth century, other inventors devised various combinations of balloon, flapping wings, and airscrew propellers.[31] Truly, Bishop John Wilkins's vision had become reality; if it seemed possible, clever mechanics would try to make it happen. The nearer success seemed to be, the more ingenuity was expended in its pursuit.

Notwithstanding all the scientific and philosophical ingenuity directed toward flying, one nineteenth century British naturalist wanted to know why the birds themselves had not been harnessed:

> Why have not these monsters of the sky been appropriated to the use of man? How comes it that he who has subdued the ocean and cultivated the earth, who has harnessed elephants, and even lions, to his chariot wheels, should never have availed himself of the wings of the eagle, the vulture, or the frigate pelican? That, having ascertained the possibility of traveling at the rate of eighty miles an hour through its void regions, he should yet allow himself to be the mere sport of the whirlwind, and not tame to his use, and harness to his car, the winged strength of some of these aerial racers, and thus stamp with reality some of the boldest fictions of the heathen poets? . . . The hint has, indeed, long been thrown out; and the perfection to which the art of falconry was carried in former times sufficiently secures it against the charge of absurdity or extravagance.[32]

Although he was behind his times, his question might be extended: why had not birds been harnessed to balloons? A number of contraptions had been suggested for guiding the flight of balloons,[33] but there is no suggestion of utilizing teams of birds as had been done in the old legends and stories. Had Western humankind become so "scientific" that only artificial wings would now be considered, albeit based on those of birds?

Gustav and Otto Lilienthal in Germany began their aeronautical work as youngsters, paying close attention to the details of birdflight in designing their flying apparatus. Inspired by a fable in which a stork instructs a small willow wren how to fly without getting too tired, the brothers tried to get close to the storks in the meadows around their hometown. When a stork would notice them, it would take off against the wind even when that meant it had to go toward the boys—a clear indication that lifting against the wind must be easier than with it, "because without compelling cause the shy bird would not advance toward us."

The brothers in their early teens were encouraged by their mother, who willingly supplied financing for their early "flying machines" even though she was then a widow on a tight budget. Others were not so supportive; Gustav reports "in order to escape the jibes of our schoolmates, we experimented at night time . . . but there being no wind on these clear star-lit summer nights, we met with no success. We were then 13 and 14 years of age respectively, and our flying experiments rather interfered with the proper discharge of our school work."[34]

As adults, the Lilienthal brothers continued their fascination with birdflight, making careful measurements as they experimented with wing shapes. They even built their own hill for takeoffs.[35] Although their ultimate goal was mechanically powered flight, their first step was to thoroughly investigate flying itself. Since nature had spent millennia perfecting birds, and the major difference between birds and people in this respect was available power, it is not unreasonable for them to have tried to imitate birds with the ultimate aim of simply adding mechanical power to a successful design.[36]

The brothers continued their experiments, scrimping on meals to pay for materials, and continued to avoid public notice. In 1871, they flew "an apparatus which was fitted with beating wings, moved by spiral springs and which was launched from an inclined plane out of the window of our lodging on the fourth floor, at 4 o'clock in the morning, so as to avoid being seen."[37] Looking back in 1893, Otto recalled, "[M]ost people in Germany considered anyone who would waste his time on such a profitless art to be a fool. . . . At that time it had just been confirmed once and for all by a particularly learned government-appointed commission that man could not fly, which did not particularly lift the spirits of those working on the problem of flight."[38] That commission, headed by no less a figure than Hermann von Helmholtz, had concluded that *human-powered* flight was not feasible, but the subtle nuance was widely ignored. Gustav and Otto were not aiming for human-powered flight. Their designs were adapted from birdflight, and tested as unpowered kites or gliders, but they intended to use motors for power both in their small models and in the eventual aircraft. By 1874:

In our loft we installed a regular workshop and laid the keel of a wing flyer. The wings were an exact copy of a bird's wings: the pinions consisting of willow canes with narrow front and wide back feathers . . . the whole thing was the size of a stork, and the propelling force was to be a light motor which, however, had first to be designed.... We also built kites in the form of birds, in order to study the behaviour of the apparatus in the wind; the surfaces of the wings being curved, in order to imitate a bird.[39]

Slowly, slowly, they gained confidence and made progress. In 1889, after more than three decades of work as boy and man, Otto published *Der Vogelflug als Grundlage der Fliegekunst (Birdflight as the Basis for Aviation)*. However, it was far from a commercial success. He had to pay the printing costs, and must have been disappointed in the meagre sales. The first printing was a thousand copies, but fewer than three hundred of those were sold in the next seven years.[40] His tables and calculations were influential both in Europe and the United States, but the number of tinkerers, mechanics, and theoretical aerodynamicists constituted a very small market. (Had he known of it, he might have taken some comfort in the comparably poor showing of another important book, Nicholas Copernicus's *Revolutions of the Heavenly Spheres*. A thousand copies were printed in Nuremburg and never sold out.)[41]

Otto's name alone appears on the published work, and only Otto addressed technical and scientific societies, although the brothers were truly partners in the joint endeavor. Perhaps this was because Otto was a trained engineer, having passed his examinations with record high honors at the Provincial Technical School at Potsdam, while Gustav was more strictly a businessman in "the building trade."

What kept the brothers at work on their flying machines, through all those long years? Their sources of motivation blend into each other— their boyhood fascination with birds nourished and sustained their adult fascination with the intellectual and ethical challenge of flight. Ethical? Yes, the men shared a deep desire for social justice, and felt that flight, among other things, would help. Otto wrote: "The borders between countries would lose their significance, because they could not be closed off from each other; linguistic differences would disappear as human mobility increased. National defense would cease to devour the best resources of nations ... and the necessity of resolving disagreements among nations in some other way than by bloody battles ... would secure for us eternal peace."[42] Alas, like so many other technological innovations heralded as panaceas, cures for the world's ills, flight did not irresistibly lead to utopia.

SCIENCE AS MANLY SPORT

American balloonist John Wise tried to bring Roger Bacon's ideas into the nineteenth century by putting mathematics to work, with careful attention to details of construction. The adventuresome boy peeps through the facade of the objective scientist:

> Soon after [Roger] Bacon's time, projects were instituted to train up children from their infancy in the exercise of flying with artificial wings, which seemed to have been the favorite plan of the flying philosophers and artists of that day. If we credit the accounts of some of their experiments, it would seem that considerable progress was made in that way. The individuals who used the wings could skim over the surface of the earth with a great deal of ease and celerity. This was accomplished by the combined faculties of running and flying. It is stated, that, by an alternately continued motion of the wings against the air, and the feet against the ground, they were enabled to move along with a striding motion, and with incredible speed.
>
> If we are permitted, for a moment, to digress from the historical part of our subject, we will show that this method of locomotion, under the present knowledge of aeronautics, could be turned to considerable account. [If a man uses a balloon to lift most of his weight, and then] provides himself with a pair of wings, made on the bird principle, with socket joints to slip over his arms at the shoulders, and a grasping handle internally of each one, at the distance from the shoulder joint of the wing, as the distance is from his shoulder to his hand, he may beat against the air with his wings, and bound against the earth with his feet, so as to make at least a hundred yards at each bound. *This the writer has often done, in the direction of a gentle wind, with the aid of his feet alone, after his balloon had descended to the earth; and, on one occasion traversed a pine forest of several miles in extent, by bounding against the tops of the trees.* Such a contrivance would be of inestimable value to exploring expeditions. Landings to otherwise inaccessible mountains; escapes from surrounding icebergs; explorations of volcanic craters; traversing vast swamps and morasses; walking over lakes and seas; bounding over isthmuses, straits, and promontories, or ex-

ploring the cloud-capped peaks of Chimborazo, could thus all be easily accomplished.⁴³ [Emphasis added]

Don't you wish you had been there to see him "bounding against the tops of the trees"!

PERSISTENCE OF VISION

Even with cloth or paper kites as examples, even when balloons provided lift, minds were drawn back to birds. How difficult it was to abandon the use of birds as models for human flight! Late in the nineteenth century, Alexander Graham Bell called for a return to the study of birds "that were pursued for hundreds of years before the invention of the balloon diverted attention from the subject." Bell reminded his contemporaries that none of the natural fliers, "from the smallest insect to the largest bird" uses the balloon principle in flight.⁴⁴

In science, one goal of experimenters and theoreticians is to isolate one factor, and hold all the others constant. Only then can one be reasonably certain that one's results are correlated to that factor and not others. (It should be remembered that correlation is not identical to cause, but that is another issue entirely.)

Historians also may become seduced by the notion that an event results from a single cause. When more than one cause contributes, the event is classed as "overdetermined." In the case of artificial flight, "overdetermined" seems almost inadequate to describe the persistence of the birdflight model. There were both technical and ideological foundations involved, and untangling them is difficult.

Birds use their wings for both propulsion and lift. Roger Bacon, Francesco Lana de Terzi, and Bartholomew Guzman suggested that lift be separated from propulsion: that lighter-than-air spheres be used for lift, and some variation on oars or sails be used for propulsion. Most aeronautical pioneers until the nineteenth century, however, continued to work with ways to power variations on the artificial "birdlike" wing. The development of hot-air Montgolfier and then hydrogen-filled balloons revived speculation as to how aircraft could be pushed and aimed in defiance of the wind.

George Cayley is credited with the first heavier-than-air design which separates lift and propulsion. Even after these two components were well recognized as distinct factors, however, controversy raged about the best methods of raising and directing aircraft. Should mechanical power be applied to flapping the wings, or to an airscrew?[45] The Lilienthals steadfastly developed their ornithopter designs, while others as steadfastly insisted that the airscrew in combination with fixed wings was the proper approach. The Wright brothers used fixed-wings, but with a twist, literally: their success depended on their ability to variably bend (warp) their wings in adjusting to flight conditions. The airscrew has now become so firmly identified with mechanical flight that it is simply known as "the propeller"—literally, that which pushes.

"DRESSING IN THE WORK-CLOTHES OF BIRDS"

The psychological and spiritual components supporting the birdflight model were very strong. The simplest psychological factor may be sheer familiarity. Many technical innovations retain visible reminders of previous versions, called skeuomorphs.[46] Early plastic objects, for example, retained the angular shapes of their predecessors made from less bendable or moldable materials. Even the names of new things often refer to the familiar: "iron horse" (railway locomotive) and "horseless carriage" (automobile) to name but two. "Wireless telegraphy" (radio) is another. We "dial" telephone numbers long after dials have been replaced by pushbuttons. We cling to familiarity, to continuity. So it was with flight; like Shun, the young Chinese emperor-to-be, we dress in the work-clothes of birds.[47]

We have noted that birds represented positive spiritual values; most Western dreamers based their designs on birds rather than insects or bats. Birds not only fly, they symbolize flight; thus there is a strong tendency to think their form and function are ideal for the purpose, even over and above the fact that they do fly.

Another source of spiritual reinforcement is the deep sense that natural forms embody a divine plan; that earthly forms mirror the intent of the deity, and artificial forms had best follow suit if they mean to be most effective. The concept that God (or nature) is the best engineer bridges the spiritual and technical.[48] Fifteenth-century architect Francesco di Giorgio inscribed a human figure on the plan view of a church: "Since man was made in the image of God, so it was believed the proportions exemplified in the human form would reflect a divine and cosmic order."[49] The nature philosophy of the Enlightenment, in the eighteenth century, also saw cosmic unity in form and function.[50]

Deeper still, there are echoes of sympathetic magic or religious imitation. To imitate a thing is in a sense to become that thing; actual physical flight is only one of the many things that birds represent. The same impulse that leads us to think that "the name *is* the thing" suggests that the shape and properties of a thing are also part of its essence. So many of the aviation pioneers, "scientific" and "eccentric," began by letting their imaginations fly with the birds they watched!

CHAPTER 6

GLIDERS, PARACHUTES, AND KITES

T he kite, the sail, the parachute—they seem so alike to us, an expanse of fabric catching the air. And as one historian put it, "the kite is a tethered glider."[1] They have each contributed to the development of flight, but each has a historical path of its own.

Once again, each of these elements has symbolic associations as well as physical reality. Unpowered flight was pursued for its own sake, and for earthly uses, as well as in exploring the properties of the air and setting the parameters within which powered flight might be realized. Windmills harnessed the air for the mundane purpose of grinding flour for our daily bread, and pumping water for our refreshment and our crops.

Kite flying for pleasure is a worldwide phenomenon; Alexander Graham Bell used kites systematically in his approach to the problems of flight, as did the Wright brothers and other pioneers. The boundary between powered flight and gliding is not sharp: many early "flights" were probably predominantly glides rather than powered flight, regardless of the experimenter's intention.

SOULS IN THE AIR

How many children, innocently playing, realize that they are acting out the faint echoes of ancient rituals? The Western youngster running across the field towing a kite is surely unaware that thousands of years ago in Asia kites had religious significance in honoring gods and heroes. Strings and pipes might have been attached to those long-ago kites, as they are sometimes in Asia to this day, to make pleasing music as the air passed over the kite's surface. In many cultures, kites were and are a strictly masculine matter, forbidden to women. Aggressive competition between kites is also common; the strings are coated with ground glass or porcelain, and the kite handlers skillfully maneuver them to cut the strings of competing kites until only one is left triumphant in the air.

In today's northern Indian province of Punjab, the spring festival of Basant Pachani also echoes ancient rites. As the yellow flowers of the mustard plant color the landscape, yellow accents adorn the local clothing: turbans, scarves, shawls, bandannas, handkerchiefs. This is the season for kite flying, kite contests, kite battles. Hundreds of thousands of kites are flown; households set aside separate rooms for kites and their construction.

Kite strings are coated with starch and powdered glass for battle. Beginning in the early morning, kites soar high, drawing their strings behind them for miles. An evenly matched battle may last all day, though lesser contests are decided sooner. With each severed string, "the strength put forth by the arms spurts into the emptiness and the slackness. This is a pain that transcends the physical. The string is some sort of umbilical cord to the birth of man. . . . " says an Indian observer. "This is a man's game" he explains, " . . . There are big kites, heavy enough to carry a child with them. Others, sharklike, all points and deadly fins, seem to harness the force of a gale, and constantly tug a man's arms out of his sockets. . . . These special kites give dominance, but they are hard to control, wanting a constant juggling, a ceaseless watch, and a complete understanding. . . . Like the first woman of the first spring, the women watch and understand without any explanation."[2]

Further east, in China, Korea, and Japan, similar festivals are celebrated. Often the aim is to sever the opponent's string; other times, large "male" kites strive to capture the smaller "female" kites and drag them into male territory. Kites are strictly seasonal in Korea now, flown only during the first two weeks of the New Year. After that, the scapegoat "kite for warding off evil" is flown and released, carrying with it all bad luck.[3]

In some parts of Asia, extra strings are attached to the kites, to make a humming noise as the kite flies. These kites may be flown all night in pleasant weather, to lull people to sleep outdoors. A change in the music serves as a storm warning.

Strength spurting into slackness, umbilical cords, battles between males in spring, scapegoats, and guardian spirits. What a complexity and wealth of symbolism! The association with fertility and new life could not be more clear.

How did kites begin, and what was their original purpose? We can only guess the details, since the origins were not recorded. Some scholars speculate that kite development began with the practice of tying a fine line to an arrow so that it could be retrieved. Joseph Needham thinks this is unlikely, since the action of retrieving a tethered arrow (standing still and pulling) is quite different from that of launching and flying a kite. Further, Needham suggests that if kites began as hunting aids, it is not likely that they would have the early religious associations that they did.[4]

Imagine how it might have happened. We can visualize such a tethered arrow used to shoot a bird, which may have fluttered and flapped its wings in its attempt to escape. The hunter would then pull at the line, just as the kite flyer does. Perhaps, then, kites were developed to mimic this action, in the hope that re-enacting the hunt would ensure success for the next one. Just as the European cave paintings of four-footed game might have been a sort of incantation to attract those animals, perhaps kite flying was a parallel attempt at sympathetic magic. Perhaps, once our long-ago thinker had devised his kite, he flew it as a simple lure. "Fly," he may have asked the kite, "and call to your winged brethren, that my family may eat." Or, perhaps the kite was meant to symbolize the return of a dead bird's spirit to the air, as a gesture of respect and supplication.

The very name "kite" is shared with an aerial acrobat; the whole family of birds called kites are known for their spectacular courtships aloft. Mating and fertility rituals are among the most ancient known to mankind; perhaps here is a clue to some part of the fabric or wooden kite's ritual significance. It would not be the first time that technology was developed to serve spiritual rather than "practical" purposes: ceramics were used to make the exaggeratedly female figurines called "Venus of Willendorf" about twenty-five thousand years ago; another fifteen thousand years went by before anyone got around to making such mundane items as ceramic pots, utensils, tiles, and bricks.[5]

Another scholar suggests that kites may have their origin among sailing folks, via the process of retrieving a sail that had come loose.[6] The partnership of the sailor, the wind, and the water is very like that of a human, spirituality, and a life's path. Think of the sail as the soul of the boat, as it fills with air and moves the vessel. Think of a human's spirituality, the ethical values of that person's culture, as the "air" which gives impetus and direction to the soul's sail.

The nautical account of the kite's origin should give us pause. Five thousand years ago, Egyptian paintings included sailboats. Mediterranean voyagers filled the sea with sailboats. If sails gave birth to kites, why did the kite not appear in Europe until the sixteenth century of the common era? Why was it brought from China, and not developed locally? On the one hand, how many times has it taken decades, centuries, or millennia to develop things that seem so obvious and inevitable in hindsight? On the other hand, we must be careful about plausible explanations which have limited application. Trying to explain "exceptions" can lead to some pretty convoluted reasoning.

The fact remains that the kite was known in Asia and the Pacific for centuries, perhaps a millennium or more, before the Europeans took much notice. The answer to our question, "What was the origin," may be "all of the above"—kites may have developed independently, and served different functions, in several cultures.

Polynesians communicated with their gods Rongo, Tane, Rehua, and Maui by means of kites. After a time, kites came to represent the souls of heroes, of men, and of the gods themselves. The stories seem a bit muddled in translation; the gods are first identified with live birds, then with kites as artificial birds. Kites (flown only by men) play the roles of both gods and goddesses, sometimes re-enacting divine sexual relations and the production of offspring.

Hawaiian myths describe kite competitions as struggles between the gods and the elements. Since the gods themselves often indulge in kite competitions, such activity among humans mirrors and imitates divine activity. Rehua, the "god of highest heaven and of health," is both a sacred bird and the ancestor of all kites. Birds, kites, souls, gods, sex, wings; the web of symbolism ties them together.

Among the Maori, kites were used for divination. In one story, a mother enlists the aid of priests to find her two missing sons. Two large kites are made and named after the sons. When the kites are flown following the appropriate rituals, they persistently hover over a particular town. The town is attacked, and the son of the chief who had killed the woman's sons is executed.[7]

Maori kites were also a ritualized weapon of war. Carefully prepared, the kite would be flown by the priest using only his right hand. Upright flight was a good omen, lopsided flight a sure indication of disaster in battle. Again with careful ritual, the kite was released to fly over the camp of the enemy. "Should any of the enemy chance to take hold of that trailing cord, which was more deadly than a 'live' wire, . . . it practically ensured the success of an attack . . . that cord possessed magic properties with which it had been endowed by the incantations" of the priest.[8]

Symbols, as Mircea Eliade reminds us, are never simple. Whether first used for hunting rituals or not, kites aloft would soon come to symbolize or represent the supernatural inhabitants of the air. The behavior of the kite would seem to mirror the behavior of aerial spirits, and control of the kite would then embody hope for control of the air or spirit. It is a short step from there to a general association of kites with deities as a group, and another short step to inclusion of kites in a wide variety of symbolic rites. With such rich spiritual associations, does it surprise you that kite flying would be restricted to particular elements of society?

Keep in mind that our ancestors were no less intelligent than we, no less interested in the deep mysteries of life. Their perspectives may not have been the same as ours, their attempts to make sense of their world may not follow the lines we might choose, but they were serious thinkers nevertheless. To the believer, religion is not Karl Marx's "opiate of the masses," but rather an honest and thoughtful search for meaning in life. The language of that search is necessarily abstract and symbolic.

CARRYING WEIGHT

Freud reminds us that "sometimes a cigar is just a cigar," and so also sometimes a kite is just a kite.

Once kites had been developed, whatever their original spiritual and emotional associations, in time they were also used for other purposes.

In Indonesia and Melanesia for example, fishermen used kites to carry the line and its baited hook away from the boat, to areas where the fish had not been frightened.[9] Pacific islanders also use kites to snare the long-nosed garfish, dangling a noose or an entangling wad of spiderweb to secure the fish's snout. This kite also served as a lure, resembling a bird enough to trigger the gar's instincts; birds hover over schools of small fish, tasty for both gar and bird.

Perhaps the most famous kite in American history is the one used by Benjamin Franklin in 1752 to draw lightning from the heavens and demonstrate that it was no more, and no less, than the same electricity one could obtain from rubbing wool or amber. His friend and fellow scientist noted that before Franklin tried his experiment, "dreading the ridicule which too commonly attends unsuccessful attempts in science, he communicated his intended experiment to no body but his son, who assisted him in raising the kite."[10] Only afterward did Franklin write of his success to Joseph Collingswood at the Royal Society in London. Franklin's letters on electricity were highly respected and widely publicized, translated into most of the languages of Europe, and into Latin for good measure. (Franklin's distaste for ridicule was shared by other pioneers such as the Lilienthal brothers and Samuel Langley, who sent up their models and prototypes in secret. Even the Wright brothers kept a low profile until they had acquired substantial experience.)

Franklin's experiments established the use of kites for scientific exploration of the upper air. Well into the twentieth century, thermometers and other instruments were still carried aloft by kites.

Kites had obvious military uses as well. They could carry messages across city walls, and they could be used in groups to lift an observer high above the field. According to Needham, these strategies go "back a long way in Chinese history."[11] Needham recounts the story of General Han Hsin, about 200 B.C.E., flying a kite over an enemy palace to estimate the length of tunnel needed to reach within. Another Chinese general "conceived the ingenious idea of frightening the enemy by flying kites, fitted with Aeolian strings, over their camp in the dead of night. The wind was favorable, and when all was wrapped in darkness and silence the forces of Liu Pang heard sounds in the air resembling *Fu Han!* Beware of Han! It was their guardian angels, they declared, who were warning them of impending danger, and they precipitately fled, hotly pursued by the general and his army."[12]

A later legend from Korea tells of a clever ruse by Gen. Gim Yu-Sin. A "falling star" was seen before an important battle, a bad-luck omen. Troop morale had fallen with the star, and prospects looked bleak for the general's cause. One of his advisors suggested attaching a lantern to a kite; the support was invisible against the night sky, and the return of the "star" to the heavens gave new hope to his army.[13]

Marco Polo's *Travels*, published about 1300 C.E., included a description of kites that he saw in China. Most editions of the *Travels* are incomplete, however, so it is difficult to say just how many people saw the description that Lynn White, Jr., suggests "describes the East Asian kite in a way almost designed to stimulate ideas about aviation: he speaks of a man-carrying kite, and lays great stress on how the kite reacts to the wind. . . . Polo tells us that when a merchant ship is about to start on a voyage, a kite is sent up for augury:

> The men of the ship will have a wicker framework, that is a grate of switches, and to each corner and side of that framework will be tied a cord, so that there are eight cords and all of these are tied at the other end to a long rope. Next they will find some fool or drunkard and lash him to the frame, since no one in his right mind or with his wits about him would expose himself to that peril. This is done when the wind is high; then they raise the framework into the teeth of the wind and the wind lifts up the framework and carries it aloft, and the men hold it by the long rope. [If the kite tips, the men on the ground haul on the rope to straighten it, then pay the rope out again] so by this means it might go up until it could no longer be seen, if only the rope were long enough.[14]

If the kite flies straight up, good fortune is predicted; if the kite fails to soar, no merchant will invest in the doomed voyage and the ship will stay in port for a year. No mention is made of the poor soul lashed to the kite which fails to soar! Presumably he drowns or fatally crashes to earth, and being "some fool or drunkard" is little missed. Perhaps this explains the delay of almost three centuries before Western tinkerers begin to explore the man-carrying capacities of the kite.

Giovanni Battista della Porta in 1589 described kites and the influence of the flowing air. "Hence may an ingenious man take occasion to consider how to make a man fly with huge wings bound to his elbows and breast." Della Porta's kite was called a "flying Sayle" by his English translators. By 1646, Athanasius Kircher, a Jesuit with strong ties to China, reported that kites capable of carrying a man were made in Rome.[15]

So near and yet so far. A "flying Sayle" might be taut on its framework, or billowing out; the one path might lead to the airplane wing, the other to the parachute. A sail, a kite, a wing, a parachute; the similarities among them are as clear to our modern eyes as they were to our ancestors; yet it seems such a long time between concept and effective application!

Della Porta's Latin was translated into both French and English, reaching thousands of fertile and curious minds. Here was an interesting thought: humans might soar with kites, rather than flap wings like birds.[16] Looking back through time, we moderns might wonder why it took Europeans such a long time to discover the kite, since it had been known in the Islamic world since at least the ninth century.[17] It seems odd that with all the communication between the Islamic and Christian worlds in those years, the kite comes to Europe via China rather than from the Middle East or even from Muslim Spain. During the long years between the ninth century and the sixteenth, there had been ample opportunity for merchants and travelers to notice this aerial wonder; why didn't anyone call attention to it?

There is a tantalizing suggestion that the kite might have been independently developed in Europe, and then abandoned. It is hard to interpret ancient texts when their names for things are not the same as ours. We see descriptions and pictures of military banners from Roman times, some of them stiffened with a rod across the top, we read of three-dimensional banners belching flame, of flying dragons and serpents.[18] Could some of these have been kites? We have no pictures from Western antiquity or the Middle Ages that we can be sure are kites, but perhaps that just tells us kites were not popular or important.

Could it have been the case that Christian Europeans somehow associated kites (the artifacts) with witchcraft, or with low-class entertainments, or with infidel heresies? Was China a more acceptable source of strange new things than the nations of Islam, since Islam was a direct threat to European Christianity and China was not? Could fear of the Inquisition have banished the kite from high-culture Christian European notice, until some easing of religious tension allowed it to surface? Is it significant that the kite first appears in slightly more tolerant Holland and England? Is there some other element of the "cultural climate" which could have been an important factor?

These are the sorts of questions that bedevil historians, and lead them to the far corners of large or exotic libraries. So far, we have no clear answers, but the hunt continues.

Sometimes the name of a thing is a clue to its history. In Chinese and English, the word for the artifact we call a "kite" is the same as the word for a particular bird it resembles. Joseph Needham believes this mirrors the kite's introduction in Europe from China.[19] If the name is to be a useful marker for the geographic spread of the artifact, there should be some pattern leading from one country to another that parallels some cultural or trade route. Let us look at some European examples.

Since the Chinese kite-artifact was introduced via Dutch merchants, one would expect the translation to be closest in that country. But in Dutch the artifact is called simply "vlieger" (flyer) and the bird which the English call a kite is a "kiekendief" (chicken thief). The translation is not equivalent, the artifact is not called by the name of the bird. To the north, the Danes, Swedes, and Norwegians each call the artifact by their name for dragon ("drage, drake"), as do the Germans ("drachen") to the south of the Netherlands.

The Italians call the artifact "aquilone" (related to aquila, eagle). The Spanish call it a "cometa" (comet) and the French—ah, those French—name it "cerf-volant" (flying stag) after an insect, the staghorn beetle, which flies at a 45-degree angle. Alas, no consistent clue, except that most of the nations on the Baltic seem to agree on "dragon," perhaps reflecting the close trade connections among those countries. The name might also reflect association with the cylindrical "draco" (dragon) banner of the Roman armies.[20]

Is this evidence that the kite is older in Europe than the Chinese import, or is it just that old names have been revived to apply to the novelty item? Is it significant that in some Turkish languages we also find correspondence between the artifact and a bird? In Osmanli the artifact is called "kartal" (eagle) and in Jagatai and Cumanian it is "sar" (sparrow-hawk).[21] Eagles, hawks, and kites are all high-flying birds, sailing on the air as they hunt and rapidly plummeting to earth when attacking prey. Needham suggests that the different European names refer to various shapes of Chinese kites, but that seems to be stretching the concept. What do you think?

WIND AND WATER

Let us turn back to the ancient thoughts of sails and wings, and consider how each interacts with the air. The wind pushes against sails; wings push against air. In each case, air must have some substance, some mass. However, it took at least four thousand years of sailing before the wind was harnessed to mills, most likely in the Middle East. Five thousand until a man was lifted from the ground. Yet Lucian of Samosata (second century C.E.) imagines a flying battalion, held aloft by their billowing garments.

Wind and water currents seem so much alike to us; yet almost a thousand years separates the development of water mills (first to second century B.C.E.) from that of wind mills. Seagoing peoples surely noticed currents in both air and water, and used fabric and wood to move and guide their ships. Sails, oars, rudders, all these were well-known technologies by the beginning of the common era. Wind and water were both harnessed for transportation. Both were harnessed to mills as well, but with an enormous time lag between water and wind. Did mental block cause the delay, or was it lack of interest?

Take some large logs. Add some tinder. You still have no fire. But a spark alone does not last long unless it is put to tinder, and the tinder ignites the larger logs. What "causes" people to invent? Aptitude, curiosity, perseverance, luck—plus perception of a need or desire, societal support for such activity, and societal interest in the result. When any of these are lacking, bright folks direct their talents elsewhere.

What makes a man (and with aeronautics it has usually been men) choose one direction over another, when it comes to invention or scientific exploration? Motivation is always complex. Ideals will influence individual choice, and also influence the choices made by society in adopting particular technologies. Arnold Pacey puts it well:

> ... whether one considers the remote past or the 1970s, one is constantly reminded that ideals, objectives ... are a reflection of more widely held attitudes. They reflect, in fact, the prevailing values, aspirations, and social or political goals in the community at large. Technology is not value-free; on the contrary, in any community or nation it is an integral part of a wider culture, and is influenced by the same values as those which find expression in art, literature, and religion, and in the economic and institutional structures of that community.[22]

In the tenth century C.E., there were some windmills in eastern Iran and Afghanistan, but windmills were not adopted by the rest of Islam even though there was not enough waterpower to grind their grain. On the other hand, once windmills were developed in England (in the twelfth century), they spread like wildfire throughout Europe. Again they were brought to Islam, but still found no welcome.[23] Whatever the reason, the European West, from the Middle Ages onwards, has been particularly receptive to new gadgets.

One new gadget, closely related to windmill vanes and helicopters, was known in Christendom as "the Chinese Top" and in China as "the bamboo dragonfly."[24] In the United States, a similar toy is called a "puddle jumper." If you have a stick topped by something resembling an airplane propeller, and you get it to spin rapidly enough, it will rise in the air. You can spin the stick between your palms, or wrap a string around it and then pull it off quickly; either method will do nicely. George Cayley (we will hear more about him later) played with such toys as part of his own adult exploration of aeronautics.

A hundred years before della Porta's "flying Sayle," in the 1470s and 1480s such men as Leonardo da Vinci and the lesser-known Francesco di Giorgio of Siena were doodling not kites but parachutes in their notebooks.[25] One look at these drawings, however, and even the least mechanically inclined of us will realize at once that there is a serious problem. No umbrella-sized "parachute" is going to be effective, and nobody imagines that a couple of streaming banners will do much to break a fall. Lynn White, Jr., thinks the young man beneath the banners has been provided with a mouthpiece to avoid damage to his teeth; di Giorgio has clearly given detailed thought to safety. The young man nevertheless looks exceedingly dubious, as if to say "Why did I let them talk me into this?" One hopes that da Vinci and di Giorgio were not drawing to scale. Sure enough, Leonardo writes, "If a man have a tent roof of caulked linen twelve yards broad and as many high, he will be able to let himself fall from any great height without any danger to himself."[26] A modern parachute is about twenty-four feet in diameter; Leonardo at least was in the right ballpark.

Not until over three hundred years later, however, was the first recorded European parachute jump attempted. Nor was that jump inspired by European ideas, but rather an imitation of a reported feat in the court of the Siamese king, where an acrobat's fall was slowed by two parasols fastened to his belt. The rigid parasol model was soon abandoned, however, in favor of the less structured fabric pocket more familiar to us today.[27]

Balloon flights made the need for parachutes distressingly clear. One could not always control the flight path of a balloon, nor ensure that it descended gently over land. A balloon blown out to sea, carrying its passengers in a light basket, was a ticket to certain drowning. Jean Pierre Blanchard demonstrated a parachute in 1785, dropping a dog safely from his balloon, and in 1793 personally made the first successful human descent via parachute. In spite of the obvious advantage of having a parachute, not all balloonists equipped themselves with this lifesaver.

PLAYING WITH THE AIR

During the seventeenth century, fascinating new work with vacuums drew men's minds toward consideration of lighter-than-air craft. In 1670, Francesco Lana de Terzi suggested raising an airship "by means of evacuated metal spheres." Demonstration in 1680 that human muscles could not possibly sustain flight in imitation of birds further encouraged concentration on lighter-than-air flying. This focus eventually resulted in the pioneering balloon work of the Montgolfier brothers, and the first manned balloon flight, near Paris, by Jean François Pilatre de Rozier in 1783. Work on heavier-than-air flight was mostly theoretical during the seventeenth and eighteenth centuries, the pastime of mathematicians and physicists rather than tinkerers and mechanicians.[28]

European adults did not completely abandon the kite, though. It stimulated a playful English country teacher's imagination, and he devised a kite system strong enough to pull a light carriage with himself, his wife, and daughters aboard. He described his invention, and the reaction of his neighbors, in a charming book titled *The Aeropleustic Art,* published in 1825. George Pocock clearly saw himself as having "reduced the Athenian's fable [Daedalus and Icarus] to a positive reality. . . ."[29]

On one occasion, he allowed the rich carriage of the Duke of Gloucester, drawn by two pair of horses, to pass his own kite-drawn wagon. Pocock then overtook the Duke's carriage and passed it. The teacher reports that the Duke "kindly overlooked" this "rude breach of etiquette." Pocock felt positively royal, as he pulled up to toll stations where tolls were levied on commoners (but not nobility) according to the number of horses pulling the vehicle. No horses, no toll, and the tollkeeper had to scramble to open the gate before the kite-drawn wagon crashed into it.

Pocock also enjoyed causing a stir in the countryside:

In the evening, when only part of the equipage is visible, and that but for a few moments, the effects are truly sublime. Its unexpected appearance and sudden departure, passing like a shadow, has often riveted the foot passenger to the spot, motionless and mute. . . .

But of all others, those evenings are the most delightful when not a breath is felt below; when all is calm and silent; when nothing of the wind is heard, but its soft play on the Kite's cordage, from the tension of which the sound resembles the changeful note of the Aeolian harp. Those nights when Luna walks in beauty and brightness through cloudless skies, are certainly to be preferred; but the novelty and astounding effect produced are much greater on a dark night; it is necessary, then, to travel with lamps to your car, and at least one transparency suspended aloft, on the string of the Kite, which light is to inform the charioteer of the exact direction and angular height of the Kite's string, that he may avoid trees, &c. This leading star, though serviceable to the director of the expedition, has often caused impediments. The eyes of all on the road have been generally fixed, and waggoners, people with carts, foot passengers, &c. have been found standing directly in the way and gaping upwards. In general their backs are towards you; for as the light in the air is always a-head of the carriage, they have turned about to look at it, just before the car approached them. This circumstance, together with its swift and silent movement, make the bugle a *sine qua non*." [Italics in original][30]

What a sight that must have been, in the days before electric lights or motors, and before "horseless carriages," for the inhabitants of the countryside. Imagine, staring up at this ghostly light that seems to travel along without support, wondering what it might portend, and being startled from your contemplation by the alarming sound of the bugle! The truly miraculous thing is that Pocock does not report injury at the hands of his neighbors, angered at being so disconcerted.

The Pocock family was inspired to compose songs in honor of their unusual motive power, drawing metaphorical parallels between their kite-drawn carriage and the divine transport of souls:

Thus soaring, thus flying along,
Etherial pleasures we find
May kind Heav'n accept of our song,
Who lends us the wings of the wind.

The pious lark sings as it flies,
And we who thus follow its flight
May hope, when our string breaks, to rise,
And soar midst the seraphs of light.
[Emphasis in original][31]

Of course, the report of such shenanigans was received with the greatest skepticism:[32]

> Those who saw that undreamt-of equipage . . . eagerly related . . . what [they] had seen. . . . Their testimonies, however, were, with few exceptions, universally discredited. Not a few argued that the thing was impossible, and that artifice had been employed to produce illusion; hence arose dispute, sarcasm, and irony, until positive assertions on the one part met with unmeasured contradiction on the other; even unto the severing of acquaintance, and the separation of friends.

Do we believe it? Pocock's contraption does not seem to have been widely copied, perhaps for good reason, and his book is now rare although it had an expanded edition in 1827. True tale or light fiction, it remains a testimony to the active imagination.

FROM THE KITE TO THE WRIGHT STUFF

Not far from Pocock's rural home, George Cayley was launching model gliders in the early nineteenth century. Cayley's gliders were serious experimental beginnings for the airplane as we know it today. They had fixed wings, not birdlike flappers; the motive power was supplied by a separate engine. They had a fuselage, the central body so familiar to us; and they had horizontal and vertical tail structures for stability and guidance.

Cayley's vision was completely different from anything known to have come before. Some sketches in Leonardo's notebooks resemble Cayley's designs, but Leonardo's notebooks had not yet been rediscovered at that time. Cayley knew he had something special, and engraved his design on a small silver disk about the size of an American quarter. On the reverse, he engraved a diagram of the aerodynamic forces involved.

Cayley's fixed-wing models flew from his hand, gliding like the paper airplanes launched by schoolchildren nowadays. This was enough to set his mind, and that of many others, firmly toward the vision of scaling up to a full-size, powered flying machine capable of carrying a pilot and perhaps passengers as well.

Cayley's models have a rightful place on a straight-line history of powered flight. Alexander Graham Bell and Samuel Langley were more or less on the fringes of that history, but as we consider the strong motives that drive men onwards, their work and attitudes deserve extended attention. Langley sought the glory of priority, Bell pursued a gentleman's serious hobby. When the Wright brothers achieved sustained powered flight, Bell graciously acknowledged their accomplishment and applauded each new development. Langley became embittered and hostile, claiming priority for himself and refusing to credit the Wrights. For both men, the effort toward powered flight was a vehicle for their own personal agendas.

When working on the telephone, Alexander Graham Bell was a driven man. He was in his twenties, in love, unable to marry until he should have a steady income. He was a teacher of the deaf and felt very much in the shadow of his father, Alexander Melville Bell, who was famous for inventing a system of "visible speech," a notation which allowed the deaf to position their mouth and tongue to produce sounds they had never heard. Young Bell needed to establish himself and his independence in every way.

Once the telephone was developed enough to be a commercial success, however, Bell entrusted the business to others, feeling secure and free to pursue whatever interests captured his attention. They were many. Chief among them was flight, which had fascinated him since boyhood.

Shortly after the dramatic demonstrations of the new telephone at the American Centennial Exhibition in 1876, and his marriage to Mabel Hubbard, Bell and his bride traveled to Britain in the fall of 1877. Mabel watched him in amazement, writing:

> What a man my husband is! I am perfectly bewildered at the number and size of the ideas with which his head is crammed. . . . Fly-ing machines to which telephones and torpedoes are to be

attached occupy the first place just now from observations of sea gulls. . . . Every now and then he comes out with "the flying machine has quite changed its shape in a quarter of an hour" or "the segarshape is dismissed to the limbo of useless things." . . . Then he goes climbing about the rocks and forming theories on the origin of cliffs and caves. . . . Then he comes home and watches sugar bubbles.[33]

Aeronautical speculations dot Bell's notebooks from time to time over the next decade or so. He began to concentrate on them in earnest by the spring of 1891, encouraged by his friend Samuel Pierpont Langley.

Both Bell and Langley, like so many others, had been caught up as boys by the compelling mystery of birdflight. Both men had absorbed their scientific training from the Boston environment, Langley about fifteen years before Bell. Langley had gone on to be professor of physics and astronomy at the Western University of Pennsylvania, beginning his careful experiments shortly before becoming secretary of the Smithsonian in 1887. The Smithsonian Institution had been founded in 1846, "for the increase and diffusion of knowledge," and research was an important part of its mission.

By 1891, Langley published his results[34] and gave public lectures on flying machines. Mabel Bell wrote to her husband, "Of course the papers treat him more respectfully than they would anyone else, still they cannot resist a sly joke now and again."[35]

Bell began his own experiments late in 1891, and continued for the next two decades. Mabel continued to support and encourage her husband in aeronautical work, pulling him back to it when his fancy began to stray. His work was the dabbling of a gentleman, though, not the highly focused effort he had spent on the telephone. As his biographer notes, "This was not a crash program of the Edisonian sort. There were no frenzied stretches of seventy-two hours without sleep. Bell slept his fill, read his newspapers, carried on correspondence about the deaf, tended to various other matters."[36]

Still, the work was serious and sustained. Bell made careful observations and measurements on various wing designs and propellers, similar to those of his friend Langley. Bell was the only colleague Langley invited to watch the first trials of his sixteen-foot steam-powered airplane model in 1896. The success of that model encouraged both men to continue. Bell told a reporter, "The problem of the flying machine has

been solved. . . . [F]ifteen years ago a man who had the temerity to de-
liver a serious lecture on the prospects of navigating the air would have
ruined his professional reputation by the indiscretion. Now the much-
derided 'cranks' are having their innings."[37] As prominent a scientist as
Sir William Thompson, Lord Kelvin, nevertheless still maintained that
such attempts "could only lead to disappointment, if carried on with
any expectation of leading to a useful flying machine."[38]

This pessimism was not just a matter of old fogies stuck in the mud.
Science is established slowly and carefully. Overturning established principles requires rigorous proofs. Anyone today who proposes a machine
which violates, say, Einstein's spacetime physics, or the laws of thermodynamics, had better be prepared to face some fairly stiff skepticism.
Scientific dismissal of powered flight was based on the work of no less a
figure than Newton himself.

Proposition 34 in book II of Newton's *Principia* leads to a formula
commonly called Newton's sine-squared law (though Newton did not
actually express it in those terms). To follow the implications for aeronautics, we begin with the concept of "angle of attack." This is the angle
between the wing surface and the oncoming stream of air. A wing exactly parallel to the oncoming airstream has a zero angle of attack; as it
tilts against the stream, the angle of attack increases. Newton's sine-
squared law says that for small angles of attack there is very little lift
unless the wing area is increased to an impractical size, but at large angles
of attack, the drag of the airstream would increase faster than the lift,
and flying would be inefficient to say the least. The assumptions about
fluid behavior which are involved in applying the sine-squared law to
subsonic flight are incorrect, but that was not recognized until much
later.[39]

To understand what happened, we have to take a bit of a detour in
aerodynamic science, back to the mid-1700s. That is about a hundred
years after Newton, about fifty years before Cayley, and almost 150 years
before Bell. Benjamin Robins is studying the behavior of solid shapes
moving through air. He is not interested in aircraft, however, but in ballistics and gunnery.

Robins even designed a peculiar instrument for the purpose, the
"whirling arm," a horizontal pole rotating around a vertical shaft. Shapes
attached to the end of the arm sped through the air, around and around,
while the speed and the force needed to maintain that speed could be
measured.

Using this, Robins proved that three-dimensional shape mattered, not just the equivalent flat surface; a pyramid whirling point first travels through the air much more easily than base first. A flat circle encounters more resistance than a sphere of the same diameter. Robins also tested flat plates at various angles of attack, measuring the resistance. This resistance is now called "drag," and is one of three important forces on an aircraft; the others are lift and thrust.[40] He published his results in 1746.

At the time Robins was working, his findings were applied only to bullets or cannonballs moving through the air or coming to a sudden stop. It was only much later that aerodynamics was considered in relation to aircraft. Once again, an "aviation pioneer" was chasing quite a different prize. Robins's whirling arm, however, was the best experimental device for aerodynamic research until the wind tunnel was developed in the 1870s.[41]

Robins's work continued the systematic research into aerodynamics which had begun around Newton's time. Much later, further aerodynamic research eventually showed the error involved in applying Newton's sine-squared law to powered flight. But that ultimate conclusion did not appear until just about the time the Wright brothers were ready to fly. Meanwhile, serious scientists were not ready to junk anything of Newton's without a great deal of evidence—and evidence, such as a successful flying machine, was obviously lacking.

By mid-nineteenth century, a pair of Englishmen were seriously attempting to design and construct a powered, heavier-than-air flying machine. John Stringfellow and William Samuel Henson made important strides toward the fixed-wing, engine-powered airplane, but nevertheless fell victim to the ridicule so easily inspired by anything less than an actual flying machine. Their proposal made them the immediate butt of "comic songs, verses, caricatures, lampoons and critical articles . . . picturing the 'Ariel [sic] Steam Carriage' flying . . . from London to Egypt and India."[42]

The Times of London weighed in with heavy even-handedness:

This is not the first time by many that such a pretention [sic] has been advanced: however failure, sometimes ridiculous, has always been the lot of the bold adventurers who had broodingly worked themselves into a determination to try out their schemes. Not one has succeeded, while all the world has at once longed for their success and derided their hopes. . . . [Y]et we are compelled, by careful inquiry, to profess our belief that [Mr Henson] has done so much towards simplifying the question on which the resolution of this momentous problem depends, and so much more towards removing the practical difficulties in the way of his accomplishment, that the earlier, if not immediate, possession of the long-coveted power of flight may now be safely anticipated.[43]

The notion of heavier-than-air flight was considered so harebrained that anyone who attempted it was automatically labeled a crackpot, an eccentric, or worse. Failure was merely confirmation of the obvious. The fear of ridicule was well-founded.

When the Aeronautical Society of Great Britain was organized in London in 1866, its purpose was to provide a forum for the presentation and discussion of papers. By its fifth year, however, the author of its annual report complained: "Now let us consider the nature of the mud in which I have said we are stuck. The cause of our standstill, briefly stated, seems to be this: men do not consider the subject of 'aerostation' or 'aviation' to be a real science, but bring forward wild, impractical, unmechanical, and unmathematical schemes, wasting the time of the Society, and causing us to be looked upon as a laughing stock by an incredulous and skeptical public."[44] Aerodynamics was a respectable science; powered heavier-than-air mechanical flight was a fool's dream. If the Aeronautical Society was a laughing stock, they had in some measure brought it on themselves. They had organized the first aeronautical exhibition in 1868, a display of equipment which with few exceptions could rightly be described as "wild, impractical, unmechanical and unmathematical."[45]

We return now to the last decade of the nineteenth century, and the work of Langley and Bell. Both men understood that aerodynamics were important to flight, and did intensive research to have a firm scientific foundation for their designs.

In spite of scientific skepticism, Bell's thoughts fixed on the kite as the key to a successful heavier-than-air flying machine. Bell was not alone in building on that foundation. Samuel Langley at the Smithsonian was also using kites, and Lawrence Hargrave in Australia had invented the box kite in 1893 as a direct response to Langley's work.[46] Improved versions of Hargrave's kite showed great promise as foundations for aircraft design. The Wright brothers, too, used box kite principles in their work, as did many other aviation pioneers.

On a winter's day in 1897, for example, one Lt. Hugh G. Wise made an ascent on a group of four "Hargrave type" kites (box kites). One newspaper sketch shows a man sitting in the central portion of a long, multi-celled box kite. It is not clear whether the artist had definite information, or was simply illustrating his own interpretation of the text description, "Four of them were used, forming two tandems." Other newspaper clippings from the 1890s describe kites being used for weather observations and for signalling at night.[47]

Bell's chief kite innovation was the use of tetrahedral units, in which four triangles were joined to make a pyramid. The triangle is one of the sturdiest geometric forms, resisting efforts to push it out of shape. The triangular shape had been used to support maximum loads on bridges with a minimum of material; the engineer Gustave Eiffel used it in his famous Parisian tower and in bracing the Statue of Liberty destined for New York City's harbor. Bell's tetrahedrons extended the triangle's two-dimensional rigidity into three dimensions.

By the mid-1890s, Bell was well established in the scientific-social community. The income from the telephone companies allowed him to have homes in Washington D.C. and in Nova Scotia. He enjoyed the outdoor life in Nova Scotia, and the physical pleasure of experimentation with kites and models. At his Washington, D.C. home, he hosted regular "Wednesday Evening" dinner gatherings, carefully orchestrating the conversation among his distinguished guests. Not only physicists and engineers, but anthropologists, astronomers, botanists, chemists, paleontologists, physicians, and politicians, as well as university presidents and other high-ranking educators, were among the participants.[48] Bell's technical "career" was a curious mixture of respectability and non-conformity. He treasured both his status in the community and his freedom to be a "crank," pushing into areas where others feared to tread. Nor did he put all his reputation-eggs into one basket: he never ceased his activities on behalf of the deaf, and he was active in both the Smithsonian Institution and the National Geographic Society.

Even after the successful Wright brothers' flight in 1903, and their continued improvements, Bell felt that he had an important contribution to make in the matter of stability.[49] The deaths of Otto Lilienthal and others had touched Bell's compassionate core, the same quality that made him such a tender and patient teacher of the deaf. Bell would not willingly risk anyone's life. It is significant that in addition to using his kites to make detailed aerodynamic measurements, Bell was confident enough of their safety to send his assistants aloft on them.[50] He envisioned an airplane constructed of tetrahedrons, which would land gently and softly with no danger to its pilot or passengers.

By this time, moreover, Bell saw himself as an "elder statesman," and in 1907 at Mabel's suggestion he organized a group of four young men to join him in the mutual adventure. (The group included Glenn Curtiss, later to make an independent name for himself as an aircraft designer and manufacturer.) They called themselves the Aerial Experiment Association. Each took a turn designing an airplane, which the group then built and tested. When the young men preferred biplane designs to Bell's favorite tetrahedrons, Bell enthusiastically worked with them.

One of the group, Lt. Thomas Selfridge, volunteered to be a passenger in the army's 1908 trials of the Wright machine at Fort Myer, Virginia. Tragically, the plane crashed, injuring Orville Wright and killing Selfridge. Bell was stunned, and Mabel devastated. She wrote to Bell, "I miss the thought of him so. . . . Casey [another of the group] called me 'little mother of us all' and so I want to be."[51] The Bells had daughters but no surviving sons; two infant sons born prematurely had died within days. The Aerial Experiment Association had temporarily filled that emotional need.

What had flying, and kites, and science in general meant to Bell after his success with the telephone? We see a complex mixture of motives, which we can try to squeeze into the ill-fitting categories of social expectations, ambition, self-esteem, male bonding, self-indulgence, and the like.

When basic economic needs are satisfied, some people indulge in physical pleasures while others seek more intellectual amusements. Some individuals enjoy working at the borders of "respectability," others prefer the security of established fields. Music, science, literature, and philosophy were considered to be among the genteel interests suitable for upper-class and upper middle-class men and women in European, British, and American eighteenth- and nineteenth-century society. Bell's aviation pursuits combined social respectability with intellectual daring, the exercise of his mind with his physical love of the outdoors.

We all need some sort of community, the approval and friendship of others; Bell found his in science and technology, in his Wednesday evening dinner-seminars, in his avocational work with Langley and the Aerial Experiment Association, in the National Geographic Society, and in the Smithsonian Institution, as well as in his work with the deaf.

Langley, on the other hand, was much more focused on the challenge of powered flight, and had much more of his ego invested in it. A life-long bachelor, Langley was undistracted by family considerations, and conversely could draw no emotional support from that direction. Langley had developed his scientific skills by studying sunspots, and continued to approach his work in a systematic, painstaking, careful fashion. The accumulation of precise data was his ticket to fame, and he brought these habits to the Smithsonian in 1887.

Langley knew he was taking enormous risks to his reputation: ten years later he wrote that "the whole subject of mechanical flight . . . was generally considered to be a field fitted rather for the pursuits of the charlatan than for those of the man of science. Consequently, he who was bold enough to enter it, found almost none of those experimental data which are ready to hand in every recognized and reputable field of scientific labor."[52] Throughout the nineteenth century, the cry of the scientist was "Data, data shalt thou pursue!" This was what distinguished a "recognized and reputable field of scientific labor" from the wild propositions of the charlatan, or more charitably, from the untutored craftsmanship and insight of the less intellectual inventor or engineer.

Langley had made his start as an architect and engineer, turning to astronomy during the American Civil War. Born in 1834, he was already mature, with a reputation built on twenty years of astronomical research, when he was inspired to begin his aerodynamic experiments in 1886. After becoming secretary of the Smithsonian Institution in 1888, Langley was laying not only his own reputation on the line, but that of the Smithsonian as well, in this field more fitted for "the pursuits of the charlatan."

Accordingly, Langley spent four years laying a foundation of experimental data, even to the point of revisiting work done at the beginning of the century. He used his own apparatus to test and discredit the application of Newton's sine-squared law, although several previous investigators had already thoroughly demonstrated that conclusion. There is nothing like declaring a field empty, and then proceeding to ignore the work already done! In fairness, though, it must be added that Langley extended the work far beyond that which had been done before, in many cases designing his own ingenious instruments for more accurate measurements.[53]

Langley's *Experiments in Aerodynamics,* the results of those four years, included explorations of wing shape, angle of attack, lift and drag, propeller shape, and the point of action for various aerodynamic forces. His observations were presented in tabular and graphical form. Langley placed himself squarely on the side of science rather than engineering or inventing: "To prevent any misapprehension, let me state at the outset that I do not undertake to explain any art of mechanical flight, but to demonstrate experimentally certain propositions in aerodynamics which prove that such flight under proper direction is practicable. . . . [T]hese researches are, as I have said, not meant to demonstrate the art of guiding such heavy bodies in flight. . . ."[54] The book was the first significant contribution to the science of aerodynamics to be published in the United States, and immediately established Langley as a prominent member of this "recognized and reputable field of scientific labor." Nevertheless, as Mabel Bell noted, the press and the public could not resist making the occasional snide comment. Langley next turned to designing aircraft, which he hoped would once and for all establish the correctness of his data and conclusions.

Langley was a proud, self-confident, one might even say arrogant, man. Although his family was financially comfortable, Langley's background did not qualify him as a member of the social elite in the Boston of his era. Children can be cruel, and Langley may have had some harsh experiences when he attended the prestigious Boston Latin School and Boston High School, where as the old jingle goes, "the Lowells speak only to Cabots, and the Cabots speak only to God." He did not go on to college, but for the rest of his life was completely (and excellently) self-taught.

At the Smithsonian he was known for his autocratic behavior, conducting inspections in full formal dress and insisting that his subordinates walk behind him. There was even some question as to whether he took credit for the work done by others—as might be expected when a man distrusts the work of others and repeats it himself as if only he were capable of doing it correctly. Although his assistant wrote, after Langley's death, "he had given his time and his best labours to the world without hope of remuneration,"[55] monetary reward is not the only satisfaction men seek.

Langley was keenly aware of the fame and social status which would come to the man who first successfully demonstrated a powered, heavier-than-air machine capable of carrying a person aloft. He had only to look at Bell and at Thomas Edison to see the rewards of successful popular invention. He was also aware of the ridicule that would come to the man who tried and failed. Langley was determined to succeed, and he kept his machines out of the public eye until he could be sure their performance would be suitably impressive.

What a contrast with the gracious and amiable Alexander Graham Bell! Yet the two men were friends, perhaps because Bell was never a competitor for the glory Langley thought would be his. Bell was the only man, other than an assistant, invited to witness the air trials of all Langley's aircraft designs: powered models at first, then full-scale machines.

Langley came very close. On May 6, 1896, one of his steam-powered machines was catapulted into the air over the Potomac, and stayed aloft for about eighty seconds. Retrieved from the water, it was again catapulted aloft and remained in the air for about ninety seconds, traveling about 2,300 feet. Nobody was aboard, but "for the first time in the history of the world a device produced by man had actually flown through the air, and had preserved its equilibrium without the aid of a guiding human intelligence."[56] Bell had witnessed the flight, and wrote, "It seemed to me that no one could have witnessed these experiments without being convinced that the possibility of mechanical flight had been demonstrated."[57]

Three years later, Langley received a letter from Wilbur Wright, who wished to pursue aeronautics in "what time I can spare from my regular business." Wilbur was forthright but modest: "I am an enthusiast, but not a crank in the sense that I have some pet theories as to the proper construction of a flying machine. I wish to avail myself of all that is already known and then if possible add my mite to help on the future worker who will attain final success."[58]

Langley was working hard on a full-scale machine of his own, but passed the letter along to the assistant secretary of the Smithsonian, who sent Wright several pamphlets and a list of sources. The brothers obtained copies of several works on "aerial navigation," including Langley's own *Experiments in Aerodynamics*. Orville later commented that "after reading the pamphlets . . . we became highly enthusiastic with the idea of gliding as a sport."[59] A sport, mind you, not a career or a scientific investigation.

It is sometimes breathtaking to consider the apparently small forks in the current of history. Wilbur Wright and his brother Orville owned a bicycle shop in Dayton, Ohio, and like many others in that business had a mechanical turn of mind. They had previously run a printing shop, and for both businesses they had designed and built much of their own equipment. Once the bicycle shop was well established, the brothers looked for other fields to exercise their inventive wits.

One possibility was the newfangled automobile. Tinkerers across the country had made all sorts of contraptions combining bicycle wheels, wagon bodies, and small motors to carry people along the roads. One of the Wrights' part-time employees, Cordy Ruse, built the first automobile in Dayton and was very proud of it. Orville was fascinated, but Wilbur recommended that Cordy "fasten a bed sheet beneath the machine to catch the parts that fell off as it lurched down the street."[60]

Wilbur and Orville might have joined the other "bicycle men" trying to improve the automobile. Instead, they turned their attention to the "sport" of flying. The connection between bicycling and flying was not as far-fetched as it may seem, however. Speed, balance, the "sense of freedom, control, [and] escape" were common elements noted by many who compared cycling to flying. Some poets made the association explicit:

> *Hurrah, hurrah, for the merry wheel,*
> *With tires of rubber and spokes of steel,*
> *We seem to fly on airy steeds,*
> *With Eagle's flight in silent speed.*[61]

Air, horses, flying; we are back to Pegasus, if not farther. The ancient myths have a powerful hold on our imaginations. Romance and challenge: what else inspires sport?

Wilbur and Orville pursued their sport with scientific attention to detail, however. They read the scientific and technical material and began to use the vocabulary in their own notebooks and letters. They made detailed, careful observations of all aspects of aerodynamics, including lift, drag, pressure points, and propeller function. They constructed their own version of the newfangled wind tunnel, and tested their ideas in it. They focused on information that would be directly useful to their designs, rather than trying to develop a complete theory of aerodynamics.

The Wrights flew their first large models and full-scale gliders as kites until they were confident of their design and their "wing-warping" method for stabilizing its flight.[62] They were also able to use a simple spring-type scale attached to the kite string to measure the net force exerted while their machine was in the air.

They were discouraged for several years by the mismatch between the observations they made on their own, and the calculations they made using scientific data from others. In some cases they were using the data incorrectly, in other cases the data were misleading or inaccurate to begin with. As they worked, the brothers gained self-confidence and technical maturity, until they reached a point in 1901 where they decided to start over, make their own basic experiments, and develop their own tables and charts. Their results quickly led to new successes: an effective glider in 1902, and the historic powered flight piloted by Orville on December 17, 1903. Their "aeroplane" flew only 120 feet, and stayed up for only twelve seconds; the entire flight could be re-enacted within the passenger cabin of today's jumbo jets.

Can you blame Langley, if he felt that the Wrights had stolen his glory? His own unmanned but powered machines had flown much longer, although they relied on catapults to get into the air rather than lifting off under their own power. He had worked as a professional, so hard, so long, so meticulously, playing by all the rules of scientific method, achieving such success with powered models, when along come these two young men in their spare time and claim victory, fame, and glory while Langley's full-scale powered and manned machine collapsed into the Potomac. And to add gall to the wormwood, the crash had occurred just nine days before the Wright's successful flight.

Swooning in ecstasy and plunging into the ocean seem an inauspicious
way to begin "Bonne Annee," a happy new year.
Courtesy Guillaume de Syon

The Wrights did not even claim to be scientists, just a couple of hardworking bicycle mechanics out for sport, although Wilbur's work was good enough to be published in the very prestigious official organ of the Aeronautical Society of Great Britain, *The Aeronautical Journal.*[63]

It was too much for Langley to bear. Langley, and the Smithsonian after his death, continued to insist that Langley had priority in powered, man-carrying, heavier-than-air flight. This acrimony kept the Wright flyer out of the Smithsonian until 1942, when the Smithsonian offered a formal apology to Orville (Langley had died in 1906, Wilbur in 1912).

For Bell, flying had been a vocation, one serious hobby among many which gave him a great deal of personal satisfaction. For Langley, flying was to be the capstone of his scientific career and perhaps the ultimate vindication of his worth; for the Wrights, it was a competitive sport, one at which they excelled and won.

Like ballooning, powered flight soon lost its elite status and acquired vulgar associations. The open construction of early airplanes provided perfect perches for illustrations of wanton (or merely seductive) young women and their amorous companions. A winsome French lass seems eerily prophetic of Slim Pickens as Major Stanley "King" Kong riding an atomic bomb to earth in Stanley Kubrick's film *Dr. Strangelove.*

LOOKING BACKWARD

In hindsight, "progress" toward airplane ingredients was excruciatingly slow, and the list of independent ingredients is daunting. Precursors for the necessary elements are easily found, but transforming them into the actual components of a successful aircraft was not so easily accomplished.

The gendarme at lower left merely emphasizes the naughtiness of the aerial activities depicted here.

Courtesy Guillaume de Syon

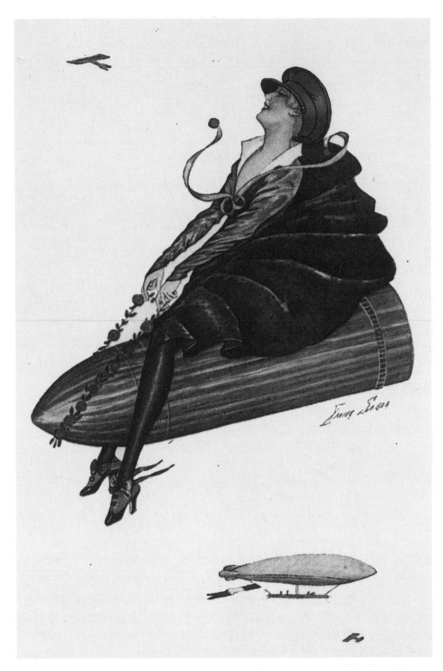

The young woman may represent Marianne, the icon of the French nation, as she rides a bomb. Her gaiety and the delicacy of the flowered reins contrast sharply with the implied intent of destruction.

Courtesy Guillaume de Syon

For the airplane, the recipe includes a propeller on a horizontal shaft, driving air rather than driven by it; fixed yet adjustable wings, with a curved upper surface; a lightweight source of sufficient motive power; long narrow wings rather than stubby ones; and an understanding of the ways of the air.

Harald Penrose chose a quotation from Milton to introduce his book on Stringfellow:

> *The invention all admired and each how he*
> *To be the inventor missed; so easy it seemed*
> *Once found, which yet unfound*
> *Most would have thought impossible.*

How many times have we all wrung our brains trying to improvise something to serve some particular purpose, only to smack our foreheads in frustrated exasperation when the "obvious" solution is pointed out to us?

CHAPTER 7

BALLOONS
AND DIRIGIBLES

SUSTAINED FLIGHT

A combination of romance, theoretical science, and practical application was involved in the development and utilization of balloons and dirigibles. The science of hydrostatics suggested that there were variations in density of air or other gases. Tinkerers explored the use of hot air and hydrogen for lift. At last, humans could remain aloft for significant lengths of time; their reports convey their unabashed delight and terror. Balloons also found several practical uses in the nineteenth century: for air mail, for scientific observation, and in wartime for communication, siegecraft, and bombing. Dirigibles were capable of long-distance passenger transportation.

A bright spring morning in the seventeenth century might have seen airborne Easter eggs. The trick required some skill, but was otherwise simple: remove the contents of an egg, place a few drops of dew (pure water) inside, and seal the opening with wax. When the sun warmed the egg, the water would evaporate and seep out through the porous shell, making it just light enough to rise into the air for a few moments, before equilibrium was re-established.

The European celebrants might have been amazed to know that in far-off China, two centuries before the birth of Jesus, eggshells had been used as miniature hot-air balloons. One may still see, in Cambodia and some Chinese provinces, balloons of oiled paper over bamboo frame-works sent aloft with a small bundle of burning tinder beneath. The tendency of such lanterns to burst into spectacular flame (oiled paper is highly flammable) may have discouraged any attempt to use them for human flight. In any event, the further development of balloons as transportation was left to the West.

By the fifteenth and sixteenth century C.E., European military accounts report that the Chinese and Mongols used paper lanterns for signalling in wartime; these might be shaped like dragons, and belch forth smoke and fire; it would not be surprising if some of these floated in the air, though nobody seems to have paid enough attention to that aspect to make a written record.[1]

CURIOSITY AND IMAGINATION

Watch a fire, see the smoke and small ashes rise. Why? Why do some things rise and others fall? The best answer the ancient Greeks could devise was that each of the four elements had its natural place, to which it attempted to return when free to do so. Earth's place was lowest, followed by water, air, and fire. The upper heavens were the location of a fifth, unchanging element, the "quintessence." Ordinary matter was a mixture of the basic four elements, in various proportions. Burning wood, for example, "freed" the fire and air in the wood to rise, and so it did, carrying small particles with it for a brief time.

Even this simple arrangement recognized that the question of why things rise is intimately related to why (and how) things fall. Rising and falling are two sides of the same observation, a vertical change of position, one thing changing its place with respect to another. Air will bubble upwards in water, water will pour downwards through air. Oil will float on water, water will sink beneath oil. In a more complex case, wood will float on water until all the air is driven out of it—it becomes waterlogged—and then it will sink.

Aristotle, whose philosophy (including physics) was not seriously challenged until the Renaissance, taught that the rate of fall would be determined by relative weights, which in turn were a consequence of the proportions of elements within any given body. A 20-pound stone, he would insist, will fall ten times faster than a 2-pound stone.

Archimedes refined Aristotle's system, introducing the concept of specific gravity, or weight per volume. We have a delightful tale of Archimedes being asked to prove whether a crown was pure gold or an alloy without destroying it. He pondered the question intensely, and noticed that when he immersed completely in his bath, the volume of water displaced was equal to his own volume. Here was a way to determine the volume of the crown! Eureka! he cried, and went running naked to the king to present the solution immediately. Find the volume of the crown, he said, and weigh it. Then find the volume of an equal weight of gold. If the crown is pure gold, the volumes will be the same.

Implications are not always immediately obvious. How often do we say "we have 20-20 hindsight"? It took almost two thousand years for scientists to realize that it was specific gravity, not "elemental" composition or relative weight, which governed the rise and fall of substances.

Galileo, in the seventeenth century, used the power of experiment to demolish Aristotle's assertions about falling:[2] "Aristotle says that 'an iron ball of one hundred pounds falling from a height of one hundred cubits reaches the ground before a one-pound ball has fallen a single cubit.' I say they arrive at the same time. You find, on making the experiment, that the larger outstrips the smaller by two finger-breadths . . . now you would not hide behind these two fingers the ninety-nine cubits of Aristotle."[3] In the course of his demonstration, Galileo mentions that air has positive gravity rather than levity ("a property possessed possibly by no substance whatever"),[4] since a volume of compressed air is seen to gain weight. If air had levity, concentrating the levity by forcing more air into a container should make the container more apt to rise and thus appear to lose weight. Galileo goes on to invoke the principles of specific gravity to explain the differential rates of fall in air, water, and other liquids.

Stimulated by Galileo's work, in 1643 Evangelista Torricelli closed a glass tube at one end, filled it with mercury, and up-ended it into an open container of mercury. Although no air could enter the tube, some of the mercury flowed out, leaving a "vacuum" in the closed end. The length of the vacuum in the tube changed from time to time, and could only be the result of changing air pressure. Torricelli had invented the barometer.

Exploration in this direction was accelerating. In 1650 the Bürgermeister (mayor) of Magdeburg, Otto von Guericke, invented an air pump. He put it to spectacular use in 1654, in front of the German Emperor Ferdinand III and a large audience. Two copper bowls, known to students today as "the Magdeburg hemispheres," were put rim-to-rim to form a hollow sphere about 14 inches (35 cm) in diameter. The pump went to work, removing most of the air from the sphere, and two teams of eight horses each tried to pull them apart with no luck whatever, although only air pressure was holding them together.

Now we are getting somewhere: air has weight, it has pressure, it can be compressed or rarified. Compressed air is heavier for a given volume, rarified air is lighter—and presumably will rise. How can we use this? And was there any other way to remove air from a vessel?

Let us go back in time again, to England in the thirteenth century. Roger Bacon, Franciscan monk, was almost single-handedly reviving the concept of science as an area of developing rather than static knowledge. Like Aristotle, his thinking ranged over the whole of human knowledge. But unlike Aristotle, Bacon also considered the uses to which knowledge could be put. In Bacon's day, it was generally accepted that there were three layers of atmosphere: one next to the earth and warmed by its heat, then a cooler layer, and finally a much hotter upper layer near the natural region of elemental fire.[5] It was on the surface of the first layer that Bacon imagined airships could float. Making an analogy between air and water, Bacon thought an airship could float on the surface of the air, much as a seagoing vessel floats on the ocean.[6]

All of these men, their achievements and speculations, laid the foundation for the eventual achievement of the Montgolfier brothers' balloon and for the scientific investigation of the properties of air, a necessary prerequisite for the Wright brothers' powered aircraft. So much for the straight-line school of history.

The full story is much more complex. None of the scientific pioneers—Aristotle, Archimedes, Galileo, Torricelli, von Guericke—had it in mind to fly. And for none of these men was the study of air their primary occupation. Roger Bacon and Francesco Lana de Terzi considered how humans might fly, as part of their broader philosophical systems. Lana de Terzi, as we saw in Chapter 4, worried about the military and social implications of human flight.

Aristotle took all of knowledge as his bailiwick, and wrote books on biology, medicine, philosophy, poetics, rhetoric, ethics, politics, and logic,

ICONISMUS XII.

terim autem , ut aliquid fiat , ideoque
Quomodo clavicula (*videatur Iconifmi* XI. *Figu-*
flatu dis- *ra* IV) noftræ phialæ, infra fimul ven-
junguntur tilio aliquo inftructa eft , per quod Sy-
phiale.

bus inflato aëre, difrumpuntur hæ
phialæ fponte fuâ , à fe ipfis. Unde
reverâ poffumus dicere, illud quod à
24 equis Imò (quando Hemifphæria *Majores*
Phial—

*Otto von Guericke used the air pump he invented to remove the air within
the two hemispheres. His experiments demonstrated the force of air
pressure outside the vessel, keeping the two halves together.*

Courtesy Library of Congress

as well as physics. He studied, and then taught, at Plato's Academy, and later
became tutor to the young man we know as Alexander the Great. I wonder
if Alexander ever asked his mentor about harnessing eagles to his chariot.

After Alexander became king, Aristotle returned to Athens and founded
his own school. Teachers and students would engage in discussion as they

strolled around the courtyard, giving the school the name "Peripatetic." Experiment was no large part of the curriculum; pure thought—reason—was the preferred mode. Aristotle's work was accepted as authoritative for thousands of years, and his cosmology was incorporated into the theology of the Catholic Church. The earth was the center of the universe, as befits the home of mankind, the crown of creation. The earth was also the center of changeability and corruption, of sin and impurity. The heavens (beyond the moon) were perfect, the abode of God.

Archimedes was primarily a mathematician and inventor. He formulated the rules of lever action, and is said to have declared "Give me a long enough lever, and a place to stand, and I shall move the earth!" He is also credited with inventing the compound pulley, which may be treated mathematically as a group of levers. While he was visiting in Egypt, he invented a screw mechanism for raising water from one level to another. Archimedes may be the prototype of the absent-minded professor so completely absorbed in thought that he was heedless of his surroundings. The story has it that when the Romans conquered his hometown of Syracuse, Archimedes was found drawing in the sand, concentrating on a calculation. Deep in thought, he grumbled at the intruding soldier, "Don't disturb my diagrams." The soldier, not recognizing a genius, killed him for the insult.

Galileo was both mathematician and astronomer as well as physicist. With Kepler and Copernicus, he is one of the major figures in what is now called "the Scientific Revolution," the shift from reliance on ancient authorities to the emphasis on experimentation and observation. The story is told that he dropped two weights from the leaning tower of Pisa, to disprove Aristotle's assertions. It is a good story, but scholars disagree as to whether it ever really happened. What is certain, however, is that Galileo actually made the experiment somewhere, and found, as he said, that the weights fell at very close to identical speeds.

Having disproved several aspects of Aristotle's science, Galileo opened the way for questioning the whole interrelated system, including the cosmology. The issue of why things fall or rise was just a small portion of Galileo's much larger work.

Evangelista Torricelli considered himself primarily a mathematician, and was appointed to succeed Galileo as mathematician at the court of the archduke of Tuscany. He continued Galileo's work in several fields of mechanics and astronomy. His important work in pure mathematics was never published, however, since Torricelli died suddenly and the man named in his will as editor of his papers died a month later.[7]

Otto von Guericke had a notable career in politics; for thirty-five years he was mayor of Magdeburg and magistrate for Brandenburg. For him as for many others, physics was a gentleman's hobby.[8]

Here again we see that history is not like a single river system, with tributary streams pouring their entire contents into the collective waterway that flows to its ultimate destination. Each of these men was pursuing his own immediate goals, intellectual, social, or financial. It is only later that we look back and see an "invisible hand" fashioning all the elements into the eventual achievement of human flight.

Biological evolution tells a similar story. Something as complex as the eye, for example, cannot appear in a single step. How can natural selection result in functional eyes, unless there is some other advantage to the various steps along the way? Similarly with birdflight: feathers, wings, and behaviors such as flapping and running gave survival benefits to the animals which had them, and only later became organized into the ingredients for flying. Just so, the steps "toward" human flight were actually taken along other roads, and only incidentally later became organized into actual mechanisms: balloons, aircraft, and space ships.

FOCUS ON FLYING—BALLOONS AND BEYOND

It would seem that the ballooning success of the Montgolfier brothers, Etíenne and Joseph, was entirely independent of any scientific foundation. Although Joseph, the older brother, told the Academy of Lyons that he was inspired by a French translation of Priestley's "Experiments Relating to the Different Kinds of Air,"[9] there are other "origin myths"— that they were inspired by smoke and clouds, or by rising steam from a pot. Which is "true"? Like the legendary apple which is said to have fallen on Isaac Newton's head and the teakettle of boiling water watched by the young James Watt, certainly the homely image of the brothers watching warm air rise and take a paper sack with it is appealing to the general public, while the proud Academy would be more receptive to a "scientific" explanation. Perhaps there is no single answer; perhaps the accumulation of stimuli eventually resulted in the Montgolfiers' inspiration and achievement.

Whatever the inspiration, the effect was stunning. The excitement can hardly be imagined by those of us quite used to large flying objects. The first public showing involved a balloon thirty-five feet in diameter, gorgeously embellished as befit such a magnificent occasion. The 23,000 cubic feet of hot air required to fill the balloon was provided by burning chopped straw and wool in a pit beneath its mouth. On June 25, 1783, in the town of Annonay:

> ... [A] great concourse of spectators assembled to witness the novel and extraordinary sight. ... When it was fully inflated ... it was found to have an ascending power of 500 pounds. As it displayed its huge dimensions, the spectators gave vent to loud exclamations and shouts of applause. In a few moments after it was filled it was released from its fastenings, and ascended majestically amidst the most deafening shouts of approbation. ...

> After this demonstration, the wonderful invention was heralded to every part of Europe with a rapidity that its importance had naturally inspired. ... other accounts give a still more glowing description of this wonderful experiment; but as the one we quote seems to be written with soberness and accuracy, we prefer it to any other.[10]

Other demonstrations soon followed, with larger balloons. In Paris, a forty-one-foot balloon impressed the members of the Royal Academy to the point that a proclamation was issued alerting the public:

NOTICE TO THE PUBLIC! PARIS, 27TH AUGUST, 1783.

On the Ascent of balloons or globes in the air. The one in question has been raised in Paris this day, 27th August, 1783, at 5 P.M., in the Champ de Mars.

A Discovery has been made, which the Government deems it right to make known, so that alarm be not occasioned to the people.

On calculating the different weights of hot air, hydrogen gas, and common air, it has been found that a balloon filled with either of the two former will rise toward heaven till it is in equilibrium with the surrounding air, which may not happen until it has attained a great height.

Vue du Jardin de la Manufacture Royale de Papiers peints de M. Reveillon,

Inflating the Balloon. An image worthy of the moment's drama, as smoke pours out of the firepit and spectators gaze in awe.

Courtesy Library of Congress

The first experiment was made at Annonay, in Vivarais, MM. Montgolfier, the inventors; a globe formed of canvas and paper, 105 feet in circumference, filled with heated air, reached an uncalculated height. The same experiment has just been renewed in Paris before a great crowd. A globe of taffetas or light canvas covered by elastic gum and filled with inflammable air, has risen from the Champ de Mars, and been lost to view in the clouds, being borne in a north-westerly direction. One cannot foresee where it will descend.

It is proposed to repeat these experiments on a larger scale. Any one who shall see in the sky such a globe, which resembles 'la lune obscurcie,' should be aware that, far from being an alarming phenomenon, it is only a machine that cannot possibly cause any harm, and which will some day prove serviceable to the wants of society.

(Signed) DE SAUVIGNY.
LENOIR.[11]

In that same year of 1783, another balloon of about the same size impressed the royal family and the aristocracy at Versailles. They were further amazed by a sheep, a cock, and a duck which were sent up with the balloon and survived. The king wanted to send a condemned criminal up next, presumably with the same who-would miss him rationale that the Chinese used to select "some poor fool or drunkard" to rise on their prognosticating kites. But Jean-François Pilatre de Rozier and François Laurent, Marquis d'Arlandes, protested that such a historic event would confer immortality on the passenger, much too precious an honor to squander on an unworthy soul. The king agreed, and on November 21, 1783, at the chateau de la Muette outside of Paris, the two men made history with the first free, untethered, sustained "artificial" flight in the world.

The marquis was a cavalry officer and aristocrat, and presumably wished to demonstrate his bravery before his sovereign, but who was this Jean-François Pilatre de Rozier? Though born to bourgeois parents—an innkeeper and his wife—he was trained in science, and ambitious. In 1780, at the age of twenty-six, he had come under the patronage of the king's brother, the Comte de Provence. Pilatre de Rozier hoped to become a member of the French Academy of Science, but was never suggested as a candidate.[12] His position at court depended on the image he maintained, at a time when physical courage was admired and intellectual diversion was fashionable among the aristocracy. What better way to advance his career than to perform a feat combining both qualities, before the assembled academicians and the social elite?

The marquis later wrote of his experience to a friend. The two aeronauts seem to have spent their time alternately gawking at the scene
below and scolding each other for neglecting the fire which kept the
balloon inflated. As they rose, the marquis "was astonished at the smallness of the noise or motion occasioned by our departure among the
spectators" and waved first his arm, and then his handkerchief. This
seemed to shake the crowd out of its paralysis, and they rushed forward.

> At this moment de Rozier called out, "You are doing nothing, and
> we do not rise." I begged his pardon, took some straw, moved the
> fire and turned again quickly; but I could not find La Muette. In
> astonishment, I followed the river with my eye, and at last found
> where the Oise joined it. Here, then, was Conflans; and naming
> the principal bends of the river by the places nearest to them, I
> repeated Poissy, St. Germain, St. Denis, Seve; then I am still at Poissy
> or Chaillot. Accordingly, looking down through the car, I saw the
> Visitation de Chaillot. M. Pilatre said to me at this moment, "Here
> is the river, and we are descending!" "Well, my friend," said I, "more
> fire;" and we set to work. . . . I said to my brave associate "Here is a
> river which is very difficult to cross" "I think so," said he; "you are
> doing nothing!" "I am not so strong as you," I answered; "and we
> are well as we are."

The pioneers continued their journey in this fashion. Suddenly the
marquis noticed large holes in the fabric; the balloon itself had caught
fire. Fortunately, Pilatre de Rozier had foreseen the possibility and brought
along water and large sponges. They were able to put out the fires, but
the holes had become large and the balloon was close to disintegrating.
They barely managed to stay aloft until they crossed over Paris and landed
safely. "The moment we touched land I held by the car [*sic*] with my two
hands; I felt the balloon press my head lightly. I pushed it off, and leaped
out. Turning toward the balloon, which I expected to find full, to my
great astonishment it was perfectly empty and flattened." The men had
narrowly escaped death.[13] But what an adventure it had been!

To the folks on the ground, the occasion was equally exciting. The
astonished witnesses included members of the aristocracy and the Academy of Sciences; the original documentation was signed by "the Duc de
Polignac, Duc de Guisnes, Comte de Polastron, Comte de Vandreuil,

D'Hunaud, Benjamin Franklin, Fanjus de St. Fond, Delisle, Leroy, of the Academy of Sciences."[14] The cool scientific reporting is shot through with their enthusiasm:

> ... It rose in the most majestic manner; and when it was about 270 feet high, the intrepid voyagers took off their hats and saluted the spectators. No one could help feeling a mingled sentiment of fear and admiration. The voyagers were soon undistinguishable; but the machine, hovering upon the horizon, and displaying the most beautiful figure, rose at least 3000 feet high, and remained visible all the time. . . . The machine was seventy feet high and forty-six feet in diameter; it contained 60,000 cubic feet, and carried a weight of from 1600 to 1700 pounds.

Seventy feet high! That may not sound like much to us, but the equivalent of a seven-story building must have been impressive indeed to folks whose most magnificent buildings were no more than four or five stories, usually only two or three. And then to see this seven-story "machine" rise in the air! "In the most majestic manner."

A few weeks after the flight, "Monsieur et Madame" (probably the Comte de Provence and his wife) hosted a magnificent party ostensibly to honor the inventor. Inventor, singular? Yes, it would appear that only one of the brothers, probably Joseph, represented the family. It may be that the other brother was rather less polished, less likely to be acceptable in aristocratic circles. Accounts differ in describing the brothers.

A "Cantate d'Appolon" was composed, words by one Monsieur Moline, music by Monsieur Mehul. There were fireworks, at least one medal was awarded, and the bust of Montgolfier was crowned with a laurel wreath, the classical reward for victory.

A few glitches marred the ceremony. The printed program, including the Cantate, misspells the inventor's name as "Mongolfier" throughout; perhaps it was just a typographical error, but it does not seem that Montgolfier himself was really important to the festivities. Report has it that "at the time his bust was to be crowned, he himself was forgotten, disoriented by the crowd, in one of the back rooms of the Museum."[15] Was he just the excuse for a party? The Cantate, however, places him among the greatest thinkers of the age:

I sing Mongolfier!
Who has extended his flight to the banks of the
Permesse!
It is his glory today that I publicize.
If he had lived in Grecian times,
All men would have rushed to build an altar to
him.
He has [glories] of all kinds,
But one alone suffices to make him immortal.
Its radiant presence surrounds him and has
spread everywhere.
Apollo of the Museum crowns him today.
Triumph, Mongolfier!
Celebrated through all time!
By your shining genius and your fortunate
audacity,
Balance in the airs, journey to master the winds!
You have the power to traverse the space of the
entire universe.
A double crown adorns your brow!
Urania from her sacred valley,
Comes to indicate your place
Between Descartes and Newton.

And you, intrepid Pilots!
More hardy than the Argonauts,
Contributing to the everlasting
Glory of the French!
In your aerial journey,
You have astonished the Nymphs of the Seine . . .
Share the honors which are enjoyed by
Mongolfier,
And from the hands of Apollo receive a laurel.[16]

In overblown fashion, the Cantate invokes Classical Greek and Roman mythology: Apollo is the most intellectual god, and the muses are
his companions. A "Museum" is a shrine to the arts and sciences they
support. Their favorite place is near the river Permesse, which flows down
from Mount Parnassus, their home. The muse Urania ("Heavenly") is

the patron of astronomy, although her name also refers to Aphrodite, goddess of love and fertility. The Argonauts were a group of Greek heroes who sailed with Jason to recover the Golden Fleece, one of those impossible tasks the ancients set each other. These are mighty comparisons indeed.

The Cantate does not seem quite so overblown, though, if you consider it a hymn to the accomplishment itself rather than to the people involved. The balloon was an extremely impressive realization of humanity's oldest dream, and European society was in a receptive mood for intellectual novelty. Science and scientific "demonstrations" were very fashionable among the aristocracy and the leisure classes of Europe and the United States in the last half of the eighteenth century. Chemistry and physics were genteel pursuits, both seriously as laboratory subjects and more lightly as polite drawing-room diversions. Scientific societies were flourishing on both sides of the Atlantic. It was no accident that scientist Pilatre de Rozier had the king's ear, and could claim the honor of the first human ascent.

The celebration was held at Pilatre de Rozier's Museum. He had established it two years previously, with "cabinets of curiosities" and scientific lecture-demonstrations for the intellectual delight of French high society.[17] Similar institutions were popular in major cities of the Western world, as the embodiment of Enlightenment philosophy. Members of the Academy of Sciences were welcome in the most exclusive salons, and Benjamin Franklin was honored for his intelligence as well as his charm.

Nor were Monsieur and Madame alone in honoring the accomplishment. An allegorical engraving prepared by the Academy at Marseilles, for instance, shows a winged female, her clothing draped in classical fashion, inscribing the name "Montgolfier" on a stone tablet held by an older winged male. At the same time, she is looking over her shoulder toward heaven, with a zodiac above indicating a point between Libra and Scorpio (November, the month of the first manned ascent). A balloon with a basket hovers above, in the midline of the picture, and a scythe lies on ground, symbolizing immortality and the defeat of death. Scientific instruments are strewn about in the foreground. Witnesses crowd behind a stockade.[18]

Experimenters in other countries quickly followed suit. As soon as the exciting news crossed the Atlantic, in 1783, scientists David Rittenhouse and Thomas Hopkinson in Philadelphia sent up balloons

Allegorical engraving published by the Academy of Marseilles.
From La Vaulx, Joseph et Étienne de Montgolfier.

Courtesy Library of Congress

of their own. In the following year a balloon 105 feet in diameter was sent up in Lyons. A smaller balloon was flown in Milan. Balloons were launched in Great Britain as well.

The courage of those who attempted night flights is remarkable. The nocturnal aeronauts had only moonlight and the earthbound streetlamps of the cities to give them any clues. Albert Smith describes his aerial view of London:

> In the obscurity all traces of houses and enclosures are lost sight of. I can compare it to nothing else than floating over dark blue and boundless sea spangled with hundreds of thousands of stars. These stars were the lamps. We could see them stretching over the river at the bridges, edging its banks, forming squares and long parallel lines of light in the streets and solitary parks. Further and further apart until they were altogether lost in the suburbs. The effect was bewildering.[19]

The Air Age was fairly launched, although for a long time balloons were used primarily as a showy novelty at festivals and carnivals, or as a vehicle for scientific exploration of the atmosphere. Their use as reliable transportation had to wait until some method of guidance could be devised. •

Meanwhile, balloons also served as a vehicle for entertainment, satire, and low humor. One British artist drew a gorgeously adorned Montgolfier-style balloon with two aristocratic passengers in the basket as it begins its ascent. They lean back, apparently joined at the hips; one comments "It rises majestically" and the other responds "I can feel it."[20] Throughout the nineteenth century, balloons were featured in comic songs, farcical plays, and futuristic cartoons. The popularity of the balloon was not limited to the upper crust. The playthings of the elite quickly became the hit of the marketplace. Fabrics, ceramics, jewelry, children's toys—all were decorated with balloon motifs.[21] The globular shape of the balloon made it an easy metaphor for the breast, and sure enough several French poems picture balloons as seductive women.[22] Fairs and festivals throughout France for a long time included balloons, often supporting aerial acrobatics and other stunts.[23] When the monarchy was restored in France, celebrants could ride a balloon "for the modest sum of '1 franc for a cavalier, and 1 franc and fifty sous with his wife.'"[24]

An elaborate vision illustrates "Three Hundred Years to Come: a New Comic Song." A busy terminal features railroad trains carrying passengers to the "Half Moon Inn" high in the sky, while "New Patent Balloon Coaches" wait to ferry others to "Air Shire" and other destinations. A small man rides a proportionately sized self-propelled teakettle, his

Satirical print. Below left, a caricature of Britain's George III complains of severe headaches caused by looking upwards; the dandified Frenchman assures him "Ha Ha, ha—why, that is our way, in France."
From Bruel, Histoire aeronautique.

Courtesy Library of Congress

scholarship indicated by the mortarboard hat he wears and the book he concentrates on, ignoring the hubbub around him. A robotic vending cart selling "Dog's meat cooked by steam" offers an unappetizing morsel with one mechanical arm to a dubiously sour-faced woman on a skateboard, at the same time with its other arm whipping off several yapping dogs. A man wearing a batwinged flying harness approaches the "Antipodean Tunnel" while thumbing his nose at "J. Doe" pursuing him with a stick.

Cover art for "Parodie du Voyage Aerien" features a balloon high above the clouds with snow-capped mountains behind them. A plainly dressed man and woman ride in the basket, which tilts alarmingly; he, mufflered and top-hatted, gives his full attention to the thermometer in his hand while oblivious to the enormous frogs sitting on the mountains. The woman watches him, her hair frazzled to match her expression, a couple of bottles of wine ignored in her market-basket. This is no picnic.[25]

Women and men with any pretension to an interest in "natural philosophy" dabbled in balloon flights. However, serious scientific exploration of the upper atmosphere via balloon was dangerous business. Jules Verne and others could mock or parody the extremes to which the explorers went, but their courage and dedication were real. Scientists risked, and lost, their lives encountering both foreseeable dangers and new phenomena. Balloons were blown out to sea or caught fire, thinning air brought on an imperceptible "rapture" and paralysis which could develop into coma and death. Even in the face of death, however, the scientists' chief focus remained the observations they had risked so much to make.

One example will suffice, from an ascent in the 1860s by Henry Coxwell and James Glaisher in Great Britain. At four thousand feet they became unwell, but continued upward to approximately twenty-nine thousand feet or higher. Their observations of external phenomena are inextricably entwined with comments on their own condition, and bear quiet witness to their determination. In Glaisher's words:

> About 1.52 P.M., or later, I read the dry bulb thermometer as minus five; after this I could not see the column of mercury in the wet bulb thermometer, nor the hands of the watch, nor the fine divisions on any instrument. I asked Mr. Coxwell to help me to read the instruments. In consequence, however, of the rotatory motion of the balloon, which had continued without ceasing since leaving the earth, the valve line had become entangled, and he had to leave

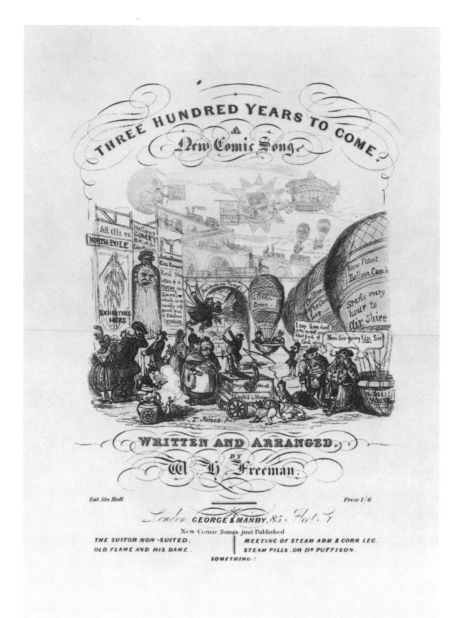

"Three Hundred Years to Come," an eighteenth- or early nineteenth-century
satirical prophecy. *From Landauer,* Some Aeronautical Music.

Courtesy Library of Congress

*"Parodie" indeed, of the focused scientific mind and the popular fascination
with balloons. From Landauer, Some Aeronautical Music.*

Courtesy Library of Congress

the car and mount into the ring to readjust it. I then looked at the
barometer, and found its reading to be 9 3/4 inches, still decreasing
fast, implying a height exceeding 29,000 feet. Shortly after, I laid
my arm upon the table, possessed of its full vigour; but on being
desirous of using it I found it powerless—it must have lost its power
momentarily. Trying to move the other arm, I found it powerless

also. Then I tried to shake myself, and succeeded, but I seemed to have no limbs. In looking at the barometer my head fell over my left shoulder. I struggled and shook my body again, but could not move my arms. Getting my head upright for an instant only, it fell on my right shoulder; then I fell backwards, my back resting against the side of the car and my head on its edge. . . . When I shook my body I seemed to have full power over the muscles of the back, and considerably so over those of the neck, but none over either my arms or my legs. As in the case of the arms, so all muscular power was lost in an instant from my back and neck. I dimly saw Mr. Coxwell, and endeavoured to speak, but could not. In an instant intense darkness overcame me, so that the optic nerve lost power suddenly; but I was still conscious, with as active a brain as at the present moment whilst writing this. I thought I had been seized with asphyxia, and believed I should experience nothing more, as death would come unless we speedily descended. Other thoughts were entering my mind when I suddenly became unconscious, as on going to sleep. I cannot tell anything of the sense of hearing, as no sound reaches the ear to break the perfect stillness and silence of the regions between six and seven miles above the earth. My last observation was made at 1.54 P.M., above 29,000 feet. I suppose two or three minutes to have elapsed between my eyes becoming insensible to seeing fine divisions and 1.54 P.M., and then two or three minutes more to have passed till I was insensible, which I think, therefore, took place about 1.56 P.M. or 1.57 P.M.

Whilst powerless, I heard the words "Temperature" and "Observation," and I knew Mr. Coxwell was in the car speaking to and endeavouring to rouse me—therefore consciousness and hearing had returned. I then heard him speak more emphatically, but could not see, speak, or move. I heard him again say, "Do try, now do!" Then the instruments became dimly visible, then Mr. Coxwell, and very shortly I saw clearly. Next, I arose in my seat and looked around, as though waking from sleep, though not refreshed, and said to Mr. Coxwell, "I have been insensible." He said, "You have, and I too, very nearly." I then drew up my legs, which had been extended, and took a pencil in my hand to begin observations. Mr. Coxwell told me that he had lost the use of his hands, which were black, and I poured brandy over them.

Coxwell had managed to pull the cord with his teeth, to open the valve and begin their descent. Eventually landing in an uninhabited area, Glaisher walked "between seven and eight miles" to shelter and human contact.[26] Other scientific ascents met similar problems, and some aeronauts did not survive.

A mix of adventure, theology, and scientific curiosity propelled the American John Wise into the air. By the end of his career, he counted "[In] nearly forty years I have made four hundred and forty-three balloon ascensions."[27] In an "Autobiographical Sketch," he tells how he was first attracted to theology, but "the more I attempted to sound its mysteries, the more I became confused in its understanding, and I gave it up in despair." His theological interest, however, led him to study "the appearance and motion of the heavenly bodies; and in their study my longings found a congenial field of thought, more, however, in the speculative than in the true mathematical direction." Wise sent up kittens in baskets attached to kites, and "wished that these little animals could . . . tell me how it looked from on high!" When he finally considered himself competent enough to try a kite large enough to carry him aloft, he prudently thought ". . . let us try how the coming down is to be effected, in case the luck of getting up should in time come to hand. The kitten aëronaut had now grown to a full-sized tabby, and her experience in such matters qualified her for the experiment. Four large-sized ox-bladders were fastened to a girth that encircled the body of the cat, and away she was launched from the gable window of the house." She made a rapid but a safe descent. Wise's next step was a Montgolfier-style "fire balloon," which

> settled on a thatched roof and set fire to it. Great were the emotions of my heart while viewing the calamity from a chink in the cow-stable. The fire-bells of the town—and these were alike the bells of the churches, the court-house and school-houses of the place— sounded the alarm of fire. The fire ranks were formed, fire-buckets were flying helter-skelter, the street-pumps were pouring out their watery contents, the roof was in a blaze, and I was trembling from head to foot in fear that the building might be destroyed. The fire was soon extinguished, but not without sundry admonitions as to what might be the consequences to that devilish boy "if he set the town on fire again with his foolish tricks."

Wise was "apprenticed to the cabinet-making trade . . . became a proficient workman, and followed it up in piano-forte making . . . " but the call of the heavens was strong. He left all such woodworking at the age of twenty-seven to become a professional balloonist "more from the scientific attractions it had than from the mere love of adventure and money-making."[28] Most likely there was still a substantial "love of adventure" cloaked in Wise's declared scientific interest. His early theological bent might have lent a touch of irony: Jesus was also a carpenter by trade, before devoting himself to the affairs of heaven.

Wise is all practicality when it comes to promoting the benefits of ballooning. Describing their use as war machines, he imagines them "moored over the investing lines [of a siege], a terrific fire of shot, shell, choke-balls of suffocating combustibles, with showers of hand-grenades, could be poured from it, so as to render the investing ground utterly untenable." More important, though, is its "commercial use as a means of transition [transportation], and for the scientific exploration of the atmosphere."[29] Our "bodily health and mental activity," he reminds us, are closely related to atmospheric conditions, and we need to have more scientific data.

As for the risks involved, Wise points out that since the balloons in the French postal service during the siege of Paris (1870–71) were made cheaply, the cloth sometimes having only one coat of linseed oil sealant "and at best only with two—and most of them [were] sent off . . . under the charge of persons who had never before sailed a balloon, and that nearly every one of the fifty-four thus sent off reached a point of safety, ballooning cannot be considered the risky business it is so universally characterised." Wise does not mention if they reached their intended destination, only that they landed safely. These are balloons, after all, not dirigibles, and the most important aspect during the siege was simply getting in and out of the city.[30]

At the end of his memoir, Wise describes various ingenious schemes for guiding balloons (none of which had been made to work) and gives a summary of the argument for heavier-than-air machines as the aircraft of the future. The argument is all the more credible since it comes from "an aeronaut of great skill and scientific attainment, who . . . did much to increase our knowledge of the upper atmosphere." This aeronaut, one M. Nadar, proclaims, "It is the screw which is to carry us through the air, it is the screw which penetrates the air as a gimlet does wood, the one carrying with it its motive power, the other its handle."

Wise concludes, however, "Unfortunately, nothing has thus far been accomplished with any of these ingenious inventions, and the balloon still continues to be the only machine we have by which it is possible to travel through the air."[31]

Alberto Santos-Dumont owns the honor of winning the prizes offered for directed, powered flight of significant duration. On October 19, 1901, he guided his balloon-based craft on a round trip from the Bois de Boulogne around the Eiffel Tower.[32] Born in Brazil, Santos-Dumont had grown up watching birds and reading Jules Verne, of whose stories he said "no one told me they weren't true." His favorite daydream was of ballooning, and he would spend long afternoons watching "the birds fly so high and soar with such ease on their great outstretched wings, . . . and you have only to raise your eyes to fall in love with space and freedom." Like other dreamers, he kept his personal ambitions to himself, for fear of being stamped "as unbalanced and visionary."[33]

Santos-Dumont spent most of his life in France, particularly Paris, living the life of a wealthy gentleman. He was a dandy and a man-about town, and for him aeronautics was a sport and a consuming passion. He took great delight in the sensuous pleasures, describing them in his journal:

> A joyous peal of bells mounted up to us. It was the noon day Angelus, ringing from some village belfry. I had brought up with us a substantial lunch of hard-boiled eggs, cold roast beef and chicken, cheese, ice cream, fruits and cakes. Champagne, coffee, and Chartreuse. Nothing is more delicious than lunching like this above the clouds in a spherical balloon. No dining room can be so marvellous in its decoration. The sun sets the clouds in ebullition, making them throw up rainbow jets of frozen vapour like great sheaves of fireworks all around the table. Lovely white spangles of the most delicate ice formation scatter here and there by magic, while flakes of snow form moment by moment out of nothingness, beneath our very eyes, and in our drinking glasses!

and

> Indeed, night-ballooning has a charm all its own. One is alone in the black void, true, in a murky limbo where one seems to float without weight, without a surrounding world, a soul freed from

the weight of matter! Yet, now and again there are the lights of earth to cheer one. . . . And when the dawn comes, red and gold and purple in its glory, one is almost loath to seek the earth again, although the novelty of landing in who knows what part of Europe affords yet another unique pleasure.

Shortly after winning the Deutsch Prize for his flight around the Eiffel Tower, he was regaling his companions at Maxim's with the tale. One ingredient in the adventure was that steering the contraption, never mind batting out flames with his hat or scrambling in the rigging, "left no hand free to check his pocket watch." Among his many friends was Louis Cartier, jeweler to the nobility and elite, who rose to the challenge. Cartier designed a "stylish and sporty" wristwatch and named it after Santos-Dumont. The Santos-Dumont wristwatch quickly became all the rage among fashionable Frenchmen, and its popularity spread abroad as well. Wristwatches had been a ladies' novelty since Queen Elizabeth I; this was a first for menswear.[34]

Short, slender, and dandyish Santos-Dumont might be, but his manly courage was never in doubt. You may have heard anecdotes about the astronauts sitting atop a giant firecracker and saying "light it!" or their trepidation in trusting their lives to complicated technology built by the lowest bidder. Think for a moment about Santos-Dumont in his wicker basket. Think of the fire roaring below the highly flammable balloon. The sensuous dandy enjoyed his picnic with the extra spice of ever-present danger. The tranquility he found aloft was all the more precious for being fragile, and his courage all the more admired because he left it unsaid.

Two years later, a Dayton afternoon newspaper's neighborhood section carried the headline "DAYTON BOYS EMULATE GREAT SANTOS-DUMONT."[35] In their own hometown, the achievement of Wilbur and Orville Wright was seen as a pale imitation of Santos-Dumont's worldwide celebrity.

The rigid dirigible airship, quiet and majestic, was further developed by Count Ferdinand von Zeppelin, a German cavalry officer who had participated in the American Civil War. It was competitive with the airplane for commercial service in the first part of the twentieth century. Docking stations were planned for the tops of tall buildings: the Chicago Tribune tower and the Empire State Building in New York City had provision for airship terminals. On a fateful May day in 1937, the

Miss Milano from Italy,
With cheeks of olive hue,
Goes sailing up among the clouds,
Up to the starry blue.
A "Dirigible" is her choice,
Steered by a soldier true;
Who wouldn't be up in the air
With such a maid—would you?

's Premium Butterine

Copyright 1910 Swift & Company

Miss Milano. Courtesy Guillaume de Syon

Hindenburg burst into flame upon landing in New Jersey, with the loss of thirty-six lives. Such casualties were unacceptable to the public, and attention turned to the fast-developing airplane. A few dirigibles (also known as Zeppelins) continued to fly for some years after that, but their hydrogen-filled structure was seen as too risky for general aviation.

Dirigibles provoked some lighter commentary as well. A series of postcards presented international "misses" in company with phallic dirigibles; the text carried thinly veiled double entendres. For example:

> *Miss Milano from Italy*
> *With cheeks of olive hue*
> *Goes sailing up among the clouds*
> *Up to the starry blue.*
>
> *A "Dirigible" is her choice,*
> *Steered by a soldier true;*
> *Who wouldn't be up in the air*
> *With such a maid—would you?*

and

Miss Johnnybull of London town
Drills with the Army Corps;
Her cheeks are rosy red, her form
You'd certainly adore.

She sails up to the starry blue,
She's fearless and she's tireless;
And when she gets up to the sky,
She sends her love by Wireless.

DEFLATED VISIONS

For more than a hundred years, balloons were the only human-made free-flying objects in the sky. On a much reduced scale, they continue to occupy aerial niches. Humbly serving the meteorologists, they are a cost-effective way to send scientific instruments aloft. And from time to time, the skies become filled with brightly-colored sport balloons, flown by pleasure-seekers and racers.

Pilatre de Rozier? He never quite achieved the immortality he sought, and died in a balloon accident in 1785, just two years after his first triumph. He was riding a tandem arrangement of his own design, with a hydrogen balloon above a hot-air balloon, to combine the advantages of each type. Unfortunately, the hydrogen was ignited by the fire under

Miss Johnnybull. Courtesy Guillaume de Syon

the hot-air balloon, and the arrangement crashed from 1,700 feet, killing both occupants. In 1981, however, his native province of Lorraine established a world ballooning center in his name.

And alas for Alberto Santos-Dumont, his beloved sport was drafted for use in war. He became depressed and returned to Brazil to commit suicide in 1932. His fame, like that of Pilatre de Rozier, had already been eclipsed by that of the Wright brothers.

CHAPTER 8

THE DREAM CONTINUES

W e have achieved the ancient dream—or have we? Aircraft of all descriptions, from balloons to jets, carry us into the sky most democratically. Those who have "the right stuff" push the envelope, piloting experimental aircraft to reach higher, faster, further. Hang gliding is a sport almost as popular as rock climbing or whitewater rafting. We have landed men on the moon, sent astronauts to live in space for months, and yet we still dream of higher frontiers. As I write, ambitious plans are being made for pressure-suited parachute jumps from a balloon at twenty-five miles up; if successful, the jumpers will exceed the speed of sound on their way down. Flying continues to be a complex and ambiguous symbol, carrying a rich assortment of associations.

In 1938, a group of cadets at Britain's Royal Air Force College compiled an anthology of poems about flight. Not about the airplane, but flight itself, for as the preface points out "when the heart is stirred by the sight of an aeroplane it has no thought of nuts, bolts, and means of propulsion; the beauty of motion is the old beauty of a bird. Wordsworth's heart leapt up when he beheld a rainbow in the sky, and Bridges wrote a lovely lyric to a passing ship; but the one had no thought of reflection, refraction, deviation or angles of incidence, nor the other of sail-area or wind-pressure."[1]

The poems in the collection range from Ovid through Milton and Goethe to Stephen Spender, and include works by unknowns who may never have penned any other lines in their lives. They were collected by the simple expedient of placing requests in several newspapers such as *The Times,* the *Christian Science Monitor,* and the *New York Herald,* and selecting from the results those which unanimously appealed to the editors. The resultant book is a powerful witness to the appeal of flight, across the millennia and regardless of geography.

A few years later, in the heat of World War II, a fighter pilot found time to exult:

> *Oh, I have slipped the surly bonds of earth*
> *And danced the skies on laughter-silvered*
> *wings;*
>
> . . .
>
> *Put out my hand, and touched the face of God.*[2]

Religion continues to drive people upward. David Noble points out that "what today we call space used to be known as heaven" and traces the paths by which "flight also resonated with the deepest impulses and symbols of religious . . . mythology." Jules Verne, the Wright brothers, and rocketry pioneers Tsiolovksy and Goddard were deeply religious, and implicitly or explicitly saw their work as bringing humankind closer to God. The American attitude toward aviation in the first half of the twentieth century is aptly captured in Joseph Corn's title, *The Winged Gospel.* Even Wernher von Braun, German rocket engineer and then shorthand symbol for the American space effort, found religion in his work.

As Americans ventured toward space in the 1960s, a deeply religious atmosphere was to be found throughout the various space centers from coast to coast. Individual astronauts expressed their religious devotion as well, several becoming ministers. "On Christmas Eve 1968, the astronauts on Apollo 8—the first manned mission to the moon—broadcast back to earth their reading of the first ten lines of the Book of Genesis." Inspired by his pastor, Edwin Aldrin took communion as his first act on the moon, later musing "the very first liquid ever poured on the moon and the first food eaten there were communion elements." Astronaut Tom Jones described the Space Shuttle as "the most magnificent cathedral you can go to church in."[3]

The space program on the ground reflects other American dreams. NASA workers may be invited to watch a launch from a special grandstand at Cape Kennedy; it is not luxurious, just ordinary bleachers, but it hosts a social miracle. NASA folks of all colors and social origins jostle with each other, climb over each other, and take pictures for each other. At one such occasion, I watched a large black man festooned with cameras work his way down among the folks sitting on the bleachers, carefully and cheerfully trying not to step on anyone—as he passed, strangers would offer him additional cameras and ask if he'd take photos for them as well. And at the lowest level, a family with two young girls asked two separate strolling female astronauts if they would mind having their picture taken with the children. Both astronauts graciously agreed; one was petite and black, the other tall willowy blonde. All this, in the heart of America's South, where less than fifty years ago blacks and whites were rigidly segregated and women knew their place—and it was not in an astronaut's uniform. The most remarkable thing about this episode is how unremarkable it was, as natural and unforced as breathing.

The sky is home to secular dreams as well; Judy Garland, as Dorothy in *The Wizard of Oz,* sang our yearning: "Somewhere, over the rainbow . . . Birds fly, over the rainbow, Why then, O why, can't I?" Flight for the wingless, along with hell freezing over and the moon turning blue, is fodder for proverb-makers expressing extreme unlikelihood. "When pigs fly" is heard among English-speakers, and "When camels fly" greeted hopes for a World's Fair in Tel Aviv early in the twentieth century. With panache, the Levant Fair of 1932 adopted the image of a flying camel as its logo.

Walt Disney put "impossible" flying at the center of *Dumbo,* one of his most beloved movies. Dumbo, an appealing baby elephant, is ridiculed for his oversized ears and further ridiculed when he discovers that he can fly with them. A group of crows, at first mocking and then sympathetic, give Dumbo a "magic feather" to account for his ability and give him confidence. Dumbo ultimately finds that it is not the feather's quality, but his own, which enables him to soar.[4] Ridicule, embarrassment, wonderful achievement and ultimate self-reliance; *Dumbo* is at once the story of human self-discovery and the story of human flight itself. To make the point explicit, in the final scene of the movie Dumbo

מגלת אסתר

כתובה בידי צבי דושניק

דפוס „אחדות" תל־אביב

*Postcard with flying camel logo of the Levant Fair, 1932. Book of Esther,
written in tiny letters, forms the "micrographia" image. Micrographia
is an ancient Jewish art form, reflecting the artist's reluctance to make
"graven images." Here, the Book of Esther was probably chosen to avoid the
ignorant or inadvertent disrespect to the name of God which would occur
with improper disposal; the Name does not appear in that Book.*

Courtesy Library of the Jewish Theological Seminary of America is shown flying just above the circus train, a pair of aviator's goggles on his forehead.

Pilots who fly close to the ground in small planes also speak in terms of romance. Here is a description of crop dusting from a Smithsonian magazine writer and avocational pilot:

> Can the magic of flight ever be carried by words? I think not. For so many millennia humans envied birds, yet in one century we have learned both to fly and to take it for granted. How can I explain . . . How the texture of life was no longer the hard edge of ground but the supple flow of air, so like the sea and so different? This happens to thousands of people a thousand times a day, but should never seem old. . . ."

> When you're at 30,000 feet in an airliner, the earth is just a painting, but when you're crop-dusting in that little space of air that's only 500 feet thick, all the shapes of land and the feel of sky are utterly poignant, and you know the depth of the world.

> There's something old-fashioned and eternal about this thing. In the air over Illinois, I was back in Lindbergh's day, while he was still flying the mail and daydreaming, way back when flying belonged only to the people who did it.

The writer had embarked on this article to explore why crop-dusting pilots, many of them well over the usual retirement age, keep working rather than retire. He found that "the truth is, . . . It doesn't matter . . . if he applies seed, fertilizer, or ground-up jelly beans in a chocolate slurry, so long as somewhere tomorrow morning, as the first sun burns the mist out of the valley, he gets to fly across a field."

As one pilot said, "Once you have it [flying] in your blood, they can take everything else away."[5]

Human-powered flight continues to entrance the creative imagination. A British manufacturer, Henry Kremer, has offered a series of prizes, and they have been spectacularly won. The first was for a one-mile figure-eight, the second for a flight across the twenty-one-mile English Channel. Designer Paul MacCready built the winning aircraft, first the *Gossamer Condor* and then the *Gossamer Albatross*. Professional bicyclist Bryan Allen provided the human power for both exploits. Leonardo da Vinci would have been proud.

Coming full circle on the ancient tale, the ultralight aircraft *Daedalus 88* left Heraklion, Crete, and flew to the volcanic island of Santorini, reproducing the legendary flight of its namesake. Kanellos Kanellopoulous, winner of fourteen Greek national cycling championships, maintained his highest level of effort for four hours to accomplish this. (Just thinking about it can give you leg cramps!) When a sudden gust of wind capsized the aircraft after seventy-four miles of flight, Kanellopoulous swam the remaining thirty feet to shore.[6]

Hang gliding, ballooning, the *Gossamer Condor,* and its offspring are extensions of the dream of individual flight, put aside but not abandoned. Dreamers and experimenters see their efforts as part of their search for inner peace or as a search for thrills and adventure.

Artificial flying objects have joined natural and supernatural ones as part of the vocabulary of artistic expression, symbols of modern times and timeless yearning. When Maurice Sendak featured a flying boy *In the Night Kitchen,* the reviewer for the *New York Times* noted that the naked child's flight around the house had sexual, incestuous implications.[7]

The dark side of flying is also still with us. "Unidentified Flying Objects," UFOs, speak to our fears. While mainstream technology fiction includes aliens at all points on the moral spectrum, UFOs seem to carry only malevolent creatures intent on vivisection, rape, and other evils.

The 1960s were a time of cultural upheaval and reassessment. American cultural expectations were turned upside down and the counterculture spread from the streets to the most elite institutions of society, gaining notoriety and respectability in equal measure. "Green" parties sprang up in Europe, the Committee for a Sane Nuclear Policy recruited middle-class mothers, the comfortable status quo rocked on its heels. It became fashionable among the avant-garde to be critical of technology.

Social revolution found its artistic expression in a new movement, christened pop (short for popular) art. Huge canvasses portrayed simple— some said simplistic—images from the everyday experiences of Western society: cans of Campbell's soup, comic book frames, advertisements, multiple images of movie icons. Oversized "soft sculptures" presented icepacks, pastries, and other commonplaces. Critics were divided into two camps: those who thought this represented the inherent values of modern society, and those who were horrified that it represented the new low in artistic taste. Both camps agreed that it mirrored the vast middle class rather than elite sensitivity.

Among the most famous pop art paintings are two which include aircraft. Both of them are fighters. In one, Roy Lichtenstein's 1963 *Whaam!* (yes, the letter a is repeated), two comic book-type panels, each about five feet high and seven feet wide, show an American single-seat fighter plane destroying an enemy exploding in flame. A cartoon dialog bubble over the American pilot's head reads in capital letters, "I pressed the fire-control . . . and ahead of me rockets blazed through the sky." Violence magnified and screaming for our attention. Is this "art"? And more important, is this "us"?

In 1965, James Rosenquist's enormous painting *F-111* was shown at a New York City gallery. It then went on to several international venues, and returned to New York to grace the walls of the venerable Metropolitan Museum of Art in February, 1968. The image of the F-111 itself, a fighter-bomber, reaches from end to end, interrupted by icons of contemporary society: a cake with its nutrients labeled, an oversized tire, some light bulbs, a child in hair curlers under a domed hairdryer, the mushroom cloud of an atomic explosion topped by a cheerful umbrella, a deep-sea diver whose helmet and air bubbles mirror the shape of the mushroom cloud, a mass of presumably canned spaghetti. All this was done in oversized billboard-style imagery; Rosenquist had previously been a sign painter.

Its sheer size, at eighty-four feet long and ten feet high, was overwhelming enough; its subject and style brought out an equally broad range of commentary. For some, it was a banality, its acceptance by the Metropolitan an occasion for shame, and evidence of a horrifying lack of standards. One review opened "Pop art at the Met? Sire, this is no longer the revolution, it is the Terror . . . " and concluded, "In sum, the appearance of a Pop mural at the Metropolitan Museum is part farce, part high drama, evoking as it does the crisis of high art in our time. The final irony, and truth, may be that perhaps the right thing has occurred but for all the wrong reasons."[8]

For others, it was a perfect symbol of modern times, just the right thing to jolt us into recognizing that we lived in an artificial, disjointed, meaningless, and frightening world. For its owner, Robert C. Scull, "it presents the essence of the United States' relationship to the world, displaying the equation of the good life of peace, with its luxuries and aspirations, and our involvement with the potential for instant war and final annihilation. I regard the painting as a milestone in the visual literature of what is perhaps art's greatest theme: the struggle between life and death. It speaks to all mankind, employing the plain language of everyday men, not the secret signs of the specialist."[9]

Here again we have a multivalent symbol and complex expression. The aircraft itself represents technological power turned to destructive uses, a reading reinforced by the addition of the all too familiar mushroom cloud. Yet the tire and the spaghetti are value-neutral, the light bulbs may represent real progress or perhaps a tyranny of the artificial over the natural. And the happy-faced little girl under the dryer, what of her? Is that her birthday cake, over there in that other panel? Why is someone so young being so artificially primped? What special occasion justifies her being given adult "beauty" treatment?

The aircraft in these paintings is only part of the total, yet surely essential, one element in a wholesale indictment of the American Dream, and by extension the Modern Dream. Flight as such is not central to pop art, yet can be part of that movement's vocabulary because it is part of our modern experience. The artist selects from the modern vocabulary, as others selected from the vocabulary of myth or the vocabulary of saintly iconography. By choosing warplanes rather than commercial airliners, the artists made stinging comments about what we have done to the dream—to all our dreams.

What are we to make of Claes Oldenburg's *Soft Screw as Balloon, Ascending?* The obvious puns leap to mind. Was this what the artist had in mind, or simply what we ourselves supply? Does it matter? Should art communicate the artist's thought, or stimulate our own? This drawing does both, by relying on a common vocabulary and succeeding to the extent that the artist can predict our response. That response is the very opposite of romance.

SEPTEMBER 11, 2001

On this date, the airplane acquired new symbolic meanings, as two civilian passenger jets were hijacked and suicidally guided into the twin towers of the World Trade Center in New York City. On another hijacked airliner, the passengers asserted control over their destiny, and prevented further destruction; a fourth plowed into the symbol of American military might.

Western technology was turned against itself, our proud material achievements became the agents of our nightmares. To some observers, it was ever thus, not only in the material world but in the spiritual and

Claes Oldenburg, Softscrew as Balloon, Ascending. *Need one say more?*

Courtesy National Gallery of Art

emotional world as well. As long as there have been dreams, there have been abuses and perversions of those dreams; the Christian Devil is a "fallen angel."

A year after the tragedy, however, a young German student at a Florida flight school could still insist that all the new security measures and the Americans' suspicion of foreigners did not outweigh his desire to fly: "I like the feeling, when you go over the clouds, and see the sun."[10]

STILL FLYING

The deep symbolic meanings of flight have been expanded and enriched, not discarded. They still contribute to our motivations and experiences. This is true not only of flight, but of our other dreams and drives as well. Those who look for the wellspring of creativity—the Hippocrene—would do well to give more than superficial lip service to ancient longings. Old dreams do not fade away, they merely adapt to current social realities.

There is a substantial literature relating technology to culture; indeed the official journal of the Society for History of Technology is called *Technology and Culture*. Most historians of technology recognize that any technology is influenced by the values and aspirations of the society in which it is embedded; there has been little attempt, however, to delve beyond economic factors in evaluating motivations. Perhaps this is because it is easy to quantify economics, and much harder to demonstrate more purely psychological factors.

GLOSSARY

::::

Aërodyne. Heavier-than-air flying craft, for example, a kite, glider, or airplane.

Aëronaut. Term applied to balloonists and other flyers; in the twentieth century, usage shifted to the term "aviator."

Aërostat. Lighter-than-air flying craft: balloon, blimp, dirigible, for example, a zeppelin.

Aëroplane, Airplane. Heavier-than-air, powered craft capable of carrying pilot and/or passengers.

Airship. *See* Dirigible.

Alexander the Great (356–323 B.C.). King of Macedonia, conqueror of the Persian Empire. When presented with the complex Gordian Knot and the associated prophecy that only the future emperor could undo it, Alexander cut through it with his sword. After years of military success, he is said to have wailed that there were no more worlds to conquer.

Astarte. *See* Ishtar.

Athena. Greek goddess of wisdom, said to have sprung full-grown from the forehead of Zeus. Athena is also the goddess of agricultural arts, household crafts, and war. She is associated with birds, particularly the owl. Her Roman counterpart is Minerva.

Bacon, Roger (1214?–94). An Englishman, a Franciscan friar, and natural philosopher who held that experimentation, rather than ancient authority, was the source of scientific truth. Bacon suggested a large hollow sphere filled with "etherial air" for flying, and claimed to know someone who contrived a mechanical flying machine.

Blake, William (1757–1827). English poet, artist, and mystic.

Bodhissatva. In Buddhism, an enlightened person or one who is destined for enlightenment.

Bruno, Giordano (1548?–1600). A Dominican monk, born in Italy and widely traveled, Bruno was a freethinking philosopher and poet. He was burned at the stake for heresy, especially the suggestion that God might have sent other saviours to other inhabited worlds.

Buraq. A winged mare, often shown with a woman's face, which carried Mohammad through six of the seven heavens.

Cyclops. In Greek and Roman mythology, a one-eyed, brutish, and cannibalistic giant.

Dirigible. A balloon that can be guided. Dirigibles are often elongated or cigar-shaped to reduce air resistance along the direction of motion. *Also called* airships.

Dante (Dante Aligheri) (1265–1321). Italian poet, most noted for his allegorical work *The Divine Comedy,* which includes tours of hell and heaven. The Classical Roman poet Virgil is his guide through hell; Beatrice, a symbol of spiritual love and beauty, guides him to heaven.

Dionysus. Greek and Roman god of wine and fertility, also known as Bacchus.

Freud, Sigmund (1856–1939). Austrian-born "father of psychiatry." His theories focused on stages in sexual development as keys to development of personality traits.

Ganymede. A handsome young Trojan prince, whom Zeus (in the form of an eagle) carried to Mount Olympus. Ganymede replaced Hebe, goddess of youth, as the gods' cupbearer. In some versions, Ganymede became Zeus's lover.

Garuda. In Hinduism, a large bird that carries the god Vishnu. Garuda is an enemy of serpents, which represent spirituality misdirected toward earth-bound concerns.

Gordian Knot. *See* Alexander the Great.

Hanseatic League. An alliance of north German cities formed in the 1100s, it rapidly dominated trade and politics in the Baltic area. Its influence lasted until the mid-1500s.

Hebe. Goddess of youth, daughter of Zeus and his wife Hera. In some places she was known as Ganymeda.

Hermes. Greek name for the messenger of the gods. Also a god of fertility, in that context shown with an enlarged erect penis. Identified with the Roman god Mercury, and often shown with wings on his cap and sandals. Hermes is sometimes identified with Apollo as well, and like Apollo associated with music and the other arts.

Hippodrome. Arena for horse racing.

Hittites. The Hittite kingdom included the present-day Turkish region of Anatolia and parts of northern Syria. Their empire flourished from approximately 2000 B.C.E. to approximately 1200 B.C.E.

Huang Ti (b. 2704 B.C.E.). Legendary Chinese emperor whose reign is said to have begun about 2697 B.C.E.

Hugo, Victor (1802–85). French poet, author of *The Hunchback of Notre Dame* and *Les Misérables,* among other works.

Ilmarinen. Finnish god-hero, a smith. Prominent character in the Kalevala, the Finnish national epic.

Innana. Sumerian goddess, daughter of Nana the moon god. *See also* Ishtar.

Ishtar. Babylonian god/goddess of love, war, and thunderstorms. Also called Innana or Astarte. In some versions, the female Ishtar has a male consort whom she abandons or murders; these versions are often associated with the ritual execution of a young man as an annual part of her worship.

Kai Kawus. Semi-legendary early Shah of Persia (now Iran).

Kelvin, Lord. William Thomson (1824–1907) was knighted in 1866 and raised to the nobility in 1892 for his work in physics and mathematics, primarily concerned with thermodynamics, hydrodynamics, magnetism, and electricity. A unit of heat, the degree Kelvin, is named for him.

Mage. Wise man, magician.

Mana, Manala. Pre-Christian Finnish abode of the dead.

Mesopotamia. Literally from the Greek, "country between rivers." Generally the region between and around the Tigris and Euphrates Rivers, considered to be the cradle of Western and Middle Eastern civilization. *See also* Sumer.

Minerva. *See* Athena.

Minotaur. Half bull, half human, monster. Poseidon, god of the sea, had given a beautiful bull to Minos, king of Crete, intending that the bull be a sacrifice. Minos decided to keep the bull, so Poseidon caused Minos's wife to fall in love with it. The Minotaur was the offspring of that union.

Momus. Greek and Roman god of ridicule and censure; also used to denote a petty faultfinder.

Montgolfier, Joseph-Michel (1740–1810) and Jacques-Étienne (1745–99). French paper manufacturers and inventors of the hot-air balloon.

Montgolfier. Hot-air balloon or "fire balloon," named after its inventors. Other balloons may be lifted by hydrogen or helium.

Newton, Isaac (1642–1727). Mathematician and physicist, also dabbled in alchemy. Popularly known for his theory of gravitation and his three laws of motion. The story that the gravitational theory was triggered by the fall of an apple onto his head is pure legend. His work in optics included the demonstration that "pure" light is composed of all the colors of the spectrum; in mathematics his best-known achievement was developing the technique known as calculus.

Odin. God of War and chief of the gods in Scandinavian and Germanic mythology; also called Wodin or Wotan. Odin rides a flying eight-legged horse named Sleipnir, and is usually accompanied by two ravens who bring him information.

Oneiric. Related to dreams.

Ornithopter. Heavier-than-air flying machine based on principles of birdflight, most notably by flapping wings.

Ovid (43 B.C.E.–17 C.E.). Roman poet who was wealthy, talented, licentious, very influential in Italian poetry during the Middle Ages and Renaissance. Several well-known English poets, including Shakespeare, were also influenced by his work.

Petrarch (Francesco Petrarca) (1304–74). Italian-born poet, lived most of his life in Avignon, France. Much of his work attempted to demonstrate continuity between Christianity and Classical Greek and Roman culture.

Prometheus. Greek Titan who stole fire from the gods and gave it to humans. For this he was chained to a rock and condemned to have a bird tear his flesh and eat his liver, which keeps growing back so that his punishment is eternal.

Robins, Benjamin (1707–51). British experimentalist in aerodynamics, specialist in ballistics and gunnery. Explored the behavior of projectiles (bullets, cannonballs, and so on) in air.

Sampo. From the Finnish epic *The Kålevala,* a gift forged by Ilmarinen. The exact nature of the Sampo is unclear; it is most likely a support of heaven. The word may be related to Sanskrit *skambha* "pillar" and Altaic *sumbur* "world mountain." The concept is related to the Tree of Life and other forms of bridge element between earth and heaven, natural and supernatural worlds. The Sampo also seems to be a miraculous mill, grinding out salt, gold, and so on. The folktale of the small mill at the bottom of the ocean, forever producing salt, may be a relic of the Sampo myth.

Silk Road (or Silk Route). The route from imperial Rome to the capital of China. Its most consistent use was during the period from the first century B.C.E. to the fifth century C.E., and intermittently thereafter. When Marco Polo took that route in the thirteenth century, the trip took approximately three years.

Sumer. Mesopotamian state roughly corresponding to the biblical Babylonia, along the Tigris and Euphrates Rivers northeast of present-day Iraq. Sumerian culture flourished from approximately 3000 B.C.E. to approximately 2000 B.C.E. Sumerians developed the cuneiform script, one of the earliest writing systems.

Tuoni. God of death, in the pre-Christian Finnish pantheon.

Ukko. Omniscient chief god of the pre-Christian Finns.

Vedas. Early Hindu scriptures in Sanskrit, written approximately 1500–1200 B.C.E.

Wayland, Weiland, Volund. Smith-hero of Germanic myth. The epic *Lay of Volund* recounts his exploits.

Watt, James (1736–1819). Inventor of the reciprocating-cylinder steam engine. The story that he was inspired by watching the action of steam rising from a teapot is a popular myth.

Wodin, Wotan. *See* Odin.

Yoga. Narrowly, refers to a certain Indian philosophy dating to approximately the second century B.C.E.; more broadly, the name is derived from the Sanskrit which signifies Union with God, and it may have earlier Vedic roots.

Yogin. An adept or initiate in the Yoga philosophy, thought to have mastered some supernatural powers such as levitation and so on. Some authors seem to use it interchangeably with shaman or other appellations for "holy man."

TIMELINE

::::

ca. 3300–1900 B.C.E.	Flourishing of Sumerian civilization in Mesopotamia.
ca. 1900–300 B.C.E.	Flourishing of Babylonian civilization in Mesopotamia.
ca. 428–347 B.C.E.	Plato, Greek philosopher and intellectual heir of Socrates.
400–350 B.C.E.	Archytas, Greek philosopher and mathematician, said to have made a wooden pigeon that could fly, but not rise from the ground under its own power.
384–322 B.C.E.	Aristotle, Greek philosopher whose teachings about the natural world (biology and physics) were accepted as dogma in the western world for almost two thousand years, until the Renaissance.
287–212 B.C.E.	Archimedes, philosopher and mathematician, developed concept of specific gravity and defined the principle of the lever.
200 B.C.E.	Approximate date of earliest recorded kites in China.
43 B.C.E.–17 C.E.	Ovid, influential Roman poet. Full name Publius Ovidius Naso. Most famous for his works *Metamorphosis* and *The Art of Love*.
0–200 C.E.	Flying phalloi [Rome, Pompeii, first and second century C.E.].
ca. 120–180	Lucian of Samosata.
800s	Kites known in Muslim countries.
1000	Approximate date of Eilmer of Malmsbury flight.
ca. 1250	Roger Bacon suggests a large hollow sphere filled with "etherial air" for flying, also claims

ca. 1250 (*cont.*)	to know someone who contrived a mechanical flying machine.
1265–1321	Dante (Dante Aligheri), Italian poet, author of *Divine Comedy.*
1300	Marco Polo publishes account of travels, including description of man-carrying kites.
1304–74	Petrarch (Francesco Petrarca) Italian-born poet, lived in France, attempted to show continuity between Classical and Christian culture.
1436–76	Johann Muller, also called "Regiomontanus," German astronomer and mathematician.
1439–1501?	Francesco di Giorgio.
1470s–1480s	Leonardo da Vinci and others doodling parachutes in their notebooks.
1505	Leonardo da Vinci compiles a small fraction of his observations on birdflight into the *Codex on Birdflight.* The first of his notations had been made about 1490.
1516	Sir Thomas More writes *Utopia* in Latin.
1535	Sir Thomas More executed for treason.
1543	Copernicus *The Book of the Revolutions of the Heavenly Spheres* first edition, Nuremberg.
1551	*Utopia* translated into English.
1589	Giovanni Battista della Porta describes the making of a kite and its action in relation to the flow of air, suggests men might fly.
1600	Giordano Bruno burnt at stake for heresy.
1609	Galileo publishes *Sidereal Nuncio (Starry Messenger).*
1610	Johannes Kepler begins to circulate *Somnium (Dream)* in manuscript (not printed/published).
1630	Kepler tries to publish *Somnium.* It is eventually published posthumously by his sons.
1632	Galileo publishes *Dialogue Concerning the Two Chief World Systems.*
1638	Galileo publishes *Dialogues Concerning Two New Sciences,* including his thoughts on the nature of air.

1643	Evangelista Torricelli invents barometer.
1646	Kites capable of carrying a man were made in Rome.
1650	Cyrano de Bergerac publishes *Other Worlds: The Comical History of the States and Empires of the Moon and the Sun.*
1661	Robert Boyle reports to Royal Society on his gas law: volume of gas inversely proportional to its temperature.
1670	Francesco Lana de Terzi suggests raising an airship "by means of evacuated metal spheres."
1680	Bishop John Wilkins publishes *Mathematical Magick.* Giovanni Borelli publishes *De Motu Animalum.*
1687	Isaac Newton publishes *Philosophiae Naturalis Principia Mathematica,* generally called "The *Principia,*" his major scientific work.
1714 or 1715	Emmanuel Swedenborg publishes design for human-powered heavier-than-air flying machine, based on birdflight.
1746	Benjamin Robins presents important aerodynamic findings in *Philosophical Transactions.*
1752	Voltaire publishes story "Micromegas;" Benjamin Franklin (1706–90) shows that lightning is electricity.
1770s–1790s	Luigi Galvani experiments with electricity's role in animal muscle activity.
1783	Montgolfier brothers launch large hot-air balloon in August; first manned flight a few months later, in November.
1804	Sir George Cayley constructs a small successful model aircraft with flat wings, a fuselage, and a tail rudder-elevator consisting of two planes (kites) intersecting at right angles.
1809–10	Sir George Cayley publishes "triple paper" on aerodynamic experiments and theory.
1818	Mary Shelley writes *Frankenstein,* drawing on recent advances in electrical and biological science.

1825	George Pocock publishes *The Aeropleustic Art*, describing carriages drawn by kites instead of horses.
1865	Jules Verne publishes *From the Earth to the Moon*.
1870s–1890s	Otto Lilienthal and others work on ornithopters
1877	Alexander Graham Bell becomes interested in "flying machines"—kites and powered aircraft.
1889	Otto Lilienthal publishes *Birdflight as the Basis for Aviation*.
1891	Langley publishes his experimental results in aerodynamics as part of the series *Smithsonian Contributions to Knowledge*.
1893	Lawrence Hargrave, inspired by Langley's work, invents box kite in Australia.
1896	Otto Lilienthal dies in glider crash.
1901	Alberto Santos-Dumont makes round trip in lighter-than-air craft, from St. Cloud around the Eiffel Tower and back.
1903	Wright brothers Wilbur and Orville make first sustained, powered, human-carrying flight in a heavier-than-air machine at Kitty Hawk, N.C.
1912	Edgar Rice Burroughs publishes *Dejah Thoris, Princess of Mars*.
1979	Human-powered flight across the English Channel by Allan Brian of England. His craft, 'The Gossamer Albatross,' weighed 17.2 kg, and the flight lasted two hours and forty-nine minutes.
1988	Human-powered flight from Crete to Santorini, reproducing legendary flight of Daedalus. Kanellos Kanellopoulus of Greece is the athlete.

NOTES

::::::
::::::

INTRODUCTION

1. George Basalla, *The Evolution of Technology,* chap. 1.
2. Charles Harvard Gibbs-Smith, *Aviation: An Historical Survey from its Origins to the End of World War II,* p. 2. Tom Crouch's excellent history of aviation, *A Dream of Wings: Americans and the Airplane, 1875–1905,* is another example of this approach.
3. See, for example, Ian Tattersall "How We Came to be Human," *Scientific American* 285, no. 6 (December, 2001): 57–63; Kate Wong, "Taking Wing," *Scientific American* 286, no. 1 (January, 2002): 16.
4. Lawrence Kushner, "What Did the Mystic Say to the Hot Dog Vendor?" *Annals of the New York Academy of Sciences* 930 (2001): 219.

CHAPTER 1. DEITIES ALOFT

1. Gen. 2:7.
2. Gaston Bachelard, *Air and Dreams,* trans. Edith R. Farrell and C. Frederick Farrell, pp. 236–37.
3. Vedic is an early form of Sanskrit. The four Vedas are holy scriptures written between 1300 and 1000 B.C.E. They may have been based on an earlier oral tradition.
4. Legend of the Prince and Princess of Bekhten. In many cases, gods seem to be bound by physical limitations, and some must be carried from place to place. The sun and moon "see everything" because they travel in the sky; other gods either take bird form or ride celestial creatures to observe widely.
5. Berthold Laufer, *The Prehistory of Aviation,* pp. 18–19.
6. *Metropolitan Museum of Art Bulletin* LIX, no. 4. (Spring, 2002): 27. Curator's note to "Masked Figure Pendant" acquisition number 1991.419.31.
7. Neil Gillman, *Sacred Fragments: Recovering Theology for the Modern Jew,* p. 1.
8. Bachelard, *Air and Dreams,* p. 68.
9. Ibid., p. 78; from William Blake, *Visions of the Daughters of Albion* (London, 1793).
10. Ibid., quoted p. 70.
11. Exod. 19:4.
12. Freud, "Leonardo da Vinci and a Memory of his Childhood," in Peter Gay, *The Freud Reader,* p. 475. I am indebted to Thomas Crouch for this reference.
13. Shamanism—the shaman ascends a ladder or pole to heaven, has a bird-type guide, and dresses in bird costume. Altaic shamans call their ritual drum "horse," and liken their ecstasy to a gallop through the heavens. (Altay is a republic in southeastern Russia.) Strictly speaking, shamanism is a religion found mostly in the far northern regions of the world, but the term has come to be

applied to all men or women who derive power through contact with the supernatural.

14. Martin Haug and Edward William West, eds., *The Book of Arday Viraf.*
15. Buraq is the Arabic word for "lightning." Illustrations usually give Buraq a woman's face and a peacock's tail.
16. *Henry V,* Act III, Scene 7.
17. *Rig-Veda,* x:lxxxi. R. C. Zaehner, *Hindu Scriptures,* p. 8.
18. Yoga, narrowly, refers to a certain Indian philosophy dating to approximately the second century B.C.E.; more broadly, the name is derived from the Sanskrit which signifies Union with God, and it may have earlier Vedic roots.
19. *Scientific American* 5, no. 36 (May 25, 1850): 358; reprinted in *Scientific American* 283, no. 1 (July, 2000): 12.
20. Jules Duhem, *Histoire des Idées Aéronautiques Avant Montgolfier,* p. 16. Other flying saints are also listed here.
21. Clive Hart, *Images of Flight,* p. 197.
22. Ibid., p. 201.

CHAPTER 2. ARTIFICIAL WINGS AND THE IMITATION OF GOD

1. William Blake, *Auguries of Innocence.*
2. Mircea Eliade, *Symbolism, the Sacred, and the Arts,* p. 5.
3. In Hart *Images of Flight,* p. 142, see Figure 80 (no date). Eros (Amor) represents carnal love, in distinction from Agape or spiritual love (English does not have separate words for these two types of love). Eros is variously portrayed as a handsome adolescent male, or as an infant; both forms are usually winged.
4. Ibid., p. 161, Figure 82, ca. 1650.
5. Ibid., p. 152.
6. Ibid., pp. 146–48.
7. Eliade, *Symbolism, the Sacred, and the Arts,* p. 3.
8. Ananda Coomaraswamy, *Figures of Speech or Figures of Thought: Collected Essays on the Traditional or "Normal" View of Art.*
9. Eliade, *Symbolism, the Sacred, and the Arts,* p. 5.
10. Eliade, *Myths, Dreams, and Mysteries; the Encounter Between Contemporary Faiths and Archaic Realities* "[T]he desire. . . " passage appears both in *Myths, Dreams* and in *Symbolism.*
11. Eliade, *Myths, Dreams,* p. 118.
12. Rosalind Williams, *Notes on the Underground: An Essay on Technology, Society, and the Imagination,* presents a parallel account of the symbolic connotations of subterranean activities and technologies.
13. Laufer, *Prehistory of Aviation,* p. 18. See also his account of Emperor Shun, p. 14. Duhem, *Idées Aéronautiques,* uses a reasonable, though still arbitrary, classification system.
14. For example, Duhem, *Idées Aéronautiques.* In fairness, it should be noted that comprehensiveness rather than contextualization is Duhem's goal. On the other hand, useful general concepts have been developed from carefully analytical comparative studies of symbolic systems, for example, Claude Levi-Strauss *Structural Anthropology, The Raw and the Cooked,* and *Myth and Meaning,* and Mary Douglas, *Purity and Danger.*
15. The story of Daedalus is much richer than can be sketched here: see Sarah

Morris, *Daidalos and the Origins of Greek Art*, for a more detailed exploration of both the myth and the word as it traveled around the Mediterranean and Aegean Seas.

16. The attribute becomes the name, much as today we might speak of "Mr Goodwrench" or "the Creator."

17. Morris, *Daidalos*, p. 193. In this version, Daedalus is credited with the invention of sails, "the wings of a seagoing ship." Morris cites Hart, *Images of Flight*, pp. 89–93, on these connections in the Greek imagination.

18. Nathaniel Hawthorne, *Pegasus, the Winged Horse*.

19. Laufer, *Prehistory of Aviation*, p. 46.

20. Richard C. Foltz, *Religions of the Silk Road*, p. 44.

21. Laufer, *Prehistory of Aviation*, p. 48.

22. "Religion By Discernment," chap. 7, *Bhagavad Gita; The Song Celestial*, trans. Sir Edwin Arnold. Available on the Internet at the Carrie website (public domain): //history.cc.ukans.edu/carrie/stacks/books002.htm

23. *The Kalevala, The Epic Poem of Finland*, trans. John Martin Crawford, Rune 19.

24. Benjamin Foster, *From Distant Days: Myths, Tales and Poetry from Ancient Mesopotamia*.

25. Peter Merin, *Conquest of the Skies; The Story of the Idea of Human Flight*, p. 28.; Laufer, *Prehistory of Aviation*. Poem on pp. 59–60, trans. "Warner."

26. Merin, *Conquest*, p. 56; see also *Encyclopaedia Britannica*, 2001 Deluxe Edition CD-ROM, s.v. "spa"; John Clark, "Bladud of Bath: The Archaeology of a Legend," *Folklore* 105 (1994); websites http://www.ldolphin.org/cooper/ch4.html and http://www.jams.swinternet.co.uk/Bath/Medieval/Bladud.htm

27. Laufer, *Prehistory of Aviation*, pp. 14–15.

28. Coomaraswamy, *Figures of Speech*, p. 10.

29. Jacques Ellul, *The Technological Society*.

30. Joseph Needham, *Science and Civilization in China*, pp. 571–72.

31. John Wise, *Through the Air: A Narrative of Forty Years Experience as an Aeronaut, Comprising a History of the Various Attempts in the Art of Flying by Artificial Means from the Earliest Period Down to the Present Time*, p. 49.

32. Laufer, *Prehistory of Aviation*, pp. 68–69.

33. Ibid., p. 13.

CHAPTER 3. TRAVEL TO EXTRAORDINARY KINGDOMS

1. Coomaraswamy, *Figures of Speech*, p. 42, note 101.

2. Plato, *Symposium*, 205 C, quoted in Coomaraswamy *Figures of Speech*, pp. 10 and 125.

3. Rupert de la Bère, *Icarus; An Anthology of the Poetry of Flight*, p. 8.

4. Théophile Gautier, *Histoire de Romanticisme*, p. 150, in Maurice Z. Schroeder, *Icarus: The Image of the Artist in French Romanticism*, p. 55.

5. Maurice Z. Schroeder, *Icarus*, p. 45, from Victor Hugo's "Mazeppa." "Il crie épouvanté, tu poursuis implacable. / Pâle, épuisé, béant, sous ton vol qui l'accable / Il ploie avec effroi; / Chacque pas que tu fais semble creuser sa tombe. / Enfin la term arrive . . . il court, il vole, il tombe, / Et se releve roi!"

6. Ibid., p. 57. "Mieux que l'aigle chasseur, . . . / Homme! monte par bonds dans l'air resplendissant. / La vielle terr, en bas, se taît et diminue." From Leconte de Lisle "In Excelsis" in *Poèmes barbares*, p. 237.

7. Joseph Brodsky, "The Hawk's Cry in Autumn" in *To Urania*. Quoted by permission of Farrar, Straus, and Giroux.

8. In Greek mythology, Endymion is a handsome youth who sleeps eternally; in some versions of the myth, Selene, goddess of the moon, had put him to sleep so that she might keep him for herself, forever young.

9. Needham, *Science and Civilization*, p. 569, note a.

10. John Lear, *Kepler's Dream with the Full Text and Notes of* Somnium, Sive Astronomia Lunaris, Joannis Kepleri, trans. Patricia Frueh Kirkwood, note 3, p. 89.

11. Ibid., p. 3.

12. Ibid., p. 77.

13. Cyrano de Bergerac, *Other Worlds: The Comical History of the States and Empires of the Moon and Sun*, trans. Geoffrey Strachan, p. viii.

14. Ibid., p. 43.

15. Ibid, p. 55.

16. de Bergerac, *Other Worlds*, chaps. 15–17.

17. Jonathan Swift, *Travels into Several Remote Nations of the World*, more popularly titled *Gulliver's Travels*, was published anonymously in 1726. The Laputans represent a mockery of intellectualism. They exploit the military/political advantages of a flying island by hovering over rebellious subjects to block the sun and rain, and in extreme case lowering the island onto them. The island flies by means of an enormous magnet beneath, which is turned to attract or repel the earth's field.

18. François Marie Arouet de Voltaire, *Candide, Zadig and Selected Stories*, trans. Donald M. Frame.

19. Jules Verne, *From the Earth to the Moon and Round the Moon*.

20. See, for example, Lester del Rey *Science Fiction Hall of Fame: the Greatest Science Fiction Stories of All Time*.

21. Susan Douglas, *Inventing American Broadcasting 1899–1922*, 305.

22. Traxler Amendment to HR 5679, debate televised by C-SPAN, July 29, 1992.

CHAPTER 4. EXUBERANT SPECULATIONS

1. Wright to Langley, May 30, 1899, in John Anderson, *A History of Aerodynamics and Its Impact on Flying Machines*, p. 206.

2. There is a large scholarly literature addressing the concept and function of mindsets and "thought communities" or "thought collectives." An early influential work is Ludwik Fleck, *Genesis and Development of a Scientific Fact*, particularly chap. 4. Other useful references include Edward Constant, *The Origins of the Turbojet Revolution;* Thomas Kuhn, *The Structure of Scientific Revolutions* and *The Essential Tension: Selected Studies in Scientific Tradition and Change;* John Servos, *Physical Chemistry from Ostwald to Pauling: The Making of a Science in America;* and Barry Barnes, *Scientific Knowledge and Sociological Theory*.

3. Alfred W. Crosby, *The Measure of Reality: Quantification and Western Society, 1250–1600*, p. x.

4. Lynn White, Jr., "Cultural Climates and Technological Advance in the Middle Ages," in *Medieval Religion and Technology*, p. 224.

5. For additional perspectives, see, for example, David C. Lindberg, ed., *Science in*

the Middle Ages and Carlo Ginzburg, *The Cheese and the Worms: The Cosmos of a Sixteenth-Century Miller,* trans. John and Anne Tedeschi.

6. White, "Introduction," in *Medieval Religion,* pp. xix–xx.
7. White, "The Iconography of Temperantia and the Virtuousness of Technology," in *Medieval Religion and Technology,* p. 186.
8. Ibid., p. 184.
9. White, "Cultural Climates," pp. 250–51.
10. White, "Iconography of Temperantia," p. 186.
11. Faith, Hope, and Charity are the three Theological Virtues; Prudence, Courage, Temperance, and Justice the four Cardinal virtues. (Cardinal from cardines = hinges; on these virtues "hinge" the "door to the good life.") White, "Iconography of Temperantia," pp. 181–204.
12. Ibid., pp. 189–90.
13. Ibid., p. 193.
14. Alfred Crosby also analyzes a painting of Temperantia, this one by Breughel the Elder (1525?–69). Crosby, *Measure of Reality,* p. 5 et seq.
15. White, "Cultural Climates," p. 223.
16. Ibid., p. 221.
17. Ibid., p. 227.
18. Spencer Weart, *Nuclear Fear,* p. 57.
19. Joseph J. Corn, "Making Flying 'Thinkable': Women Pilots and the Selling of Aviation, 1927–1940," *American Quarterly* 31 (1979): 556–71.
20. Weart, *Nuclear Fear,* p. 147.
21. Ibid., p. 151.
22. Laufer, *Prehistory of Aviation,* p. 22; also Needham *Science and Civilization,* p. 570.
23. Quoted in Phil Scott, *The Pioneers of Flight: A Documentary History,* p. 23.
24. Ibid.
25. Evelyn Charles Vivian, *A History of Aeronautics,* pt. 1, chap. 1.
26. Laufer, *Prehistory of Aviation,* pp. 12 and 13.
27. E. Seton Valentine and F. L. Tomlinson, *Travels in Space: A History of Aerial Navigation,* p. 15.
28. John Wilkins, *Mathematical Magick,* "To the Reader," unpaged introduction preceding the Table of Contents.
29. Ibid., p. 192.
30. Ibid.
31. Clive Staples Lewis, *The Screwtape Letters.*
32. Wilkins, *Mathematical Magick,* p. 193.
33. Ibid., p. 195.
34. Ibid., p. 194.
35. Ibid., p. 197.
36. Ibid.
37. Ibid.
38. Ibid., pp. 200–203.
39. Ibid., p. 201.
40. Ibid., p. 204.
41. Ibid.
42. Ibid., pp. 204–206.
43. Ibid., p. 208.

44. Ibid., pp. 209–10.
45. Ibid., pp. 214–16.
46. Ibid., p. 217.
47. Ibid., p. 213.
48. Wise, *Through the Air,* p. 56.
49. Ibid., p. 24.

CHAPTER 5. HUMAN-POWERED FLIGHT: ORNITHOPTERS

1. Lynn White, Jr., "Eilmer of Malmsbury, an Eleventh Century Aviator," *Medieval Religion,* p. 60.
2. Ibid., p. 62.
3. Isaiah 40:31.
4. White, "Eilmer," p. 66.
5. Ibid., p. 65.
6. Ibid., p. 67.
7. Laufer, *Prehistory of Aviation,* p. 66, describes ibn Firnas's other achievements, which give credibility to the account of this flight attempt.
8. Ibid., p. 67
9. Ibid., pp. 67–68.
10. See, for example, Laufer, *Prehistory of Aviation;* Wise, *Through the Air;* D. A. Reay, *The History of Man-Powered Flight.*
11. Reay, *History of Man-Powered Flight,* p. 7. No date is given for Aleman's attempt.
12. Blanche Stillson, *Wings: Insects, Birds, Men,* p. 196.
13. Anthony B. Wight, *Daedalus: The Long Odyssey from Myth to Reality,* Yale-New Haven Teachers Institute, http://www.yale.edu/ynhti/curriculum/units/1988/6/88.06.10.x.html
14. Sources include John Anderson, *History of Aerodynamics,* p. 80.
15. Ibid.
16. In Chhung, the "h" is doubled in the source text.
17. Needham, *Science and Civilization,* p. 574; Laufer, *Prehistory of Aviation.*
18. Needham, *Science and Civilization,* p. 575.
19. Ibid., p. 576.
20. Charles V, Holy Roman Emperor, 1500–58; Charles V of France, 1338–80; Charles IV (or V) Leopold of Austria, 1643–90.
21. Anderson, *History of Aerodynamics,* p. 22. See also Stillson, *Wings,* chap. 18, "The Labors of Leonardo da Vinci."
22. Quoted in Stillson, *Wings,* p. 213.
23. Giovanni Borelli, *De Motu Animalium.*
24. Henry Söderberg, *Swedenborg's 1714 Airplane: A Machine to Fly in the Air,* pp. 4–6.
25. The journal ran only six issues, 1716–17.
26. One famous American Swedenborgian was John Chapman, better known as "Johnny Appleseed." Chapman wandered around planting apple trees and carried Swedenborgian tracts, torn into sections, in his saddlebags. He would leave a section with a host family, swapping it for another when he returned on subsequent visits.
27. Swedenborg to Oetinger, in Söderberg, *Swedenborg's 1714 Airplane,* note on p. 65.

28. Swedenborg's "Soul-seeking" interpretation from the *Encyclopaedia Britannica*, 2001 Deluxe Edition CD-ROM, s.v. "Emanuel Swedenborg, Swedenborg's philosophy of nature."

29. Söderberg, *Swedenborg's 1714 Airplane*, pp. 17–23.

30. Swedenborg, *Journal of Dreams 1743–1744*.

31. Gibbs-Smith, *Aviation*, chap. 5. See also Wise, *Through the Air*, chap. 14.

32. John Mason Good, *The Book of Nature*, 1839, quoted in Jen Hill, *An Exhilaration of Wings: The Literature of Birdwatching*, p. 113.

33. Wise, *Through the Air*, pp. 143–44.

34. Otto Lilienthal, *Birdflight as the Basis of Aviation: A Contribution Towards a System of Aviation*, p. xii.

35. Anderson, *History of Aerodynamics*, p. 158.

36. Ibid., p. 159.

37. Lilienthal, *Birdflight*, p. xvi.

38. Quoted in Anderson, *History of Aerodynamics*, p. 156.

39. Lilienthal, *Birdflight*, pp. xviii, xix.

40. Anderson, *History of Aerodynamics*, p. 157.

41. Arthur Koestler, *The Sleepwalkers*, p. 191.

42. Anderson, *History of Aerodynamics*, p. 161.

43. Wise, *Through the Air*, pp. 51–52. Mt. Chimborazo is the highest peak of the Ecuadorian Andes (20,702 feet [6,310 miles]). Many attempts were made to climb Mt. Chimborazo in the eighteenth and nineteenth centuries; the first to reach the summit was the British mountaineer Edward Whymper, who climbed the peak twice in 1880. The geographer, naturalist, and explorer Alexander von Humboldt reached 18,893 feet in 1802, *Encyclopaedia Britannica*, 2001 Deluxe Edition CD-ROM, s.v. "chimborazo."

44. Laufer, *Prehistory of Aviation*, p. 13.

45. Anderson, *History of Aerodynamics*, p. 118. "Also appearing in the third annual report [Aeronautical Society of Great Britain, 1869] were statements by both Wenham [inventor of the wind tunnel] and Stringfellow that the airscrew would be the "best method of propelling through the air," despite the fact that no real experience had proved that. The publications of the society were peppered with debates concerning the best propulsive mechanism—a propeller or a beating wing." Wise also adresses this issue, in the last chapter of *Through the Air*.

46. Basalla, *Evolution of Technology*, pp. 106–108.

47. Chapter 2, section "Kings and Wings."

48. Steven Vogel, *Cat's Paws and Catapults: Mechanical Worlds of Nature and People*, explores the relationships of "the mechanical worlds of nature and people."

49. Philip Steadman, *The Evolution of Designs: Biological Analogy in Architecture and the Applied Arts*, pp. 17 and 18.

50. Ibid., p. 125, citing C. C. Gillespie.

CHAPTER 6. GLIDERS, PARACHUTES, AND KITES

1. Clive Hart, *Kites: An Historical Survey*, p. 17.

2. Dharam Jit Singh, *Classic Cooking From India*, pp. 142–44.

3. Hart, *Kites*, p. 48 for modern kite festivals in Asia; p. 25 for Korean customs.

4. Needham, *Science and Civilization*, p. 576.

5. Sheridan Bowman, ed., *Science and the Past*, p. 16.
6. A. C. Haddon, *The Study of Man*, in Hart, *Kites*, pp. 251–52.
7. Hart, *Kites*, p. 55, citing Elsdon Best, *Games and Pastimes of the Maori*, p. 76.
8. Hart, *Kites*, p. 58, citing Best, *Games*, pp. 70–71.
9. Needham, *Science and Civilization*, p. 576.
10. Joseph Priestley, *The History and Present State of Electricity*, 2d ed., p. 171. Priestley is better known for his experiments in chemistry, and he discovered oxygen at about the same time as did the Frenchman Antoine Lavoisier.
11. Needham, *Science and Civilization*, p. 574 and Figure 708, between pp. 590 and 591. "A train of kites bearing aloft a military observer . . . Rheims 1909." Needham refers to Vivian, *A History of Aeronautics*, p. 189. The train is of box kites, though, not invented until 1893 (in Australia, by Hargrave). The Sung (also Song) dynasty in China reigned from 960–1279 c.e., the Ming from 1368–1644.
12. Laufer, *Prehistory of Aviation*, p. 34.
13. Hart, *Kites*, p. 34.
14. Needham, *Science and Civilization*, p. 589; White, "Eilmer," p. 71.
15. Needham, *Science and Civilization*, p. 580.
16. Ibid., also cites G. B. della Porta, *Pneumaticorum Libri II* Naples, 1601. Ital. Tr. *I Tre Libri de' Spiritali*. Naples 1606.
17. Needham, *Science and Civilization*, p. 580.
18. Duhem, *Idées Aéronautiques*, pp. 194–202, speculates as to its origins and why it did not spread widely in Europe. Duhem suggests that the kite did indeed spread from Asia through Tartar and Arabic influence into Spain and that descriptions of magicians' flying machines in the fifteenth century are in fact kites. He cites the case of Konrad Kyeser, *Bellifortis* Codex 328, in the Weimar library, which shows pictures from 1405 and 1410. He describes the use of kites as entertainment, painted as dragons and mythical snakes. (Another example given is a supposed Parisian panic at the appearance of a "flying serpent" in 1579.) Duhem suggests that the notion of kite flying is known, but it does not register as anything more than cheap entertainment for use by road shows.

   I am indebted to Guillaume de Syon (personal communication) for the suggestion that kites may have been associated in the popular mind with witchcraft. Witch-hunting was prevalent between 1450 and 1700; the classic polemic against witches, the *Malleus Maleficorum* (*Hammer of Witches*), appeared in 1486.
19. Needham, *Science and Civilization*, p. 580 (note).
20. Gibbs-Smith, *Aviation*, chap. 2.
21. Turkish translations from Laufer, *Prehistory of Aviation*, p. 37.
22. Arnold Pacey, *The Maze of Ingenuity: Ideas and Idealism in the Development of Technology*, introduction and quotation from p. 21.
23. White, "Cultural Climates," p. 223.
24. Needham, *Science and Civilization*, p. 583.
25. Lynn White, Jr., "The Invention of the Parachute," *Medieval Religion and Technology*.
26. Laufer, *Prehistory of Aviation*, p. 15.
27. White, "Invention of the Parachute."
28. Needham, *Science and Civilization*, p. 579, "some of the greatest European mathematicians devoted attention to the theory of kites (e.g., Newton, Desgauliers, d'Alembert, Euler)."
29. George Pocock, *The Aeropleustic Art, or Navigation in the Air by the Use of Kites or Buoyant Sails*, preface to 1827 edition.

30. Ibid., p. 32.
31. Ibid., p. 31.
32. Ibid., introduction.
33. Robert Bruce, *Bell: Alexander Graham Bell and the Conquest of Solitude*, p. 255.
34. Samuel P. Langley, *Experiments in Aerodynamics.*
35. Bruce, *Bell*, p. 358.
36. Ibid., p. 359.
37. Ibid., p. 361.
38. Ibid., p. 363.
39. Anderson, *History of Aerodynamics.* pp. 39–40.
40. Ibid., pp. 28–29.
41. Ibid., p. 122.
42. *The Times of London*, March 30, 1843, quoted in Harald Penrose, *An Ancient Air: John Stringfellow of Chard, The Victorian Aeronautical Pioneer*, p. 51.
43. Ibid.
44. Anderson, *History of Aerodynamics*, p. 115.
45. Ibid., p. 177.
46. Lawrence Hargrave, "Cellular Kites," *Engineering* 56 (Oct. 27, 1893): 523–24.
47. Papers of Octave Chanute, Box 16, Library of Congress.
48. Bruce, *Bell*, pp. 312–13.
49. Ibid., p. 445 et seq.
50. Ibid.
51. Bruce, *Bell*, p. 451.
52. Samuel P. Langley, and C. M. Manly, *Langley Memoir on Mechanical Flight*, p. 2, quoted in Anderson, *History of Aerodynamics*, p. 165.
53. Anderson, *History of Aerodynamics*, pp. 169, 171, 173.
54. Langley, *Experiments in Aerodynamics.*
55. Langley and Manly, *Langley Memoir*, quoted in Anderson, *History of Aerodynamics*, p. 186.
56. Ibid., p. 188.
57. Quoted in Anderson, *History of Aerodynamics*, p. 188.
58. Wilbur Wright to Samuel P. Langley, May 30, 1899, quoted in Anderson, *History of Aerodynamics*, p. 206.
59. Quoted in Anderson, *History of Aerodynamics*, p. 207.
60. Tom D. Crouch, *The Bishop's Boys: A Life of Wilbur and Orville Wright*, p. 114.
61. Minneapolis *Tribune*, Sept. 14, 1895, quoted in Crouch, *Bishop's Boys*, p. 115.
62. Anderson, *History of Aerodynamics*, p. 207.
63. Ibid., p. 217.

CHAPTER 7. BALLOONS AND DIRIGIBLES: SUSTAINED FLIGHT

1. Needham, *Science and Civilization*, pp. 597–98, section 27, subsection 7.
2. Galileo Galilei, *Dialogues Concerning Two New Sciences*, pp. 78–79.
3. Ibid., pp. 64–65.
4. Ibid., p. 78.
5. Layers of air from Clive Hart, *The Dream of Flight: Aeronautics from Classical Times to the Renaissance*, p. 21.
6. Wise, *Through the Air*, p. 50.
7. Stillman Drake, *Galileo at Work: His Scientific Biography*, p. 469.

8. Otto von Guericke was born Nov. 20, 1602, in Magdeburg, Prussian Saxony [now in Germany] and died May 11, 1686, in Hamburg. From 1646 to 1681 he was bürgermeister (mayor) of Magdeburg and magistrate for Brandenburg.

9. Valentine and Tomlinson, *Travels in Space*, p. 17.

10. Wise, *Through the Air*, p. 70.

11. http://www.ulib.org/webRoot/Books/_Gutenberg_Etext_Books/etext97/haer010.txt. Appendix C: Proclamation published by the French government on balloon ascents, 1783.

12. *Dictionary of Scientific Biography.*

13. Wise, *Through the Air*, p. 71, "from a letter written by the marquis d'Arlandes to M. de St. Fond concerning this first aerial voyage, dated November 28, 1783."

14. Wise, *Through the Air*, pp. 75–76.

15. Henri comte de La Vaulx, *Joseph et Étienne de Montgolfier*, plate lxix. (The translations are the author's.)

16. Ibid., plate lxix. (The translations are the author's.) "Cantate d'Appolon a Monsieur De Mongolfier [*sic*] a l'occasion de son Buste couronne le 9 Decembre 1783, au Musee etabli par M. Pilatre De Rozier, Sous la Protection de Monsieur et de Madame. Les Paroles font de M. Moline, & la Musique de M. Mehul." The blurb for this planche (plate) (in French) seems to indicate fireworks, awarding of medal, etc. "Mais ce qui'il y eut de singulier dans ce gala des sciences, c'est qu'il arriva, ce qui si souvent a lieu en pareille occasion, que le moment ou le publique applaudit aux efforts du genie n'est pas toujours le moment ou celui que l'on fete est le plus heureux; ainsi, pendent que l'on couvroit des fleurs le buste du celebre M. de Montgolfier, il etait lui-meme oublie, confondu parmi la foule, dans un des derniers salles du Musee." [The French Revolution occurred in 1789.] The Cantate: "Recitatif: Je chante Mongolfier! / Qu'il etende son vol aux rives du Permesse! / C'est sa gloire en ce jour que je dois publier. / S'il avoit esiste dans le tems ou la Grece. / A chaque hommen celere erigeoit un autel, / Il en eut eu de toute esepece; / Mais un seul eut suffi pour le rendre immortel / Qu'il repande en tous lieux l'eclat qui l'environne! / Appollon au Musee aujourd'hui le couronne. "Air: Triomphe, Mongolfier! Fois celebre en tout tems! / Par ton brillant genie & ton heureuse audace, / Balance dans les airs, cours maitriser les vents! / De l'univers entier tu peux franchir l'espace. Qu'une double couronne embellisse son front! / Uranie, au facre Vallon / Vient de me designer ta place / Entre Descarts & Newton. "Ariette: Et vous, intrepides Pilotes, / Plus hardis que les Argonautes, / Soyex a jamais / La gloire des Francais! / Dans votre cour aeriene [*sic*], / Vouse avez etonne les Nymphes de la Seine ... / Partagez les honneurs dont jouit Mongolfier, / Et des mains d'Appolon recevez un laurier."

17. Luc Robene, *L'homme à la conquête de l'air: Des aristocrates éclaires aux sportifs bourgeois*, p. 120.

18. Compte de La Vaulx, *Joseph et Étienne de Montgolfier*, plate lxvii, "gravure allegorique publiee par l'academie de marseille a la gloire des freres Montgolfier."

19. John Bacon, *Dominion of the Air: The Story of Aerial Navigation.*

20. Francois-Louis Bruel, *Histoire aeronautique par les monuments peints, sculptes, dessines et graves, des origines a 1830*, plate 104.

21. Robene, *L'homme à la conquête de l'air*, p. 128.

22. Ibid., pp. 140–42.

23. Ibid., p. 399.
24. Ibid., p. 403. (The translations are the author's.)
25. Bella C. Landauer, *Some Aeronautical Music From the Collection of Bella C. Landauer*. The materials are undated. The clothing in these plates resembles middle-class and vendor-class dress of the late eighteenth and early to mid-nineteenth century.
26. Bacon, *Dominion of the Air*.
27. Wise, *Through the Air*, preface.
28. Ibid., pp. 27–31.
29. Ibid., p. 35.
30. Ibid., p. 37.
31. Ibid., p. 150.
32. *Scientific American* 283, no. 1 (July, 2000): 12.
33. Nancy Winters, *Man Flies: The Story of Alberto Santos-Dumont, Master of the Balloon, Conqueror of the Air*, quoted pp. 14–15.
34. Ibid., p. 45 et seq.
35. *Daily News*, quoted in Crouch, *Bishop's Boys*, p. 272.

CHAPTER 8. THE DREAM CONTINUES

1. De la Bère, *Icarus*, p. ix.
2. John Gillespie Magee, Jr., "High Flight."
3. David Noble, *The Religion of Technology: The Divinity of Man and the Spirit of Invention*, quotations on pp. 115, 120, 134, 139, and 142. For another spiritual perspective on spaceflight, see Wynn Wachhorst, *The Dream of Spaceflight: Essays on the Near Edge of Infinity*.
4. *Dumbo*, Walt Disney Productions, 1941.
5. Michael Parfit, "The Corn was Two Feet Below the Wheels," *Smithsonian Magazine* 31, no. 2 (May, 2000), pp. 59–66.
6. Anthony Wright, Yale Curriculum.
7. *New York Times*, Dec. 7, 1970, 43:1.
8. Sidney Tillim, *Artforum*, in Steven Henry Madoff, *Pop Art: A Critical History*, pp. 258–62.
9. Robert C. Scull, "Re the F-111," in Madoff, *Pop Art*.
10. Some excellent historical studies that invoke emotional factors are Rosalind Williams, *Notes on the Underground*; David E. Nye, *American Technological Sublime*; Howard E. McCurdy, *Space and the American Imagination*; and David Noble, *Religion of Technology*.

ANNOTATED BIBLIOGRAPHY

::::

American Heritage History of Flight. New York: American Heritage, 1962.

Anderson, John. *Introduction to Flight: Its Engineering and History.* New York: McGraw-Hill, 1978.

————. *A History of Aerodynamics and Its Impact on Flying Machines.* Cambridge: Cambridge University Press, 1997.

Armstrong, Edward A. *The Folklore of Birds; An Enquiry into the Origin & Distribution of Some Magico-Religious Traditions.* 2d ed. New York: Dover Publications, 1970.

————. *The Life and Lore of the Bird in Nature, Art, Myth and Literature.* New York: Crown, 1975.

Arouet de Voltaire, François Marie. *Candide, Zadig and Selected Stories.* Translated with an introduction by Donald M. Frame. Bloomington: Indiana University Press, 1961.

Bachelard, Gaston. *Air and Dreams.* Translated by Edith R. Farrell and C. Frederick Farrell. Dallas: Dallas Institute Publications, 1988. See particularly chaps. 1, 10, and 11.

Bacon, John. *Dominion of the Air: The Story of Aerial Navigation.* London, New York: Cassell and Company, Limited, 1902. This book is available on the Internet, as part of the Gutenberg e-text project, at: ftp://ftp.ibiblio.org/pub/docs/books/gutenberg/etext97/dmair10.txt

Baker, David. *Flight and Flying: A Chronology.* New York: Facts on File, 1994.

Barnes, Barry. *Scientific Knowledge and Sociological Theory.* London and Boston: Routledge & Kegan Paul, 1974.

Basalla, George. *The Evolution of Technology.* Chap. 1. Cambridge: Cambridge University Press, 1988.

Best, Elsdon. *Games and Pastimes of the Maori.* Wellington: Whitcombe and Tombs Ltd., 1925.

Bhagavad Gita; The Song Celestial. Translated by Sir Edwin Arnold. Introduction by Sri Prakasa. Illustrated with paintings by Y. G. Srimati. New York: Heritage Press, 1965. Text of Arnold's translation also available on the Internet, via the Carrie website (public domain) at: http://www.contrib.andrew.cmu.edu/~eclectic/o/gita/b-g.html

Borelli, Giovanni. *De Motu Animalium.* N.p., 1680–81.

Bowman, Sheridan, ed. *Science and the Past.* Toronto and Buffalo: University of Toronto Press, 1991.

Brodsky, Joseph. *To Urania.* New York: Farrar, Straus, and Giroux, 1988.

Bruce, Robert. *Bell: Alexander Graham Bell and the Conquest of Solitude.* Boston and Toronto: Little, Brown and Company, 1971.

Bruel, François-Louis. *Histoire aeronautique par les monuments peints, sculptes, dessines et graves, des origines a 1830; deux cents reproductions en noir et en couleur; texte par Francois-Louis Bruel.* Paris: A. Marty, 1909.

Constant, Edward W. II. *The Origins of the Turbojet Revolution.* Baltimore and London: Johns Hopkins University Press, 1980. See especially chaps. 1, 6, and 8.

Coomaraswamy, Ananda. *Figures of Speech or Figures of Thought: Collected Essays on the Traditional or "Normal" View of Art.* Second series. New Delhi: Munshiram Munoharlal, Publishers, 1981.

Corn, Joseph J. "Making Flying 'Thinkable': Women Pilots and the Selling of Aviation, 1927–1940." *American Quarterly* 31 (1979): 556–71.

———. *The Winged Gospel: America's Romance with Aviation, 1900–1950.* New York: Oxford University Press, 1983.

Courlander, Howard. *Treasury of African Folklore.* New York: Crown, 1975.

Crosby, Alfred W. *The Measure of Reality: Quantification and Western Society, 1250–1600.* Cambridge and New York: Cambridge University Press, 1997.

Crouch, Tom D. *The Bishop's Boys: A Life of Wilbur and Orville Wright.* New York and London: W. W. Norton & Company, 1989.

———. *A Dream of Wings; Americans and the Airplane, 1875–1905.* Washington D.C. and London: Smithsonian Institution Press, 1981, 1989.

———. *The Eagle Aloft: Two Centuries of the Balloon in America.* Washington, D.C.: Smithsonian Institution Press, 1983.

de Bergerac, Cyrano. *Other Worlds: The Comical History of the States and Empires of the Moon and Sun.* Translated and introduced by Geoffrey Strachan. London: Oxford University Press, 1965.

Deisch, Noel. "The Navigation of Space." *Popular Astronomy* 38 (1930): 77–88. Good overview of fictional and philosophical background.

de la Bère, Rupert et al. *Icarus: An Anthology of the Poetry of Flight.* London: Macmillan & Co. Ltd., 1938.

del Rey, Lester. *Science Fiction Hall of Fame: The Greatest Science Fiction Stories of All Time.* 3 vols. New York: Avon Books, 1970. Short stories and novellas chosen by the Science Fiction Writers of America. The material included was written between 1929 and 1965, considered the "golden age" of science fiction by most fans of the genre.

Dhalla, Viraf Minocher. *Symbolism in Zoroastrianism.* Bombay: K. R. Cama Oriental Institute, 1994.

Dictionary of Scientific Biography. New York: Charles Scribner's Sons, 1980.

Douglas, Mary. *Purity and Danger: An Analysis of Concepts of Pollution and Taboo.* Harmondworth: Penguin, 1970.

Douglas, Susan J. *Inventing American Broadcasting, 1899–1922.* Baltimore: Johns Hopkins University Press, 1987.

Drake, Stillman. *Galileo at Work: His Scientific Biography.* Chicago: University of Chicago Press, 1978.

Duhem, Jules. *Histoire des Idées Aéronautiques Avant Montgolfier.* Paris: F. Sorlot, ca. 1943. This is a very thorough treatment of the subject, including various legends and saints' stories, myths, and early speculations and attempts.

———. *Musée Aéronautique avant Montgolfier.* Paris: F. Sorlot, 1943.

Eliade, Mircea. *Myths, Dreams and Mysteries; the Encounter Between Contemporary Faiths and Archaic Realities.* Translated by Philip Mairet. New York and Evanston: Harper Torchbooks, Harper & Row, 1961, ca. 1960. N.B.: "[T]he desire . . . " passage appears both in *Myths, Dreams* and in *Symbolism, the Sacred, and the Arts.*

———. *Shamanism: Archaic Techniques of Ecstasy.* Bollingen Series LXXVI. Princeton: Princeton University Press, 1964.

———. *Symbolism, the Sacred, and the Arts.* Edited by Diane Apostolos-Cappadonna. New York: Crossroad, 1990.

Eliot, Alexander. *The Universal Myths: Heroes, Gods, Tricksters and Others*. With contributions by Joseph Campbell and Mircea Eliade. New York: Meridian Books. 1976.

Ellul, Jacques. *The Technological Society*. Translated from the French by John Wilkinson. New York: Random House (Vintage Books), 1964.

Fleck, Ludwik. *Genesis and Development of a Scientific Fact*. Translated by Fred Bradley and Thaddeus J. Trenn. Chicago and London: University of Chicago Press, 1979. Originally published as *Entstehung und Entwiklung einer wissenschaflichen Tatsache*. Basel, Switzerland: Benno Schwabe & Co., 1935.

Foltz, Richard C. *Religions of the Silk Road*. New York: St. Martin's Press, 1999.

Foster, Benjamin. *From Distant Days: Myths, Tales and Poetry from Ancient Mesopotamia*. Bethesda: CDI Press, 1995. This book is available on the Internet at: http://www.gatewaystobabylon.com/myths/texts/classic/mythetana.htm

Frontisi-Ducroux, Françoise. *Dédale: mythologie de l'artisan en grèce ancienne*. Paris: François Maspero, 1975.

Galilei, Galileo. *Dialogues Concerning Two New Sciences*. Translated by Henry Crew and Alfonso de Salvio. New York: Dover Publications, 1954. This book was first published in 1638.

Gay, Peter. *The Freud Reader*. New York: W. W. Norton, 1989.

The Genesis of Flight: The Aeronautical History Collection of Colonel Richard Gimbel. The Friends of the United States Air Force Academy Library. Seattle: University of Washington Press, 2000. This book offers an excellent introductory essay and an abundance of annotated illustrations of flying-related items dating from approximately 3000 B.C.E to 1914.

Gibbs-Smith, Charles Harvard. *Aviation: An Historical Survey from its Origins to the End of World War II*. London: Science Museum (Her Majesty's Stationery Office), 1979.

————. *Flight Through the Ages: A Complete, Illustrated Chronology from the Dreams of Early History to the Age of Space Exploration*. New York: Crowell, 1974.

Gillman, Neil. *Sacred Fragments: Recovering Theology for the Modern Jew*. Philadelphia and Jerusalem: Jewish Publication Society, 1990.

Ginzburg, Carlo. *The Cheese and the Worms: the Cosmos of a Sixteenth-Century Miller*. Translated by John and Anne Tedeschi. Baltimore and London: Johns Hopkins University Press, 1980. Presents the thoughts and experiences of an intelligent but uneducated person struggling to understand the new cosmology, in the context of his faith and the constraints of his society.

Godwin, Bishop Francis. *The Man in the Moon*. Edited with an introduction and annotations by John Anthony Butler. Ottawa, Canada: Dovehouse Editions, 1995.

Good, John Mason. *The Book of Nature*, 1839. Excerpted in Jen Hill, *An Exhilaration of Wings: The Literature of Birdwatching*. New York: Viking, 1999.

Haddon, A. C. *The Study of Man*. London, 1898. In Hart, *Kites*.

Hargrave, Lawrence. "Cellular Kites." *Engineering* 56 (Oct. 27, 1893): 523–24.

Hart, Clive. *The Dream of Flight: Aeronautics from Classical Times to the Renaissance*. London: Faber & Faber Limited, 1972.

————. *Images of Flight*. Berkeley and London: University of California Press, 1988. The sexual connotations of various types of flight in pictorial art are well documented and described. See especially Chapter 1: Upward Flight, Freedom; Chapter 2: Downward Flight, The Annunciation and Tintoretto; Chapter 4: Flight Into Union, Sexuality and Ecstasy; and Chapter 5: The Flying Saint.

————. *Kites: An Historical Survey*. Revised and expanded 2d ed. New York: Paul P. Appel, Mount Vernon, 1982.

Haug, Martin, and Edward William West, eds. *The Book of Arday Viraf.* 1872. Reprint, Netherlands: Amsterdam Oriental Press, 1971.

Hawthorne, Nathaniel. *Pegasus, the Winged Horse.* New York: Macmillan, 1963. Originally published in Hawthorne's *A Wonder Book* with the title "The Chimera."

Heinlein, Robert A. *The Green Hills of Earth: Rhysling and the Adventure of the Entire Solar System.* With an appreciation by Mark Reinsberg. Chicago: Shasta Publishers, 1951.

———. *The Man Who Sold the Moon: Harriman and the Escape from Earth to the Moon.* Introduction by John W. Campbell, Jr. Chicago: Shasta Publishers, 1950.

———. *Waldo, and Magic Inc.* Garden City, N.Y.: Doubleday, 1950.

Hughes, Thomas Parke. *American Genesis: A Century of Invention and Technological Enthusiasm, 1870–1970.* New York: Viking, 1989. An exploration of the cultural and social context of invention.

Jablonski, Edward. *Man With Wings: A Pictorial History of Aviation.* Garden City, N.Y.: Doubleday and Company, 1980.

The Kalevala, the Epic Poem of Finland. Translated by John Martin Crawford. New York: J. B. Alden, 1888. The Kalevala is also available on the Internet at: http://www.sacred-texts.com/neu/kveng/kvrune19.htm/

Koestler, Arthur. *The Sleepwalkers.* New York: Grosset & Dunlap, 1963. History of the "Scientific Revolution" in astronomy and physics, focusing on Kepler, Copernicus, and Galileo.

Kuhn, Thomas S. *The Structure of Scientific Revolutions.* 2d ed., enlarged. Chicago and London: University of Chicago Press, 1970.

———. *The Essential Tension: Selected Studies in Scientific Tradition and Change.* Chicago and London: University of Chicago Press, 1977.

Kushner, Lawrence. "What Did the Mystic Say to the Hot Dog Vendor? Six Neo-Kabbalistic Metaphors for Cosmic Design." In *Annals of the New York Academy of Sciences* 950, pp. 215–24.

Landauer, Bella C. *Some Aeronautical Music From the Collection of Bella C. Landauer.* Paris, 1933. The materials are undated: the clothing resembles middle-class and vendor-class dress of the late eighteenth and early to mid-nineteenth century.

Langley, Samuel P. *Experiments in Aerodynamics.* Smithsonian Contributions to Knowledge, no. 801. Washington, D.C.: Smithsonian Institution, 1891.

Langley, Samuel P., and Manly, C. M. *Langley Memoir on Mechanical Flight.* Smithsonian Contributions to Knowledge, vol. 27, no. 3. Washington, D.C.: Smithsonian Press, 1911.

Laufer, Berthold. *The Prehistory of Aviation.* Vol. XVIII, no. 1, Publication 253, Anthropological Series. Chicago: Field Museum of Natural History, 1928. Laufer has a good bibliographical essay on p. 85 et seq.

La Vaulx, Henri, comte de. *Joseph et Étienne de Montgolfier.* Annonay, 1926.

Lear, John. *Kepler's Dream with the full text and notes of* Somnium, Sive Astronomia Lunaris, Joannis Kepleri. Translated by Patricia Frueh Kirkwood. Berkeley and Los Angeles: University of California Press, 1965.

Levi-Strauss, Claude. *Structural Anthropology.* Translated from the French by Claire Jacobson and Brooke Grundfest Schoepf. New York: Basic Books, ca. 1963.

———. *The Raw and the Cooked.* Translated from the French by John and Doreen Weightman. Chicago: University of Chicago Press, 1983.

———. *Myth and Meaning.* New York: Schocken Books, 1979.

Lewis, Clive Staples. *The Screwtape Letters*. New York: Macmillan, 1946.

Lilienthal, Otto. *Birdflight as the Basis of Aviation: A Contribution Towards a System of Aviation*. Compiled from the results of numerous experiments made by O. and G. Lilienthal with a biographical introduction and addendum by Gustav Lilienthal. Translated from the 2d ed. by A. W. Isenthal. London and New York: Longmans, Green, (W. Clower & Sons) 1911, p. xvi.

Lindberg, David C., ed. *Science in the Middle Ages*. Chicago: University of Chicago Press, 1978. Scholarly history of the foundations and development of various scientific disciplines, and of scientific thought, in this period. See especially chaps. 2, 3, 6, 7, and 15.

Lucian of Samosata. "Icaromenippus, an Aerial Expedition." In *Marcus Aurelius and His Times; The Transition from Paganism to Christianity* . . . New York: W. J. Black for the Classics Club, 1945.

———. "The True History." In *The Works of Lucian of Samosata, Complete with Exceptions Specified in the Preface*. Translated by H. W. Fowler and F. G. Fowler. Oxford: Clarendon Press, 1905.

Luck-Huyse, Karin. *Der Traum vom Fliegen in der Antike*. Stuttgart: Franz Steiner Verlag, 1997.

Madoff, Steven Henry. *Pop Art: A Critical History*. Berkeley, Los Angeles, London: University of California Press, 1997.

Magee, John Gillespie, Jr. "High Flight." 1941.

McCurdy, Howard E. *Space and the American Imagination*. Washington, D.C.: Smithsonian Institution Press, 1997.

Merin, Peter. *Conquest of the Skies; The Story of the Idea of Human Flight*. London: John Lane, 1938.

Miller, Walter M. *A Canticle for Liebowitz*. Philadelphia: Lippincott, 1960.

Morris, Sarah. *Daidalos and the Origins of Greek Art*. Princeton: Princeton University Press, 1992. This is a specialist's book. The ability to transliterate Greek and understand German is a plus for the intrepid reader. The tale Morris spins and the connections she demonstrates, however, are fascinating and well presented.

Moskowitz, Sam. *Explorers of the Infinite*. Cleveland and New York: World Publishing Co., 1963. The author is among the most respected historians of "science fiction."

Needham, Joseph. *Science and Civilization in China, by Joseph Needham with the Research Assistance of Wang Ling*. Vol. 4, part 2. Cambridge: Cambridge University Press, 1965. Needham's work is considered the premier and most comprehensive treatment of the subject in English.

Noble, David. "The Ascent of the Saints: Space Exploration." Chap. 9 in *The Religion of Technology: The Divinity of Man and the Spirit of Invention*. New York and London: Penguin Books, 1999.

Nye, David E. *American Technological Sublime*. Cambridge, Mass.: MIT Press, 1994.

Pacey, Arnold. *The Maze of Ingenuity: Ideas and Idealism in the Development of Technology*. Cambridge, Mass. and London: MIT Press, 1974.

Penrose, Harald. *An Ancient Air: John Stringfellow of Chard, The Victorian Aeronautical Pioneer*. Washington, D.C.: Smithsonian Institution Press, 1989.

Pocock, George. *The Aeropleustic Art, or Navigation in the Air by the use of Kites or Buoyant Sails*. Bristol, 1827.

Priestley, Joseph. *The History and Present State of Electricity*. 2d ed. N.p., 1769.

Reay, D. A. *The History of Man-Powered Flight*. Oxford and New York: Pergamon Press, 1977.

Robene, Luc. *L'homme à la conquête de l'air: Des aristocrates éclaires aux sportifs bourgeois.* Paris: L'Harmattan, 1998.

Rowland, Beryl. *Birds with Human Souls.* Knoxville: University of Tennessee Press, 1978.

Schroeder, Maurice Z. *Icarus: The Image of the Artist in French Romanticism.* Cambridge, Mass.: Harvard University Press, 1961.

Scott, Phil. *The Shoulders of Giants: A History of Human Flight to 1919.* Reading, Mass.: Addison-Wesley, 1995.

———. *The Pioneers of Flight: A Documentary History.* Princeton: Princeton University Press, 1999.

Scull, Robert C. "Re the F-111; A Collector's Notes." In Steven Henry Madoff, *Pop Art: A Critical History.* Berkeley, Los Angeles, London: University of California Press, 1997. Originally published in *Metropolitan Museum of Art Bulletin* (March, 1968): 282–83.

Sendak, Maurice. *In the Night Kitchen.* New York: Harper & Row, 1970.

Servos, John. *Physical Chemistry from Ostwald to Pauling: the making of a science in America.* Princeton: Princeton University Press, 1990.

Singh, Dharam Jit. *Classic Cooking From India.* Boston: Houghton Miflin Company, 1956.

Smithsonian Magazine 31, no. 2 (May 2000): 59–66.

Söderberg, Henry. *Swedenborg's 1714 Airplane: A Machine to Fly in the Air.* New York: Swedenborg Foundation, 1988.

Steadman, Philip. *The Evolution of Designs: Biological Analogy in Architecture and the Applied Arts.* Cambridge: Cambridge University Press, 1979.

Stillson, Blanche. *Wings: Insects, Birds, Men.* London: Victor Gollancz Ltd., 1955.

Swedenborg, Emanuel. *Journal of Dreams 1743–1744.* Edited from the original Swedish by G. E. Klemming; translated into English, 1860, by J. J. G. Wilkinson; edited by William Ross Woofenden. New York: Swedenborg Foundation, 1977.

Tillim, Sidney. *Artforum.* 1968, 46–49. In Madoff, *Pop Art.*

Tyler, Hamilton A. *Pueblo Birds and Myths.* Norman: University of Oklahoma Press, 1979.

Valentine, E. Seton and F. L. Tomlinson. *Travels in Space: A History of Aerial Navigation; with an introduction by Sir Hiram Maxim.* New York: Frederick A. Stokes, 1902.

Verne, Jules. *From the Earth to the Moon and Round the Moon.* Introduction by Arthur C. Clarke. New York: Dodd, Mead & Co., 1962.

Vivian, Evelyn Charles. *A History of Aeronautics, by E. Charles Vivian, with a Section on Progress in Aeroplane Design by W. Lockwood Marsh.* London: Collins, 1921. This book is available on the Internet, as part of the Gutenberg e-text project, at: http://www.ulib.org/webRoot/Books/_Gutenberg_Etext_Books/etext97/haero10.txt

Vogel, Steven. *Cat's Paws and Catapults: Mechanical Worlds of Nature and People.* New York and London: W. W. Norton, 1998.

Wachhorst, Wynn. *The Dream of Spaceflight: Essays on the Near Edge of Infinity.* New York: Basic Books, 2000. From the Foreword by Buzz Aldrin: "*The Dream of Spaceflight* is not just for space buffs, it is for everyone who sees the mystery of the cosmos as analog to the human soul."

Weart, Spencer. *Nuclear Fear.* Cambridge, Mass., and London: Harvard University Press, 1988.

Wells, H. G. *War of the Worlds*. New York and London: Harper & Brothers, ca. 1898. Reprinted and anthologized many times. See also Hadley Cantril, *The Invasion from Mars: A Study in the Psychology of Panic. With the complete script of the famous Orson Welles Broadcast.* With the assistance of Hazel Gaudet and Herta Herzog. Princeton: Princeton University Press, 1940.

White, Lynn, Jr. "Cultural Climates and Technological Advance in the Middle Ages." In *Medieval Religion and Technology.* Berkeley, Los Angeles, London: University of California Press, 1978. Originally published in *Viator* 2 (1971): 171–201.

———. "Eilmer of Malmsbury, an Eleventh Century Aviator." In *Medieval Religion and Technology.* Berkeley and Los Angeles: University of California Press, 1978. Originally published in *Technology and Culture* 2 (1961): 97–111.

———. "The Iconography of Temperantia and the Virtuousness of Technology." In *Medieval Religion and Technology.* Berkeley, Los Angeles, London: University of California Press, 1978. Originally published in Theodore K. Rabb and Jerrold E. Siegel, eds., *Action and Conviction in Early Modern Europe: Essays in Memory of E. H. Harbison* (Princeton: Princeton University Press, 1969).

———. "The Invention of the Parachute." In *Medieval Religion and Technology.* Berkeley and Los Angeles: University of California Press, 1978. Originally published in *Technology and Culture* 9 (1968): 462–67.

———. *Medieval Religion and Technology.* Berkeley, Los Angeles, London: University of California Press, 1978.

Wight, Anthony B. *Daedalus: The Long Odyssey from Myth to Reality.* New Haven: Yale-New Haven Teachers Institute, 1988. http://www.yale.edu/ynhti/curriculum/units/1988/6/88.06.10.x.html

Wilkins, John. *Mathematical Magick: or, The WONDERS that may be performed by mechanical geometry. : In two books . . . : Being one of the most easie, pleasant, useful (and yet most neglected) part of mathematicks. Not before treated of in this language.* London: Printed for Edw. Gellibrand at the Golden Ball in St. Pauls Church yard, 1680.

Williams, Rosalind. *Notes on the Underground: An Essay on Technology, Society, and the Imagination.* Cambridge, Mass.: MIT Press, 1992. Explores the relationship of mythic elements to technological development and social structure.

Winters, Nancy. *Man Flies: the story of Alberto Santos-Dumont, Master of the Balloon, Conqueror of the Air.* Hopewell, N.J.: Ecco Press, 1998.

Wise, John. *Through the Air: A Narrative of Forty Years Experience as an Aeronaut, Comprising a History of the Various Attempts in the Art of Flying by Artificial Means from the Earliest Period Down to the Present Time.* Philadelphia, New York, Boston, Chicago: To-Day Printing and Publishing Company, 1873. Also reprinted by Arno Press, 1972.

Zaehner, Robert Charles, trans. *Hindu Scriptures.* New York: Everyman's Library, Alfred A. Knopf, 1992. Rig-Veda is available on the Internet at: http://www.magna.com.au/~prfbrown/rig_veda.html

INDEX

⁙